THE LIFE OF WALTER SKIRLAW

MEDIEVAL DIPLOMAT
AND
PRINCE BISHOP OF DURHAM

GLYNNE JARRATT

Highgate of Beverley

Highgate Publications (Beverley) Limited
2004

ACKNOWLEDGEMENTS

In researching and writing this book I would like to thank all those who have contributed in some way to this end, especially Dr. R. G. Davies, Mr. L. Trewartha, Mr. M. G. Snape, and the Reverend D. W. Perry. I am especially grateful to my wife, Christine, and sons, Christopher and Jonathan, for their support and encouragement during the years I have spent on this project, which made it all possible. Special thanks are due to Dr. John Markham of Highgate Publications Limited and Margaret and Ian Sumner for their helpful suggestions on the script.

All photographs were taken by the author apart from the one of the St. Martin-le-Grand plaque which was taken by Jonathan Jarratt. I am grateful for the permission to photograph inside various buildings given by the Dean and Chapters of Durham Cathedral and York Minster, the Vicars of Howden Minster, Preston Bissett and Skirlaugh Church, and the Master of Balliol College, Oxford. With regard to the prints of seals etc., every attempt has been made to obtain permission to reproduce copyright material. If any proper acknowledgement has not been made, copyright holders are invited to inform the author of the oversight.

Front Cover: Statue of Bishop Walter Skirlaw, York Minster
St. Augustine's Church, Skirlaugh
Back Cover: Durham Cathedral

British Library Cataloguing in Publication Data.
A catalogue record for this book is available from the British Library.

© 2004 Peter Glynne Jarratt

Peter Glynne Jarratt asserts the moral right to be identified as the author of this work.

ISBN 1 902645 38 3

Published by

Highgate of Beverley

Highgate Publications (Beverley) Limited

Contents

Acknowledgements	page ii
Contents	page iii
Introduction	page iv
Chapter One: The Young Skirlaw	page 1
Chapter Two: Skirlaw, the Rector and Archdeacon	page 12
Chapter Three: Skirlaw in the King's Service	page 26
Chapter Four: Skirlaw, the Diplomat	page 42
Chapter Five: Bishop Skirlaw	page 57
Chapter Six: Skirlaw and the Diocese of Durham	page 67
Chapter Seven: Skirlaw and the Religious Activities of Durham	page 82
Chapter Eight: Skirlaw and the Palatinate of Durham	page 97
Chapter Nine: Skirlaw, his Buildings and Bridges	page 106
Chapter Ten: Skirlaw's Chapel	page 135
Chapter Eleven: Death of Bishop Skirlaw	page 146
Chapter Twelve: Skirlaw's Will	page 159
Chapter Thirteen: Skirlaw Remembered	page 179
Appendix A: John Danby	page 189
Appendix B: John Skirlaw	page 190
Bibliography	page 191
Notes	page 199
Index	page 217

Introduction

The aim of this book is to bring together the facts known about Walter Skirlaw (medieval spelling of 'Skirlaugh'), who was born in the village of Skirlaugh in Holderness in the East Riding of Yorkshire, and who was Bishop of Durham in the late fourteenth and early fifteenth centuries. I am particularly pleased to have completed this book in time for the six hundredth anniversary of the opening for worship of his church here in Skirlaugh.

Books and documents on various aspects of medieval life make reference to Skirlaw's role as a diplomat in shaping the history of England at that time. The Church also had a profound influence on life in those days and Skirlaw rose to high office in the land. He made his mark for posterity by funding many buildings and other structures, most of which are still present and in use today, including the church of St. Augustine, Skirlaugh.

Skirlaw lived during a period when many events of great significance happened in the history of England. He was born in the reign of Edward III. During Skirlaw's lifetime the Hundred Years War started, the Black Prince won his spurs at the battle of Crécy, the Order of the Garter was founded, the Black Death came and went, Langland's *Piers Ploughman* was written, the first Stuart king of Scotland was enthroned, Richard II became king of England, the Peasants' Revolt took place culminating in the death of Wat Tyler, John of Gaunt was born and died, the Scots beat the English at Otterburn, Chaucer produced his *Canterbury Tales*, Henry Bolingbroke landed on the coast of East Yorkshire and ousted Richard to become King Henry IV, John Wycliffe, the Oxford theologian, translated the Bible into English and with his heretical views established the Lollard movement, Dick Whittington became lord mayor of London, and an archbishop of York was executed for treason.

CHAPTER ONE
THE YOUNG SKIRLAW

Walter Skirlaw is thought to have been born in the village of Skirlaugh in Holderness in the East Riding of Yorkshire and took his surname from the name of the village. The A165 road passes through, linking Kingston upon Hull with Bridlington and Scarborough. Skirlaugh also links with Rise and Hornsea via the B1243. It is around the junction of the A165 and B1243 that the village is now clustered. In terms of distance Skirlaugh is about eight miles (13 kilometres) from Kingston upon Hull, Beverley and Hornsea.

Holderness is a generally flat, low-lying, part of East Yorkshire which is situated to the east of Kingston upon Hull and Beverley, from north of Hornsea down to Spurn Point, bounded by the North Sea and the Humber estuary. Skirlaugh is situated on undulating ground which rises to some 65 feet (20 metres) above sea level. The Lambwath Stream divides the village into two parts, North Skirlaugh and South Skirlaugh, and in the past they were known as two separate villages when they were about a mile apart.

In the Domesday Book (1086), Skirlaugh was referred to as Schireslai and was also anciently written as *Schyrlake*, i.e. 'skyre', meaning a divide or cut, and, 'lake', which in its broad sense can be construed as a sewer, dyke, drain, or current of water. The term 'lake' would no doubt relate to the Lambwath Stream which divides the village. There were other lakes, ponds or marshes in the area used as fisheries by Swine Priory situated three miles south,[1] most of which have since been drained. Kent, however, states that the name Skirlaugh is an Anglo-Scandinavian hybrid, meaning 'bright clearing'.[2] In 1609 Skirlaugh was described as 'a bare and barren place'.[3]

In medieval times, North Skirlaugh and South Skirlaugh were part of the parish of Swine; much of the land in North Skirlaugh lay in the Rise Estate of the Fauconberg family, whereas in South Skirlaugh the land was held by the abbot of Thornton Abbey in Lincolnshire and the prioress of Swine Priory.[4] The prioress of Swine had the concern of the spiritual well-being of the two villages. It was not until 1867 that the two villages, together with Rowton, Arnold, Benningholme and Grange, and Marton split from Swine and formed the separate parish of Skirlaugh.[5] From that date, the church of St. Augustine, which was formerly the chantry chapel of Swine church, became the parish church of Skirlaugh.

Over the centuries the name of the village has changed from 'Schireslai' from the Domesday Book, to 'Skirlaw' and other similar spellings in the Middle Ages, to 'Skirlaugh' as it is now written. The spelling of the name using *sk* as against the more English *ch* or *sh* is indicative of the former Scandinavian occupation of this area.[6]

It was in the village of South Skirlaugh that Walter Skirlaw was born around the year 1330.[7] The date of his birth is not known, as parish records and registers were not generally kept in Edward III's reign, and Swine appears to be no exception.

When Skirlaw became bishop of Durham he adopted a coat of arms of six willow wands interlaced to form a cross (described in more detail in Chapter Six). Because of this, tradition has it that his parents were peasants, his father gaining a living making sieves (used for measuring grain etc.), bolters (used for sifting flour) or baskets, woven from willow wands.[8] Willow trees would abound round the ponds and marshes of Skirlaugh. Until recent years, South Skirlaugh had a windmill, and it could be therefore that Walter's father was a flour miller, and may have managed a windmill or water mill.[9] Holderness was known for the quality of the flour produced; the flour sieves there were called *tiffanies* because they had the fineness of tiffany silk.[10] Until the Black Death, the East Riding was the north's prime corn-growing district. Since then, much of the land had been turned to pasture mainly because of the shortage of labour which resulted from the Black Death.[11] The Cistercian monks of Meaux Abbey, situated some two and a half miles west of Skirlaugh, were great sheep farmers and owned some 11,000 sheep on their various estates in 1280 (although the numbers subsequently declined).

An alternative theory is that Walter Skirlaw's family were builders and the coat of arms adopted by him relates to the interwoven willow stems used as wattle in building walls, roofs and fences. Skirlaw himself was very interested in aspects of building and was described as a 'great architect' by one commentator, as will be seen in Chapter Nine.

Families living in medieval villages were usually allotted strips of land out of the landlord's estate with which to work and gain sufficient income to subsist. Apart from this, the more enterprising villagers would also employ their particular skills to increase their income and standard of living. The holding was usually passed on to the eldest son, while other sons might go into the Church or some other occupation away from home, after being sent to an appropriate school. Daughters would usually take on domestic service at home or elsewhere, although it was customary for wealthier families in those times to send them to a nunnery or similar establishment.[12] In the case of the Skirlaw family, it is probable that, if they were peasants, they occupied a sizeable strip of land, which may have been under the ownership of the priory of Swine in South Skirlaugh, and that the father gained additional income from his skills as a sieve-maker or builder.

However, it is argued by some authorities that Walter Skirlaw was of middle or upper class parentage, although it is surprising that no such connections have been established. Records relating to landed gentry and leading members of the community and government are usually available in some form and detail. The fact that his sister, Joan, was a prioress signifies the likelihood that the family was of some standing in the neighbourhood. It may be that the Skirlaw family was connected in some way to Lord Fauconberg of Black Hall, Rise (now part of the Bethell estate), two miles east of Skirlaugh, who owned land in North Skirlaugh. Over the generations, Walter was a recurring name in the Fauconberg family.[13]

Another possibility is that the Skirlaw family was related to John Thoresby, who became archbishop of York in 1352, and many of whose relatives came from Holderness, Howdenshire and North Lincolnshire. The archbishop took as much interest in the education and career of Walter Skirlaw as he did of his other known relatives. He was very active in securing good positions for his 'household', including Walter, in the Church and government. Thoresby himself came from North Thoresby a few miles south of Grimsby in Lincolnshire. His known relatives included the Ravensers, who originated from the lost town of Ravenser in Holderness near Spurn Point at the mouth of the Humber. Thoresby was also connected to the Waltham family, who came from Waltham in Lincolnshire, and the Ferribys from the village of (North) Ferriby in Howdenshire in East Yorkshire.

There seem to be no records relating to the Skirlaw family apart from those relating to Walter and some (or possibly all) of his brothers and sisters. The eldest son, thought to have been called William, married Ellen (Elena); he perhaps continued to occupy the family home in Skirlaugh and may have inherited his father's trade. Walter Skirlaw, as a younger son, was schooled with the aim of taking a university education and eventually obtaining a position in the government or Church. The youngest son may have been John; he was not as academically inclined as Walter, but his education was sufficient to gain him a position in the lower orders of the Church (see Appendix B). Philip Skirlaw may have been yet another brother; his calling was the sea and he joined the crew of fishing vessels round the coast of England.[14] Walter's sister Joan was admitted to the priory of Swine, where in time she became prioress. It is interesting to note that Joan was prioress of Swine Priory at the time Walter Skirlaw drew up his will.[15] She also witnessed one of the codicils attached to his will on 1 August 1404 (see Chapter Twelve).[16] Her name is not among the list of prioresses given by either Torre or Burton,[17] but is included by Fallow.[18] Walter Skirlaw's will included a legacy to a cousin, Robert Custeby, who at the time of Walter's death was a schoolboy[19]. Another kinsman, William Skirlaw, was a warden of Skirlaugh Chapel under the patronage of Walter as bishop of Durham. The date of William's institution was 2 May 1404 (see Chapter Ten); he subsequently resigned his position in 1410.[20] It seems possible that this William was the son of William and Ellen and therefore Walter Skirlaw's nephew. There was also a Peter Skirlaw, a chaplain in Swine during Walter Skirlaw's life, who may have been related.[21] Another relative was John Danby, who was appointed clerk to the parish of Bosham in the diocese of Chichester. Aspects of his career are summarised in Appendix A. A comparison of their careers shows that both John Danby and John Skirlaw took posts at Fauconers, Good Easter in Essex, and this suggests that they could have been the same person.

Attempting to establish relationships in and from medieval times is not always straightforward. Sons might adopt a surname relating to the place in which they were born, later dropped in favour of a family name or mother's name. Members of the same family might therefore adopt different surnames, which can be very confusing.[22] Walter Skirlaw's name is sometimes written as Walter de Skirlaw,[23] which might indicate his place of origin. It could be, however, that his brother William was called William de Swine, or somewhere else, depending on where he was born or where he lived. From records kept at the York registry, various spellings of the surname 'Skirlaw' can be found during the fifteenth and sixteenth centuries in wills which have been registered there of men who lived in Beverley, Long Riston and Hornsea (Beck) in Holderness.[24] *Shirlaw* prevails and this name might be an alternative spelling of *Skirlaw*. One source suggests that *Shirley* is the English spelling of the more Scandinavian surname *Skirlaugh*.[25] The names *Skirlaugh* and *Skirlaw* can be traced again in the nineteenth century from the International Genealogical Index of the British Isles, which may indicate a continuance of the Skirlaw family lineage.

Walter Skirlaw is said by one authority to have attended Swine Priory for his early schooling.[26] However, priories did not usually educate children and he may have been taught more locally at South Skirlaugh chapel by a priest. In those days attendance at school usually began at the age of seven with the teaching of the rudiments of Latin pronunciation and reading. Children became conversant by singing plainchant and learning the psalms. For his secondary education Skirlaw may have attended Beverley Grammar School at the Minster, which was also the choir school[27] and where Latin grammar would be taught. As a schoolboy Skirlaw's life would be very disciplined. The usual regime was to rise early each day when pupils would recite the Creed, three Paternosters and five Aves. They would then make their beds and wash before going to church, doing so in an orderly fashion without running, jumping or talking, and without carrying bows, staffs or stones. They would make a sign of the Cross on entering the church, then process to the choir, bow to the Cross, and file to their pews keeping their eyes towards the altar. The boys were not to smile, laugh nor deride poor singers, answer back or poke each other. On leaving their pews they bowed to the altar, and those who knew their Latin but spoke in English or French were rapped with a ruler. A boy in possession of dice would receive a blow for every spot. On feast days boys were forbidden from going into the town and were not allowed to visit the homes of rustics (country folk). Boys were taught from the Bible, Latin texts and medieval texts such as the *Elegies of Maximian*.[28]

Further studies may have taken place at Meaux Abbey, where the Cistercian monks maintained a comprehensive library of biblical texts, commentaries and patristic works.[29] Having mastered sufficient Latin, Skirlaw would then have acquired enough training for ecclesiastical or secular service, and to be considered for acceptance as an undergraduate at one of the two English universities, Oxford or Cambridge. Education to this standard needed financing and, if sufficient funds were not available from the family, it might be that the Church or some other benefactor assisted.

It would have been during Skirlaw's time at a grammar school that the Black Death descended upon the country around 1349 when he was in his mid-teens. He was fortunate in surviving the terrible plague which afflicted people of all ages and walks of life. Many men in high positions in Church and government died, as did agricultural workers. Skirlaw may have recognised the opportunities which could accrue to him as a result of the plague, if he continued his education at a university. John Thoresby, who was elected archbishop of York in 1352, was soon leading a recruiting drive for clergy, the impact of the Black Death having seriously weakened Church discipline.[30] Skirlaw may well have been one of those recruits.

According to one source, after completing his schooling, Walter Skirlaw, being 'very untoward',[31] ran away to Oxford, only resuming relations with his family after he became bishop of Durham.[32] How far this is the truth is open to conjecture. He must have obtained some financial and educational backing to have been able to continue his education at Oxford, if indeed that is where he went for his undergraduate studies. It could be that his schooling was incomplete before he left for Oxford, and he may have attended a grammar school there controlled by the University, which appointed two masters of arts to superintend each school. The main aim of these schools was to bring pupils' written and spoken Latin to an appropriate standard to enter the university. There was no university entrance examination, but an entrant without these Latin skills would not find his time at the university profitable.[33]

The University of Oxford ranked on a par with other European universities such as Paris, Salerno and Bologna, although it had not developed on the same lines. The universities on the continent had evolved from the twelfth century, when higher education moved from the monasteries to cathedral schools, and so facilitated the bringing of secular education to the developing towns and cities. Paris University was an example of this type of development. Had this pattern been followed in England, cathedral schools at towns like York and Lincoln would have had universities in medieval times. In fact York University was not formed until 1962 and the university at Lincoln was not established until 1996,[34] although Bishop Grosseteste College was founded in the city for teacher training by the Anglican Church in 1862.

The University of Oxford (like Cambridge) is not situated in a cathedral town. According to Rashdall's thesis, it became a seat of learning on the migration of some of the masters and students from Paris in 1167, and so established itself as a *studium generale*.[35] This meant that its educational standards were recognised by other European universities as of equal status, and so academics could be accepted as teachers in any other university with this standing. As the language used in teaching was mainly Latin, transferability was no problem. The ultimate jurisdiction of such universities was through papal authority and this also applied to Oxford. The patronage of the crown and to some extent the bishop of Lincoln assisted Oxford, then situated just within the diocese of Lincoln, in increasing its position and strength as a university. In fact it is claimed that Robert Grosseteste was the first chancellor of Oxford in 1221.[36] He was educated at Oxford (and probably Paris) and later became bishop of Lincoln.[37]

The approach to education in medieval Oxford was based on Christian theology. Skirlaw's foundation studies were not confined to this narrow area but would also embrace logic and mathematics. The college library contained books in manuscript in the relevant areas, but students themselves would be fortunate to possess any but the basic texts, handed down from previous undergraduates. As books were not easily obtainable such volumes as the library possessed were chained to the desk in which they were kept. Fellows or teachers were able to borrow such books to read in their own rooms, although they were usually very large and heavy to carry. Other books were retained in a chest for sole distribution to fellows.[38]

A university student during Skirlaw's time needed cash to spend on items such as rent, personal items, travelling, clothing, lecture fees, books, and contributions towards food and cooking. He would also have to give sums from time to time to the beadle of his faculty to contribute towards such events as special feasts and gaudies. The estimated breakdown of expenses for one student for one term noted in 1424 by the principal of his own college included the following:

Commons (share of college food)	6s	3¾d
Battels (college board and provisions)		5¼d
Gaudy (college feasts)	1s	0d
Lecture	1s	8d
Manciple (catering staff) and cook	1s	0d
Barber		1d
Laundress		1d
Shoes		7d
Shirt		8d
Belt		1d
Candles		1d
Clogs		4d
Book		6d
Journey home	1s	8d

His total expenses for the year were reckoned to be £3. 13s. 4d. Some students were known to live on as little as £2. 10s. per annum.[39]

Skirlaw was described as a 'sizar' by one authority, which indicates that he was a poor student who would receive an allowance from his college to enable him to study.[40] This allowance may have taken the form of a reduction in tuition fees, and he may have also acted as a servant to the college.[41] A 'loan-chest' system was also operated by the University, which provided students with credit facilities, which could give welcome temporary support to them. Without such facilities some students who fell into debt would not have been able to continue their studies.[42] In 1360 William Selton, canon of Wells, bequeathed 100 marks[43] to the University, to assist members who had financial problems. This became the *Selton and University Chest*. The borrowing limits were: heads of halls sixty shillings; masters, if studying, forty shillings; bachelors, if studying, two marks; and scholars, one mark. Other similar bequests followed.[44]

Because of the dearth of appropriate texts for the course, Skirlaw and other students would need to rely on lectures given by teaching or regent masters of the college. For students to meet for these lectures, the master hired a room in the town or in a hall of residence. The teachers or regent masters of undergraduates were often graduates who were continuing their studies towards a master's degree or doctorate. Such teaching was built in as part of the master's degree course. It was also found to be cheap way of running undergraduate courses as the student paid his fees, but the teaching cost nothing. Every student had to enrol with a master who maintained an attendance register.[45]

Skirlaw, as an undergraduate, would follow a daily routine starting between five and six o'clock in the morning. He would attend an early mass and then join lectures until ten or eleven o'clock when the bell rang for dinner. Grace was said before and after the meal, usually by the first student to arrive at the table. Students brought their own cutlery and plate, but the table cloth and other utensils were provided. During the meal a passage was read from some learned tract. After dinner there was time for exercise before the next lecture or disputation. Alternatively students may have participated in 'repetitions', when they expounded on a previous lecture. Supper was at five o'clock, after which students were free to pursue recreations, which could include visits to the local taverns. Before bed at nine o'clock students congregated in the hall for a *collatium* or *biberium* (evening assembly, usually with a reading and night-cap).[46]

Skirlaw studied canon and civil law for a period of six years ending in 1358 when he graduated Bachelor of Civil Law (BCL).[47] It is probable that he was accepted as an undergraduate at either Balliol College, originally instituted as a house for poor students to study arts,[48] or Merton College, which produced some notable bishops and archbishops during the fourteenth century.[49] However, there are no records of his attendance at either. Balliol College is the more likely, as most of the college income in medieval times came from northern counties including Northumberland, Yorkshire and Lincolnshire, whereas other undergraduate colleges such as

Merton and Oriel drew the bulk of their income from more southern sources.[50] Also Skirlaw was commemorated in stained glass in Balliol College (see Chapter Twelve).[51]

During his early studies Skirlaw was appointed by Archbishop Thoresby to a series of posts at York. He was licensed by the pope as a notary in 1353 and a record of his notarial sign is preserved in the archbishop's register. Each clerk had his own individual sign, often in the shape of a cross, which was drawn in documents or contracts written by him to indicate their authenticity. In addition to the sign he also added his signature, and in the final clause of Latin documents, which the notary attested and authenticated with his signature, the *E* in the *ET EGO* was elaborate and individually recognisable to him. *(An example of Skirlaw's sign, E and signature is shown on Plate 1.)*[52] To become a proctor and notary a clerk would have to spend a period of up to seven years in articles to a senior proctor. Skirlaw's year of birth may well have been about 1330 if he took articles at sixteen for seven years.[53]

An example of his duties as a notary is to be found in the archiepiscopalian records at Durham. Skirlaw was Archbishop Thoresby's notary to a document of appropriation by the archbishop and papal legate, with the consent of the chapter of York, of the church of Hemingbrough, to the prior and convent of Durham. In consideration the priory and convent were to pay an annual pension of 100s of silver, 66s 8d to the archbishop and 33s 4d to the chapter of York. The document was witnessed and sealed in the archbishop's manor near Westminster.[54]

The archbishop appointed Skirlaw his domestic chaplain in 1354 and 1356, secretary in 1359 and proctor in 1361. During that year he funded Skirlaw to attend the papal Curia in Rome, describing him as 'our beloved clerk'.[55] Thoresby may have found him a place at Balliol in the same way as he did for other protégés such as John Waltham (nephew), William Ferriby (relative), John Wycliffe (the Lollard) and John Hugate. If Skirlaw was not a relative of Archbishop Thoresby, it is not clear how they became acquainted, but it may be that they had met when Skirlaw was still at

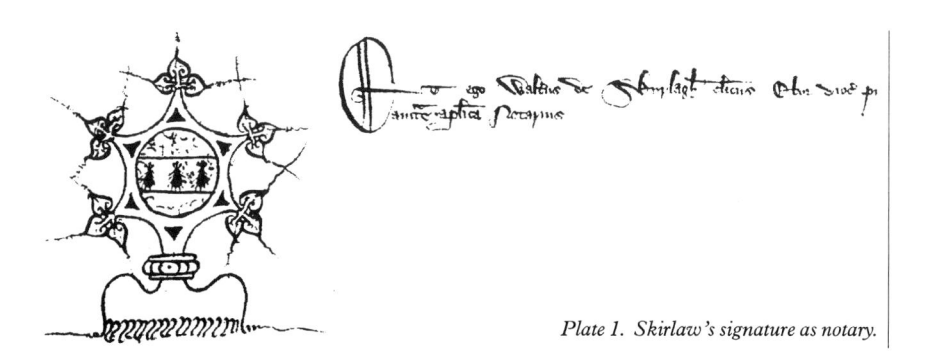

Plate 1. Skirlaw's signature as notary.

school (at Beverley Minster?), or at Swine Priory, and that Thoresby had encouraged him towards a career in the Church. Thoresby may also have offered some financial backing towards his higher education. Whatever the case, he became a member of Thoresby's inner circle of friends and associates, and was highly regarded by him. Thoresby, who died in 1373, was an Oxford graduate who served the government as keeper of the privy seal, went on diplomatic missions abroad, and later became archbishop of York. His career bore a marked resemblance to that which Skirlaw would follow.

If Skirlaw studied for his first degree at Oxford he may well have witnessed or have been personally involved in the riots that took place on St. Scholastica's Day, 10 February 1355. The account goes that two students, who were priests, engaged in a bitter argument with the landlord of the Swyndlestock Inn at Carfax. They finished by throwing a large pot of ale in the landlord's face, and then started to beat him up. The landlord's friends who witnessed the incident summoned the assistance of other Oxford people to get rid of the students by ringing St. Martin's bell. In retaliation the students rang St. Mary's bells to augment their numbers against the townspeople. The chancellor of the University went to the scene and tried to pacify the two sides, but was obliged to retreat without success. The following day, the town's mayor rode out to Woodstock to complain to Edward III about the students' behaviour. Meanwhile the townspeople and others attacked the students in Beaumont Fields, beating them up and killing several. A number of students fled to their halls only to find that the townspeople had set some of them on fire. Many students then retreated from the town. The bishop of Lincoln in due course used his powers to send the mayor and other colleagues to prison. On 27 June 1355 a new charter was drawn up which gave the chancellor greater powers; the townspeople were required to pay the University a substantial fine, as were the mayor and bailiffs who also were required to attend mass for the souls of the clerks slain in the riot every St. Scholastica's Day. This penance was only abolished in 1825.

On 9 February 1359 Skirlaw was granted a licence for further study for one year at the University of Oxford, where he took his Master's degree. According to one authority, Wood, he was then elected to one of the scholarships (fellowships) on the foundation of William of Durham to study Theology and Canon Law.[56]

It was William of Durham who founded the first Oxford college at Durham House,[57] for fellows from the Durham diocese (set up in 1286 and later extended by Bishop Hatfield to those of the York diocese[58]). Subsequently Durham House was named University College. William of Durham was a scholar of some standing who attended Paris University until 1229, when he left following a riot between clerks and townsmen, which resulted in the dispersal of the students.[59] He had been archdeacon of Caux, in Normandy, and of possibly Durham as well, and later in 1235 became archbishop-elect of Rouen. He died in 1249, and in his will bequeathed 310 marks to the University of Oxford for the purchase of property to provide income to be used to maintain ten or more students studying for Master's degrees in divinity.[60] Various properties were acquired in Oxford and further legacies were invested in additional premises to accommodate fellows of the College during the first half of the fourteenth century.[61] The College was not open to undergraduates at that time.

During the same period, one of University College's first benefactors bequeathed property situated in Holderness not far from Walter Skirlaw's birthplace. This was Philip Ingelberd of Beverley, who probably studied at Oxford between 1306 and 1311, obtaining an MA and a DTh.[62] Ingelberd became rector of Keyingham in Holderness in 1306, and remained there until his death nearly twenty years later. During this time he accumulated property including a mill in the Keyingham area together with some land at Paull, a few miles away, which it is thought originated with the family of William Pagula (Paull).[63] (William studied at Oxford around the same time as Philip, gaining degrees in canon and civil law and in theology, became vicar of Winkfield, Windsor, wrote a number of ecclesiastical texts, and died around 1350.[64]) The income from Philip's legacy was to support two scholars or masters from the area around Beverley or from Holderness. A number of scholars with names relating to this area certainly came to the College and would have taken advantage of the support provided by the income from Philip's legacy.[65] Walter Skirlaw may well have been among them.

There is no proof that Skirlaw attended University College, as student records are only available from the 1380s,[66] but evidence suggests that he did study there for his doctorate (see Chapter Twelve).[67] The first recorded Master of University College was Roger Aswardby, who held the position the in years 1361-1362, when it is likely that Skirlaw was a student. The names of Aswarby's successors as Master in the fourteenth century do not survive.[68] There were two faculties of law at the university, civil law and canon law, and it seems likely that Skirlaw studied in the faculty of canon law for his doctorate. The curricula of the two faculties and the opportunities open to those qualifying were very similar, although theology and canon law were considered the 'divine' or 'superior' sciences.[69] It was not until 1373 that Skirlaw became a Doctor of Canon Law (DCnL)[70] when he was around forty years of age. His ecclesiastical career had begun some sixteen years earlier when he was granted *letters dimissory (l.d.)*[71] to all holy orders on 13 January 1357.[72] Skirlaw studied longer than was usual for his degrees. It was normal then for scholars to take at least sixteen to eighteen years to acquire a doctorate[73]. Skirlaw appeared to take altogether around twenty-one years — six years for his BCL, and fifteen years for his MA, DTh and DCnL.

In medieval times a university qualification in canon or civil law was almost a prerequisite to a career in ecclesiastical administration. The English Crown too employed academic lawyers not only in its office of the privy seal but also in its diplomatic service which included involvement in negotiating and drafting truces and treaties. Almost half of the Oxford men appointed to the episcopate at Skirlaw's time were lawyers of one discipline or another.[74] In order to equip him in practical areas of administration, Skirlaw may also have taken classes at Oxford in *dictamen*, which was a course of accounting, letter-writing and basic legal drafting.[75] Thus Skirlaw was well placed for a career which in fact spanned both ecclesiastical and diplomatic roles.

Plate 2. Preston Bissett Church.

CHAPTER TWO:
SKIRLAW, THE RECTOR AND ARCHDEACON

The *letters dimissory* to all holy orders granted on 13 January 1357 provided the first stepping stone for Skirlaw to pursue a calling to the cloth, and gave him the bishop's authorisation to be a candidate for ordination.

Thus accepted as a suitable candidate Skirlaw was admitted as a clerk in holy orders and became rector of Preston Bissett in 1357. Skirlaw's appointment may have been made by the bishop of Lincoln or by the patron of the benefice (then the head of the Greynsby family[76]), subject to the influence of the papal provisions of right of appointment. The University of Oxford might also have submitted a list of suitable candidates to the appointers, and the influence of archbishop Thoresby at the University of Oxford should not be forgotten. Subsequently Skirlaw was ordained acolyte and sub-deacon by *letters dimissory* on 17 March 1358, and as deacon on 22 December. Skirlaw served as rector of Preston Bissett for four years.

Preston Bissett lies in a parish of some 1,520 acres watered by a tributary of the Great Ouse, as it meanders its way to the Wash at King's Lynn. The village is situated in the north of the parish, while towards the south-east lies the hamlet of Cowley.[77] The parish is about four miles south-west of Buckingham, which was within the diocese of Lincoln until 1837, when Buckinghamshire became part of the diocese of Oxford.

The church of Preston Bissett, dedicated to St. John the Baptist *(Plate 2)*, is situated in an elevated position in the centre of the picturesque village on a site where there has been a place of worship for 900 years. The nave, chancel and tower of the present building were started in 1310. The aisles and clerestory were added together with a large east window in the chancel in 1350, some eight years before Skirlaw arrived. Further alterations to the structure took place during the nineteenth century although the essential characteristics of the medieval church remain today.[78] The walls of the aisles were of an unusual construction, built on the interior so that they actually lean outwards in 'ark-like' form. Skirlaw's name is included in a list of rectors spanning the period from 1259 to the present day in a framed plaque on the west wall inside the church near the south entrance *(Plate 3)*. Apart from this church, the rector of Preston Bissett also had charge of a chapel at Cowley where services were held every week.[79] It is not known where the rectory was situated in Skirlaw's time, although it may have been in what is now a field known as 'Parson's Close', where the foundations of an ancient chapel can be seen.[80] Another possible site is on the land of the present rectory built in 1840.

It is possible that Preston Bissett was chosen for Skirlaw's parish because it was a journey of only about twenty miles along the Roman road to Oxford. He could therefore continue his degree studies at Oxford

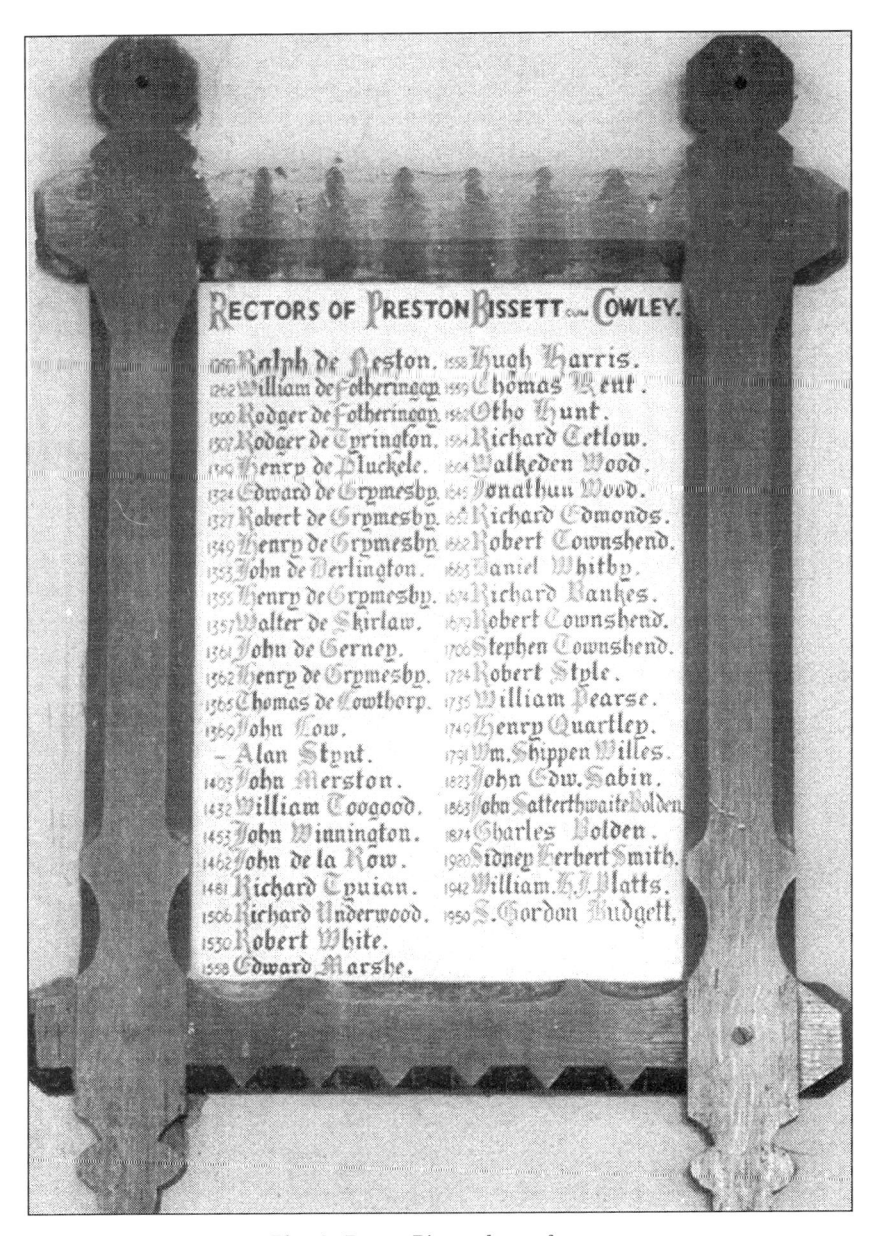

Plate 3. Preston Bissett, plaque of rectors.

towards his BCL and afterwards his DCnL without too much inconvenience. However, Skirlaw may also have had papal permission to reside at the University itself for some of the time, as was the case with other similar appointments. Wherever he lived, during his various absences from the parish Skirlaw would need to hire a substitute (at a lower salary) for many of the parochial duties.[81] Apart from his mission to the Curia, it is not known how much time Skirlaw actually spent at Preston Bissett.

Skirlaw's income from the living would depend on the tithes, land and oblations which brought in revenue, and the amounts he would need to pay out to substitute clergy during his absences from the parish. The tithes levied for his support would amount to one-tenth of the grain harvest and also one-tenth of other products such as animals and fruit.[82]

In early 1359, the archbishop of York, John Thoresby, sent Skirlaw on a mission to the Curia at Avignon, where he stayed for about a year dealing with matters concerning the archbishop.[83] Thoresby recognised Skirlaw as a man of outstanding ability, as a trusted administrator and lawyer, and as someone who was destined for higher office. On 30 November 1359, before he arrived back from Avignon, Skirlaw was appointed archdeacon of the East Riding of Yorkshire,[84] by papal provision at the request of Thoresby, and so resigned his position at Preston Bissett. He had still not completed his doctorate at Oxford. He was admitted as archdeacon on 21 January 1360, taking over from William Walcote, who had held the position from 1352.[85] Skirlaw was sent by Thoresby on further missions to the Curia after he became archdeacon, between 1360 and 1363.[86]

His new position ranked him just below the archbishop and carried with it an administrative post as assistant to the prelate. In Skirlaw's case Thoresby described him as his secretary. An archdeacon was called the 'archbishop's eyes'; he carried out the archbishop's duties under his authority, and represented the backbone of the diocesan administration. In accordance with the position of archdeacon, Skirlaw became a canon of York with the expectation of a prebend[87] in 1362, and on 30 November 1370 he was appointed canon of York and prebendary of Fenton, a parish some fifteen miles south of York. An appointment with a prebend entitled a canon to an income from the named parish, often as a proportion of land or tithe. Such positions were much sought after by the clergy. As prebendary, Skirlaw was the rector of Fenton but without any duty to his parishioners, and therefore the cure of souls was delegated to a vicar. Skirlaw's duty lay with the greater Church as canon of York Minster, where he had a stall in the choir and was a member of the chapter. At York the institution of prebendal vicars lay with the dean and chapter as ordinaries within their peculiar jurisdiction.[88] Skirlaw also contributed towards the cost of rebuilding the choir of York Minster in 1370 (see Chapter Nine).

Skirlaw was given a house in Beverley, and certainly spent time there. On 19 September 1380, he set off from Beverley on a diplomatic mission to the Marches of Scotland with John of Gaunt, whom he met at York, returning to his house in Beverley 'late' on 10 November.[89]

Skirlaw's main duty as archdeacon was to supervise the churches in his area of the diocese. His ordinary right was the duty of holding yearly visitations in the archdeaconry, which were in theory superseded every third year by episcopal visitations. Skirlaw may not have been very popular with parishioners for bringing men and women before the church courts for various offences, where he would act as the judge. It is said that the summoners of some archdeacons and their officers were less concerned about the repentance of a sinner than the fees they might collect. Archdeacons often had a bad reputation and their practices were seen as corrupt. Their power over all ranks of people was such that they were feared greatly. They often used the weapon of excommunication with great effect. If the offender failed to submit within forty days, the archdeacon could have his bishop, or in Skirlaw's case the archbishop of York, issue a 'significance of excommunication' to the chancellor, which could be followed by imprisonment. Newcourt's description of an archdeacon in the fourteenth century was that he was 'bound yearly to visit all his archdeaconry throughout; there to inquire into all crimes and misgovernment of the people, as well the clergy as the laity, by churchwardens and others; and to reform whatsoever they found otherwise than well, either committed heinously against the laws of God, or the ordinance of the Prince for a quiet common-weal,[90] dissonant to God's laws, Man's laws, and the politick order of the World; or by pains and penalties, according to humility and humble subjection of the offender, and repentance of his offense.'[91]

Chaucer's Friar had these words to say on the powers of an archdeacon:

An archdeacon dide execucioun	*An archdeacon did execution*
In punysshynge of fornicacioun,	*In punishing of fornication,*
Of wicchecrafte, and eek of bawderye,	*Of witchcraft, and also of bawdry,*
Of diffamacioun, and avowtrye,	*Of defamation, and avowry,*
Of chirche reves, and of testamentz,	*Of church reeves, and of testaments,*
Of contracts, and lakkeof sacramentz,	*Of contracts, and lack of sacraments,*
Of usure, and of symonye also.	*Of usury, and of simony also.*

Chaucer also gave this description of the summoner:

Of cursyng oghte ech gilty man him drede,	*Of cursing ought each guilty man him dread,*
For curs wol slee right as assoillyng savith,	*For curse would slay right as assoiling[92] saveth,*
And also war hym of a *Significavit*.[93]	*And also award him of a Significavit.*[94]

Of course, Chaucer's view of the archdeacon's summoner as a repulsive and unscrupulous man may be extreme and much would depend on the attitude of the archdeacon towards his duties. Many archdeacons, like Skirlaw, were learned men of integrity who endeavoured to fulfil their office to the best of their ability.

Other duties of the archdeacon included responsibility for holding deanery chapters for parish clergy once a month.[95] He would be responsible for inducting incumbents into benefices on receipt of episcopal mandates. Because Skirlaw was involved with other duties not only relating to the archbishop's administration but also to the government of the country, the duties of induction would often be taken by one of his deputies or the rural dean.[96]

Archidiaconal visitations became rare in Skirlaw's time, and formal procurations absolved the parishes of the archdeaconry from any expensive and unwelcome burden. Archdeacons often obtained papal indults authorising them to visit churches by deputy and receive procurations[97] up to a stated daily maximum. Even so there seems to be no evidence that visitations by deputies ever actually took place. However, the archdeacon appointed his own official, usually one of his parochial clergy, to collect the procurations and undertake that sinners when discovered were fined. Archdeacons who received payments in lieu of visitations were unlikely to take much interest in church fabric and maintenance, which was their responsibility. Consequently many churches ended up in a dilapidated state.[98]

There is some evidence that Skirlaw did perform the duties of an archdeacon from time to time. For instance, in October and December 1375, Skirlaw was involved in official business for the archbishop of York, Alexander Neville, at Cawood Castle, one of his residences, and was a witness to the appropriation of a church.[99] In April 1376 he was witness to the ordination of a vicarage[100] and in June 1377 Neville commissioned Skirlaw and John Waltham, canon of York Minster, to judge a dispute over a rectory.[101] Skirlaw was commissioned by Neville to carry out an exchange of benefices in March 1378.[102]

Again in 1382/83 a dispute arose between Robert Marrays (former rector of Huggate) and Thomas Etton (the current incumbent), concerning a breach of faith. William Marrays (abbot of St. Mary's, York) and Skirlaw were chosen by both parties to settle the affair. This concerned thirty marks owing out of a total sum of eighty marks previously awarded on Etton's institution to Huggate on 7 September 1375, by reason of exchange with Marrays of the church of Uldale in the diocese of Carlisle.[103]

Skirlaw, John Waltham and John Clifford were appointed by Neville in March 1379 to investigate the suitability of a Carthusian foundation proposed by Sir Michael de la Pole for a site in Kingston upon Hull and reported their findings in April.[104] In due course de la Pole was able to establish an hospital by letters patent, on 1 March 1383. The hospital was for 'thirteen poor men and thirteen poor women, feeble and old,' to be built on some of his land in Myton near Kingston upon Hull to be named 'God's House of Hull', or as it is presently called 'The Charter House'. A number of conditions were written into the endowment including that the master should be a priest aged at least thirty, who should live in the house and conduct daily services at which the residents should attend. The master's appointment should be made by Sir Michael de la Pole or his heirs or their appointees, or failing that the prior of the nearby Carthusian Priory of St. Michael (established by Sir William de la Pole, Michael's father), followed by the Mayor, then the archdeacon of the East Riding. Income for the hospital came from an endowment of land and properties.[105] The Charter House still exists today, although it has since been rebuilt in 1779/80.

As archdeacon and official[106] of the archbishop of York, Skirlaw represented Neville in Parliament as proctor in April 1379 and November 1380. He also represented the chapter at York in Parliament in January 1377, April 1379, January 1380, October 1380, September 1382 and November 1384.[107] Skirlaw was given similar appointments by Bishop Thomas Appleby of Carlisle in January 1379 and Bishop Houghton of St. David's in 1382. These duties gave Skirlaw valuable experience of the way Parliament was conducted, and brought him into contact with many of the country's leaders. On some occasions Skirlaw was accompanied by Richard Ravenser, John Waltham and others as proctors for the York chapter. The fact that Skirlaw also had a residence in London at that time was convenient when Parliament was held at Westminster.

Apart from the archdeacon of the East Riding, there were four other archdeacons in the York diocese, York (West Riding), Cleveland, Richmond and Nottingham. The East Riding archdeaconry, like the others, possessed a small peculiar jurisdiction of its own whose incumbency was annexed to the office. This consisted of the church of All Saints, Mappleton, in Holderness.[108] Skirlaw, as archdeacon, would have been involved as patron of Mappleton, with the institution of a new incumbent, Johs. Fitzpeter Sutton, in 1369.[109] The area of the archdeaconry was and still is very similar to the geographical area of the East Riding. In 1362, as well as becoming canon at York, Skirlaw was granted the canonry of Howden in the East Riding of Yorkshire by papal provision with the expectation of a prebend. This was granted in addition to the York appointment he already held.

His position as archdeacon came under serious threat from the Crown in 1364, when a royal writ was served on him, and proceedings were taken to deprive him of his appointment in favour of the queen's secretary. This was an example of the conflict which could take place from time to time between the king's wishes and those of the Church. Thoresby, who was instrumental in appointing Skirlaw to the archdeaconry, would not oppose the Crown in its action in the court and Skirlaw failed to appear, presumably because he would be likely to lose a case brought by the Crown. Fearing that Skirlaw would take his case to the papal court, a royal writ was issued to prohibit him from leaving the country, and so prevent him from taking his case to the Curia. Eventually, he was successfully smuggled out of the country, disguised as a servant in striped clothing, with the aid of a Peter Stapleton and other supporters. His income as archdeacon was sent abroad to him by another friend who was the prior of Drax, and this helped to finance his stay in Avignon. When the Crown became aware of his escape, he was outlawed from England, put outside the king's protection and his estate forfeited, and those who gave him assistance were also punished. During the six years of his absence, John Hermesthorp assumed the duties of archdeacon of the East Riding.[110]

During his exile at Avignon, Skirlaw sued in the papal courts and eventually succeeded in obtaining an inhibition forbidding the archbishop from admitting the queen's secretary to the archdeaconry. A notice to that effect was posted on the doors of York Minster. Skirlaw may also have continued studying for his doctorate using the facilities of the flourishing law school at Avignon University, and at the same time would have gained experience in the workings of the papal court. In 1370 he was allowed safe conduct to return to England and, pardoned of his outlawry, was able to resume his position as archdeacon.[111]

Avignon at the time of Skirlaw's visits was the centre of the Christian world with the Papal Court established there from 1305. During this period, the town's walls and other fortifications were in the course of reconstruction under the direction of Pope Innocent VI, but were not completed until 1376 during the reign of Gregory XI. They had previously been pulled down on the orders of the king of France in 1226, but it was later considered necessary to renew them to keep out plunderers and the Rhône floods. At the time of Skirlaw's exile the pope was Urban V, who was instrumental in beautifying the papal gardens, planting an adjacent orchard and in 1367 building the Roma, a pleasure gallery, which has since been destroyed. Where in Avignon Skirlaw resided during his six year's exile is not known. He may well have found lodgings in the town, where the houses were mainly owned by the papal administration, or in the surrounding villages. As a visitor Skirlaw may have been received by Pope Urban V in the Consistory Hall of the Old Palace. When his case came up before the Curia, it would be heard in the Great Audience Hall built by Jean de Louvre in the New Palace. This was the hall in which the Court of the Rota held its sessions. The judges sat at a round bench, where they assigned ecclesiastical benefices, heard hundreds of appeals, and corresponded throughout Europe, dealing with up to 8,000 letters and 10,000 petitions a year.[112]

In May 1374, Pope Gregory XI wrote to the archbishops of Canterbury and York and to King Edward III on the subject of the English Church and its ecclesiastics, in particular relating to certain rights of patronage, rights belonging to the king, and other rights the churches of the realm, about which the king had previously written to the pope. These were to be the subject of a meeting held at Bruges between the pope's ambassadors, the bishops of Pampeluna and Senigaglia, Giles Sancii Muuionis (the provost of Valencia), and the English representatives of the Church and realm. Therefore, on 4 May 1374, Pope Gregory XI wrote informing Archdeacon Skirlaw that he was sending his ambassadors as nuncios to meet him in Bruges.[113]

Skirlaw was given the duty of visiting the pope's palace at Avignon to collect the letters and convey them to the archbishops and king. In due course he also attended the meeting at Bruges with others, who may have included the new archbishop of York, Alexander Neville. Skirlaw was later involved in a further meeting with the pope's representatives in London relating to the same issues. Neville appointed Skirlaw his official of the court of York on 19 July 1374 and sent him to summon the clergy of the northern province, including abbots and priors, to a convocation at York. At the convocation which took place in September 1374,[114] Skirlaw conveyed to the clergy the matters discussed at the Bruges meeting, in particular relating to the rights and liberties of the English Church.[115] In October Skirlaw attended the conferring of the pallium[116] on Neville. In the same month he was also present at the submission of the late Archbishop Thoresby's executors in London.[117]

In 1375 Skirlaw and six others, including a Thomas Beverley, were commissioned to investigate information received by the king relating to defects in the king's hospital of St. Leonard, York.[118] Richard Ravenser was appointed master of the hospital in 1365, a post which he held until his death in 1386.[119] This institution, like other royal chapels and hospitals, was exempt and immune from all jurisdiction of the ordinary institution, and was the oldest and largest hospital in the north, originally endowed by King Athelstan in 936. The hospital cared for over two hundred people who were poor, sick, old and infirm. The defects at St. Leonard's concerned the possessions and income of the hospital, and the conduct of all its staff. The inquisition was to include a visitation of the hospital and an enquiry into the deficiencies of the staff, 'to correct defects and excesses, punish delinquents, restore all lands, rents and possessions withdrawn, concealed, dissipated, alienated and eloigned,[120] all liberties, immunities, exemptions and privileges lost, and all pensions and corrodies[121] sold and charges imposed, and do all things that concern the visitation of the hospital and the correction of the premises.'[122]

The results of the investigation are not known although presumably the appropriate action was taken to deal with any deficiencies. However, St. Leonard's, like many other hospitals, had certainly suffered a financial crisis precipitated by the Black Death. Following the large number of resulting deaths, the income from land had diminished dramatically. Also in the latter half of the fourteenth century, the economic situation saw agricultural depression and inflation combined with a high demand for labour and manufactured goods, reducing St. Leonard's income from its manors and the Petercorn,[123] a major source of revenue. At the same time the number of wealthy merchants in the area increased.

Several of the masters of the hospital in the late fourteenth and early fifteenth centuries including Ravenser, resorted to the sale of corrodies to these wealthy merchants and landowners. They took the form of agreements to maintain a person or couple in their old age or infirmity for the remainder of their lives in return for a cash payment or transfer of land. When Ravenser was master he was aware of the risks of selling corrodies. Actuarial calculations were inadequate and the hospital was plunged into deeper financial trouble, causing squabbling between masters and brothers. There were always suspicions that cash was finding its way into the wrong hands. Further problems arose because other sources of revenue had diminished, income was not sufficient to cover outgoings, and further funds were needed. Many of the hospital residents and others supported by it were poor and unable to contribute towards the benefits they received (referred to as cremetts[124]). The investments were not producing a sufficient return, and Richard Ravenser needed to improve methods of assessing the amount of capital required to produce sufficient regular funds to cover the keep of future beneficiaries.[125]

Skirlaw also was appointed canon of Beverley and prebendary of St. Andrew's altar in the collegiate church of St. John (now referred to as Beverley Minster) in 1376.[126] In the choir of the minster the prebendary of St. Andrew's altar sat at the eighteenth pew on the south side.[127] He would also have a seat in the chapter house, now no longer standing. Later that year Skirlaw entered the royal service and received the deanery of St. Martin-le-Grand in London. From this time Skirlaw's duties and diplomatic missions were centred on London, which became his main base. During his prolonged absences from the archdeaconry, Skirlaw would require a licence from the archbishop or the pope. Aymar Robert, for example, who was archdeacon from 1343 until his death in 1352, had been granted a licence of absence for five years during which period a deputy was appointed.[128] Skirlaw's years in London will be examined in the next chapter.

In February 1376, Skirlaw was a party to a transaction in which Richard Ravenser, canon of Beverley Minster and prebendary of St. Martin, agreed to exchange a plot of land next to his manse on the north side of the minster, measuring 108 feet by 48 feet, for another plot of land on the other side of his property, measuring 147 feet by 19 feet. The former would enhance the position of the manse and extend the garden, and the latter, being next to the road, could be developed into shops and houses which would in time provide income for the fabric of the church. The canons who represented the other party to the transaction were Richard Beverley, Richard Chesterfield, Richard Lynceford, Henry Snaith and Skirlaw. The transaction was witnessed by John Scarborough, clerk to the diocese of York and notary public, and approved by Archbishop Alexander Neville, at Cawood Castle.

In June 1376, Richard Ravenser, Robert Beverley and Skirlaw, as canons of Beverley Minster, paid 60s to the king for a licence for permission to transfer ownership of certain lands and rents in Beverley and North Burton (Burton Fleming), and for the reversion of a property in North Burton on the death of Alice Milner, to the chapter of the minster. The income was to be used to maintain the fabric of the minster, in particular the chantry of St. Michael recently founded there.[129]

A second licence was granted in July 1378 relating to St. Michael's altar, for the transfer to Richard Ravenser of two-thirds of the manor of Bentley, near Beverley, and the reversion on the death of Joan, the widow of Thomas of Bentley, knight, of the other one-third, the whole yearly value of the manor being £8. This licence set out that the chantry was to be for two chaplains to pray for the soul of Ravenser, the two queens, Isabella and Philippa, Edward III, and others, and was in part satisfaction of a licence issued by Edward III up to the value of £10.[130] Until its suppression in the late 1540's masses were still being recited for Ravenser's soul (and presumably the others) at the chantry.

Skirlaw was also party to an agreement to found a chantry at the altar of St. Michael at Beverley Minster in 1378.[131] In consequence a licence was granted in October 1380 to Richard Ravenser and Skirlaw costing 40s to celebrate divine service daily at the altar.[132]

In 1377, Beverley had a tax paying population of 2,663 adults (and an estimated 4,000 inhabitants in total[133]), which made it the eleventh largest town in England at that time, and therefore a place of great importance. It was a centre for the cloth and wool trade, and had an active trading community. The minster was considered a very important building, and in 1348 the archbishop of Canterbury had issued an edict urging people to contribute to the cost of building the church, offering relief from purgatory in return.

The town was still ruled by the traditional regime of twelve custodians, who were rich inhabitants such as Adam Coppendale, Thomas Beverley, John Gervays (the vintner), Thomas Gervays (the goldsmith), and John Ake (the draper and mercer). The town was also very much under the influence of the archbishopric of York and the canons of Beverley Minster. The archbishop was lord of the manor of Beverley, and owned a substantial amount of property in the area, including a manor house near the minster. Most other substantial English towns in the late fourteenth century were governed by a single alderman, two chamberlains, a recorder and a council of twenty-four.

Beverley Minster chapter, like the archbishop, possessed extensive land in the area, and its income was partly based on its agricultural rents and corn tithes. The minster's right to collect four thraves[134] of grain from each working plough in the East Riding is said to have been granted by King Athelstan in the tenth century. The minster also received income from those seeking sanctuary, as well as from the pilgrims who came in large numbers to the shrine of St. John of Beverley. The archbishop's close interest in Beverley and the minster was the cause of constant strife with the canons of Beverley, who did not want the archbishop as overlord. The only establishments in the diocese of York with higher incomes than Beverley were York Minster, Durham Cathedral Priory, St. Mary's Abbey, York, and the Cistercian abbeys of Fountains and Furness.

The minster was run by fifty-seven clergy comprising a provost, eight canons, nine vicars-choral, seven chantry chaplains, nine canons' clerks, one precentor's clerk, a clerk of the charnel, seven *berefellarii*,[135] two incense bearers, eight choristers, two sacrist's clerks, and two vergers or bell-ringers. The presidency of the chapter was usually taken by the senior canon.

The provost was the head of the collegiate church of Beverley Minster and was appointed to administer its lands and revenues. He owned lands in his own right by virtue of his position and maintained a household of servants. The post was very important and was usually given by the Crown in return for services rendered. The provost had no status in the chapter, and neither did three other officials of the minster (the chancellor, precentor, and sacrist or treasurer to the college) who were officers ranking below the canons. The provost lived in private apartments in the communal living accommodation in the bedern, which was situated in St. John's Street, Beverley. The canons moved out of the communal building to houses adjacent to the minster about the time Skirlaw became canon at Beverley. As archdeacon, Skirlaw was already living in a house given for that office.

Skirlaw and the other prebender canons were responsible for ensuring that the services ran smoothly, and that feast days and other special days were observed. Each was responsible for his own altar dedicated to a particular saint. A cluster of parishes was attached to each prebender canon. These canons were recruited from high levels of society and were not always resident. Vicars-choral were delegated to perform their tasks during their absences, each supported by a clerk. Skirlaw's vicar-choral in 1381 was Henry Beswick. Prebends awarded to canons were quite substantial and amounted to an average of £40 a year, which in present-day figures would be in the region of £16,000, while the provost received around £110 a year (£45,000 in current terms).

In 1381, whilst Skirlaw was archdeacon of the East Riding of Yorkshire and canon of Beverley Minster, the town was in a state of turmoil. There was evidence of corruption in the town's government, and an ecclesiastical dispute arose between the archbishop of York and the canons of the minster. The provost, Master John Thoresby, had recently died.. He was the nephew of the late Archbishop Thoresby of York. It is known that the archbishop took a special interest in his nephew's career, and no doubt he had some influence in his appointment as provost in 1371.[136] The canons at the time were Richard Ravenser, who was deputy provost (St. Martin's Altar) and also related to Archbishop Thoresby; Richard Chesterfield (St. Peter's); Nicholas Louth (St. Katharine's); William Burstall (St.

Michael's); Richard Thearne (St. Stephen's); Walter Skirlaw (St. Andrew's); John Wellingborough (St. Mary's), who was closely connected or possibly related to archbishop Thoresby;[137] and Henry Snaith (St. James'), who was followed by Hugh Ferriby on his death in February 1381. Ferriby was probably a member of the Ferriby family, also related to Archbishop Thoresby.[138]

Alexander Neville succeeded Thoresby as archbishop of York at the age of 42 in 1373. He was very unlike the highly professional administrators who had gone before him. He appears to have been arrogant, ambitious, of fiery disposition, and lacking application to detailed business. He announced on 26 February 1381 that he would make a formal visit to the canons and clergy of the minster 'for the recreation of your souls', on 26 March. When the notice was received by the Beverley clergy on 2 March, their reaction was that Neville was seeking to take over the jurisdiction of their affairs by exercising his deemed right to be the church's ninth canon. It had arrived only a few weeks after the death of the provost Master John Thoresby, and may have been a deliberate attempt to oust the Thoresby connection from the minster's valuable financial prizes. Robert Mansfield became the next provost.[139]

The chapter lodged an appeal with St. Paul's Cathedral in London on 20 March to confirm that the canons held full capitular justice over the business of their church. This did not stop Neville from visiting the minster on 26 March as intended. The canons of the minster were summoned by the archbishop to present themselves and their vicars before him. The custom (confirmed by the Apostolic See) was that the chapter and canons were free from all visitations, except for one visit by the archbishop of York in person during his time in office. The proposed visit by the archbishop was not his first, and an appeal against the visitation was also made to the pope. However, the archbishop insisted on visiting the minster and demanded the presence of various men and women who fell within the jurisdiction of the chapter. Those who failed to appear were excommunicated by him.

The archbishop then summoned the other members of the minster clergy who had failed to present themselves during mass at his visitation. The long list which was fixed on the stalls and called by the crier included: prebendaries Richard Ravenser (St. Martin's), Richard Chesterfield (St. Peter's), Nicholas Louth (St. Katharine's), William Birstall (St. Michael's), Henry Snaith (St. James), Richard Thorne (St. Stephen's), Master Walter Skirlaw (St. Andrew's), and John Wellingborough (St. Mary's), and their respective vicars, precentor Ralph Wallace, chancellor Robert Leconfield, sacrist Roger Ripon, the seven *berefellarii*, seven chantry priests, and twenty-one clerks of the second form. The only persons who presented themselves apart from the archbishop's staff were the precentor, one *berefellarius* and one chantry priest. The others who had been summoned were pronounced contumacious,[140] and the meeting was adjourned to a later date. When the vicars were asked why they had not appeared at the visitation, they replied that they dare not go against their masters' (the canons') wishes and in derision left the chapter house. The archbishop called them back, warned them of their disobedience, and ordered Richard Ravenser and John Wellingborough to be summoned personally together with all the canons and the statutes and ordinances they relied upon for their non-attendance.

Only two canons, Nicholas Louth and Richard Thorne, purged their contempt and acknowledged the archbishop's right to visit, but none of the vicars would do so. When the archbishop attended matins at Beverley Minster, the vicars were not in attendance and, in order to conduct the service properly, vicars from York were called in to sing. In due course the canons, Louth and Thorne (and Chesterfield, who later joined them), were warned to keep canonical residence and ensure the church was properly served so that it should not be defrauded of divine service. The absent canons, Ravenser, who led the rebellion, and Wellingborough, were similarly warned, and, because they failed to attend were sentenced to excommunication. The immediate result for Neville was to oust two of the (at least) four members of the Thoresby connection with Beverley Minster. Skirlaw escaped attention as he was abroad on king's business for most of the period. He played a rather passive role in the strike so cannot be seen to have taken up any active position against Neville. Skirlaw continued to serve Neville during the rest of his time as archdeacon of the East Riding of Yorkshire. Hugh Ferriby did not take up his office as canon of St. James' altar until after the event and was therefore not involved in the dispute.

In due course, the matter of excommunication was presented in the king's court, and Richard II rebuked Neville for using persecution and armed force against the Beverley chapter. However, the archbishop would not accept the decision of a secular court in a spiritual matter. Neville considered himself the legal as well as the spiritual heir of St. John of Beverley. Beverley Minster was not a royal foundation, but a creation of the Blessed Bishop John of York who was later known as St. John of Beverley.

As a result of their struggle with Neville, the canons who were excommunicated were deprived of their prebends, which meant they lost of a small amount of income as they had sources from other institutions. For the vicars choral including Skirlaw's vicar, Henry Beswick,[141] the loss of income meant the loss of their livelihood itself. Ravenser came to their rescue, however, and until his death in 1386 maintained them at Lincoln, where he was the archdeacon.[142] He had taken a prominent part in the quarrel between Archbishop Neville and the chapter of Beverley, and his residence at Lincoln became a 'cave of Adullam'[143] for the excommunicated clergy of Beverley.[144] Henry Beswick was reinstated at Beverley in 1388.[145]

Neville was concerned that the lion's share of the exceptional wealth of Beverley Minster was being siphoned towards a small group of usually absentee possessioners,[146] and felt that a greater share of its wealth should come to York. However, the Beverley canons did plough back a considerable amount of their personal fortunes into the adornment of Beverley Minster itself, and Skirlaw and Richard Ravenser had endowed lands to the minster in 1380. There had been friction and rivalry between Beverley and York for many years, and this incident did nothing to improve relations between the two institutions.

In view of the strength of the Beverley canons' opposition to the attack of 1381, Neville formed a political alliance with Sir Michael de la Pole, which proved ill-fated when de la Pole fell from grace in 1386. In the previous year, when Skirlaw had been elevated to the bishopric of Lichfield and Coventry, Neville had selected John de la Pole, younger son of Sir Michael de la Pole, who was only twelve years old at the time, to take over the Beverley prebend of St. Andrew's.[147] His appointment brought considerable discredit to his father and Archbishop Neville.

On 3 February 1381, Skirlaw and Richard Chesterfield were appointed the executors of Henry Snaith, the Beverley Minster canon who was also a king's clerk and canon of St. Paul's, Lincoln and Howden, and who died that same month before the visitation of Neville.[148] It is interesting, that in his will he gave £10 towards the chapter house at Howden, which Skirlaw built some twenty years later, after he became bishop of Durham (see Chapter Nine).[149]

In 1381, Skirlaw became archdeacon of Northampton,[150] taking over from Henry Piel on 8 May. He also became treasurer of Lincoln[151] in that year, in addition to the other appointments already mentioned, and others he had acquired whilst dean of St. Martin-le-Grand. Skirlaw exchanged his treasurership with Peter Dalton on 22 March 1383 for a prebend in the church of St. Martin-le-Grand, London (see Chapter Three).[152] One authority questions Skirlaw's appointment as archdeacon of Northampton — did he really hold two such appointments at once?[153]

Only one record relates to Skirlaw's position as archdeacon of Northampton, authorising him as archdeacon of Northampton and commissary of John, bishop of Lincoln, to arrange for an exchange of benefices between Thomas Badby, dean of the king's free chapel of Shrewsbury in the diocese of Coventry and Lichfield, and Richard Bromley, parson of the church of Ashby Folville in the diocese of Lincoln.[154] In February 1383, Skirlaw, as treasurer of Lincoln, was appointed proctor in parliament for bishop Buckingham, along with Richard Ravenser as archdeacon of Lincoln. In May 1385 Ravenser, a great friend and colleague of Skirlaw's, drew up his will to include a legacy to Skirlaw in the form of a book of chronicles.[155]

When Skirlaw became bishop-elect of Coventry and Lichfield in December 1385, his position as archdeacon of the East Riding of Yorkshire was taken over by William Waltham, a descendant of the Thoresby family.[156] Skirlaw, who was now in his early fifties, had served an eventful twenty-six years as archdeacon.

CHAPTER THREE
SKIRLAW IN THE KING'S SERVICE

While continuing his duties as archdeacon of the East Riding, Skirlaw was called to London by Edward III to take on royal duties which could lead to high-ranking positions in the government and Church, a call he could not refuse. It seems that Skirlaw entered royal service as a king's clerk on (or before) 5 October 1376. Soon afterwards, on 27 November 1376, he received the deanery of the king's free chapel of St. Martin-le-Grand, a collegiate church within the city walls of London, not far from St. Paul's Cathedral.[157] It was usual for these two prominent appointments to go hand in hand.

He was no doubt an ideal candidate because of his qualification as a doctor of laws, his practical experience as archdeacon, and his understanding of the papal courts. During his travels at home and in France, Skirlaw had met many high-ranking people with whom the government might wish to do business. It is likely that the archbishops of York, Thoresby (who had government experience as chancellor between1349 and 1356) and later Neville, would have mentioned Skirlaw's outstanding abilities to the king. This method of recruitment by recommendation, sometimes by magnates and bishops but often by kinsmen and neighbours, was normal in the Middle Ages and appeared to work well. In fact many of the royal clerks during this period were from the York diocese or north Lincolnshire and were recommended by Thoresby.[158]

The chapel of St. Martin-le-Grand can be traced back to 1068 when William the Conqueror confirmed a grant of lands made by one Ingelric to the church of St. Martin, which he and his brother Girard had built at their own cost as a foundation for secular canons.[159] During the reign of Henry I, the chapel was established as a royal free chapel, which conferred freedom from the authority of the pope and the bishop of London. Instead, authority was held by the king who usually had the support of the pope, and any attack on the privileges of the chapel was deemed to be an attack on the royal dignity. As a collegiate church its status was similar to that of a cathedral, with an endowed chapter of canons and prebendaries, but without a bishop. The dean received his stall in the choir and his place in the chapter by the royal hand only.[160] Records of staff at the college during Skirlaw's time showed a canon, seventeen vicars, a sacrist, and a clerk. The college held a number of lands, manors and prebends including Good Easter, Maldon, Newport, Chrishall and Witham.[161]

The college ran a grammar school which Geoffrey Chaucer, the author of *Canterbury Tales*, may have attended in the 1350's.[162] In all probability Skirlaw would have known Chaucer in later years, and worked with him when they both served the king and country in similar roles as king's clerk and diplomat. Because St. Martin's was exempt from the ordinary ecclesiastical jurisdiction and at the same time was situated in London, it developed a peculiarly close attachment to the royal household. It thus became a centre of administrative and judicial business, a corporation of officials rather than a religious house.[163] St. Martin-le-Grand also acted as a court of error or appeal, and dealt with other matters which were heard by the king's justices, in particular relating to erroneous judgements in the City of London courts.[164] When Skirlaw became dean, the king's justices were Robert Bealknape and Roger Fulthorpe. In one instance, on hearing a case relating to a dispute between the prior of the hospital of Jerusalem and Bishop Houghton of St. David's, they quashed the previous proceedings in the husting, the highest court in the City of London.[165] This church also rang the curfew by which fires had to be covered or extinguished by a fixed hour in the evening in medieval London.[166]

The church was situated in Aldersgate ward in St. Martin's Lane (now named St. Martin-le-Grand, EC1) and was originally established on the east side of the street, though according to one map the college property eventually extended to the west side as well.[167] Among the many traders, craftsmen and merchants, the saddlers' fraternity flourished in an area round the church. There were merchants handling imported leather and linen and then selling the finished product. There were joiners (fusters), who fashioned the wooden quarters and saddle trees, lorimers in iron and copper producing the ornate bits and bridles, and painters who resided in nearby Cripplegate Without adding decoration to the saddles.[168] St. Paul's Cathedral was only a short distance away. As a result of the Reformation, the collegiate church was surrendered to Henry VIII with the prebends going to the king's clerks, in particular of the king's wardrobe.[169] In 1548, in the reign of Edward VI, the college church was pulled down, a wine tavern and many 'highly prized' houses were built there and in the precinct, some of which were occupied by canons who had previously served the college.[170] The remains of the by then disreputable quarter that had developed were finally destroyed in the Great Fire of London in 1666.[171] The General Post Office was built on the site in 1829 but was later demolished in 1912 and replaced by more modern commercial buildings including Empire House (a block of offices on the east side of St. Martin-le-Grand), where a plaque has been placed commemorating the location of the former religious house *(Plate 4)*.[172]

For some considerable time before Skirlaw's appointment to St. Martin-le-Grand, the college had been falling into a state of disrepair. Deans were appointed for their legal and administrative skills. Their attention was reserved largely for their royal duties and their own personal interests. Peter de Savoy, who was recorded as dean in 1294, 1301 and 1308, spent most of his time abroad. A report in 1323 criticised the running of the college — staff were not serving the institution properly and books and ornaments were lacking — and the dean was dismissed. In 1331 the dean

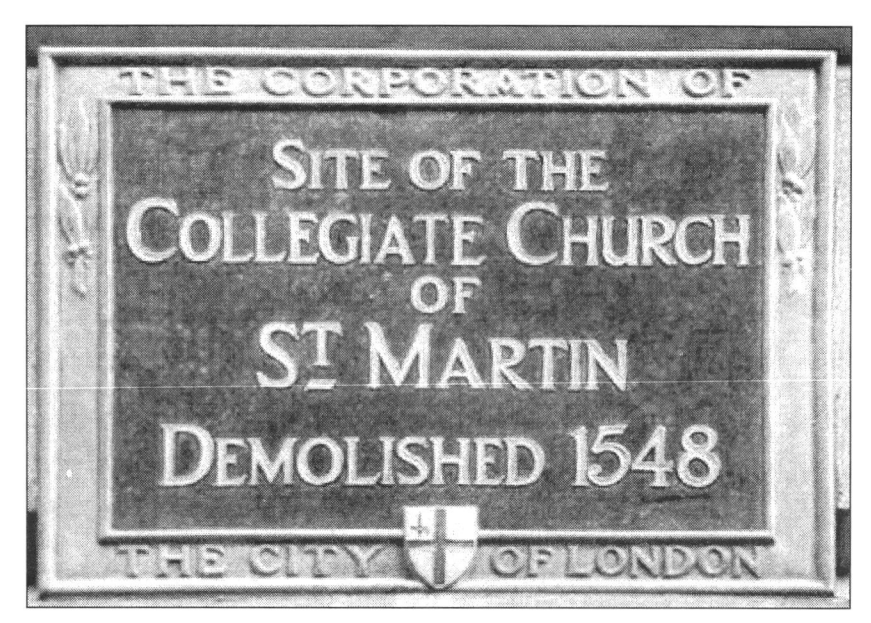

Plate 4. St. Martin-le-Grand, plaque.

and chapter complained that the air in the church and dwellings of the college was corrupted by the stench of dung-heaps raised by neighbours near the wall of the close. Another enquiry in 1343 showed further dilapidations to the college, while the Black Death in 1349 brought desolation and waste to its lands. Income was not sufficient to cover ordinary expenditure and urgent repairs could not take place.

The buildings were only saved through the generosity of the dean, William Wykeham, who restored the church and cloisters in 1360 and also built a beautiful chapter house. Some sixteen years later, Skirlaw followed William Moulsoe as dean at a time when the college was back on a relatively sound basis, although cash resources continued to be strained. He also benefited from the work done by William Wykeham.[173] On the death of William Moulsoe, another commission was instituted to investigate the reports of many defects in the chapel of St. Martin-le-Grand. They related to the books, vestments and ornaments of the chapel as well as to the properties of the deanery. The commission also investigated whether enough money was available to make good these deficiencies, and if the chapel had any funds which could be allocated for these purposes. The commission was composed of the king's clerks, William Burstall, Richard Ravenser, John Freton and Nicholas Drayton.[174]

It was customary for king's clerks to occupy the town houses of bishops where they often carried out many of their duties. The bishops rented and provided board or lodgings for ministers and other high officials of the government. When John Fordham was keeper of the privy seal (1377-1381), he and other chancery clerks lived and worked in the house of the bishop of Lichfield at the east end of the Strand, near the church of St. Mary-le-Strand. Clerks also worked at Westminster, and Skirlaw may have stayed for some time in buildings erected in 1346 near Westminster Hall and Westminster Palace.[175] However, it is more likely that he used the dean's accommodation at St. Martin-le-Grand for a while. It is also evident that Skirlaw, during his stay in London, rented the house (or inn) of the bishop of Bath and Wells in the parish of St. Clement Danes near Temple Bar. The house was located in the area of Surrey Street, Norfolk Street and Arundel Street between the Strand and Temple Place.[176]

In late September 1376 Edward III contracted a serious illness which lasted over four months, and because of his failing health he drew up a will. On the 7 October 1376, soon after being appointed king's clerk, Skirlaw was summoned to the royal manor at Havering-atte-Bower in Essex and, in the presence of the king, witnessed the signing of his will. The other witnesses were Sir John Burley, Sir Richard Storey, Sir Philip Vache, William Street (controller of the wardrobe), and John Beverley and John Salisbury (esquires of the chamber). The archbishops of Canterbury and York, who were named as supervisors, were also likely to be present.[177] The following day Skirlaw together with John of Gaunt, duke of Lancaster, the bishops of Lincoln and Worcester, Sir Roger Beauchamp (chamberlain), Sir Robert Ashton (treasurer[178]) and Nicholas Carew (keeper of the privy seal) witnessed the submission of a petition by the king to the chancellor John Knyvet, for the pardon of William Latimer. He had been impeached by the Commons as a bad adviser and appropriator of funds, but had since returned to favour on payment of fines to the king.[179]

Edward III died at his manor at Richmond (Surrey) on 21 June 1377.[180] Worn down from war, business and pleasure, the king also appears to have suffered from senile dementia towards the end of his life. He had been king for over 50 years, but the triumphs of the earlier part of his reign with his resounding victories against the French in the Hundred Years War at Crécy and Poitiers and elsewhere had long since faded. By the end of his reign the lands gained in France had been almost all retaken by the enemy. By 1375 only the town of Calais and its marches and the Gascon coastal strip south of Bordeaux were left. Only the initiative of Pope Gregory XI and the brokering of a truce in 1375 prevented the French from inflicting further humiliations on the English. Towards the end of his life, Edward's friends and supporters had deserted him and he died a broken man.

It may have been around the time that Skirlaw witnessed Edward's will, that he was also witness to a declaration by the king on the succession. His eldest son, the Black Prince, the victor at Crécy and Poitiers, had died the year before and the declaration stipulated that Richard, son of the Black Prince, should become heir to the throne, thereby preventing other possible claims. The charter, which appears to be in draft form, is somewhat incomplete due to a fire at Ashburnham House, where it was stored in the Cotton Library in 1731. The names of some of the witnesses and much of the wording of the charter have been burnt away.[181] Richard was only ten years old when he became king.

As king's clerk and dean of St. Martin-le-Grand, Skirlaw appears several times in the Calendar of Patent Rolls. For example, pardon was granted to William, son of Stephen Withernwick, for the death of Richard Grunset whom he killed in self-defence, and for breaking out of prison at Kingston upon Hull, at the supplication of Skirlaw.[182] He also obtained a pardon for William Batchelor for the death of John, the son of John Gardiner. In November 1376 Skirlaw, together with the archbishop of Dublin, the bishop of Worcester, Robert Bealknap and Nicholas Drayton, was commissioned by the king to visit the free chapel of St. Stephen, Westminster, of the king's foundation and patronage. They were to investigate and report on the many defects in the buildings, books, vestments and ornaments of the institution, and on shortcomings relating to the members themselves.[183]

In February 1377 Edward III appointed Skirlaw, together with the earls of Warwick and Suffolk and John Sheppey, to a commission on his behalf to decide an appeal on a matter of arbitration between Robert Knolles and Richard Wigan. A previous judgement had been made against Robert Knolles by Robert Ashton, without full information.[184] Two months later, the king appointed his son, Thomas of Woodstock, to hear the appeal instead of the original commission, as they were by then occupied with other matters required of them by the king.[185]

Meanwhile, on 6 March 1377, Skirlaw was promoted to chancery clerk dealing with diplomatic affairs, much of which were concerned with foreign negotiations (see Chapter Four). John Bouland was removed from the post under privy seal writ, and another writ granted Skirlaw forty marks a year to mark his promotion.[186] His appointment would be made by the king with advice from his chancellor, John Knyvet. Skirlaw's duties brought him into close contact with Edward III, and continued when Richard II came to the throne in 1377. The duties of the chancery clerk during Edward III's reign were many: negotiating loans for the king, supervising the supplying and fitting out of ships, the purchasing of provisions, and the export of wool; and arranging various subsidies for the government. As Skirlaw was appointed by the king, he would be the chancellor's deputy in charge of the departmental rolls.[187] He would also be in charge of the great seal whenever the chancellor was absent.

According to Wilkinson's analysis, the majority of chancery clerks during Edward III's reign came from the counties of Yorkshire (7), Lincolnshire (5), Lancashire (3), Nottingham (5) and Northumberland (3) under the influence of the House of Lancaster and of a closely connected group of northern lords. Political strife appears to have influenced the most important changes in the position of chancery clerk, in particular when they became receivers of petitions in Parliament. Wilkinson concludes that patronage and political influence affected the appointment and promotion of chancery clerks, and their position vis à vis the chancellor and members of the council. Richard Ravenser (archdeacon of Lincoln), who was still important and active in government, was among those who received petitions at the time Skirlaw became a chancery clerk.[188]

During the years before Richard II reached manhood, England was ruled by his uncle John of Gaunt, who, as regent, ran the country together with an appointed council for the boy king. Gaunt was unpopular with many people, including the businessmen of the City of London, the Church leaders and the commoners of Parliament. England in the 1370s and early 1380s was somewhat leaderless, overtaxed and still at war with France. It is against this background that Skirlaw's diplomatic skills were tested. Skirlaw gained a reputation as a loyal and trustworthy servant of the Crown. Soon after Richard II came to the throne, the work of chancery clerk became more specialised and more important and the number of assistant clerks under him doubled.[189]

The Crown had for many years taxed the clergy and Church property to help finance the war with France, in all but two instances basing the assessment on that used in the 1291 *Taxatio*. This had a number of drawbacks among them the exemptions granted from taxation, the exclusion from assessment of property given to the Church after 1291, and the exclusion of many unbeneficed clergy, who received their income from stipends rather than endowed property. In 1371 the government decided to experiment with a new poll tax imposed on both clergy and laity. One aim was to tax those clergy who had either been untaxed or undertaxed in relation to their incomes in the past. This tax was a failure, as there was widespread hostility towards it and many unbeneficed clergy avoided payment.

Pope Gregory XI, understanding the difficulties of payment of taxes arising from the effects of the Black Death, granted a special indulgence to those visiting the church at St. Martin-le-Grand on certain feast-days from 1372 for the next 20 years. Certain additional sources of funds were also given to the college, which helped to improve the cash flow.[190]

A graduated tax was introduced in 1377 where every beneficed person was to pay 1s, and any other cleric over fourteen years of age who was not a mendicant[191] was to pay 4d. The tax introduced in 1379 was more sophisticated with fifteen different rates applied to the clergy depending on their rank and income. The lists of the clergy of the City of London and their assessments for 1379 have survived. The tax was to be delivered in two equal amounts by 7 July and 8 September that year.[192]

Walter Skirlaw as dean of St. Martin-le-Grand was assessed on a property value and income figure of £333 6s 8d and was required to pay tax of £3. Most of the twelve canons listed were due to pay 5s tax, the thirteen vicars listed 2s each, and the four clerks 4d each. One of the canons listed was John Skirlaw (Skyrlowe), who was prebendary of Fauconers in Essex. Presumably this is the same John Skirlaw, a relative of Walter Skirlaw's, who was appointed to the chapel of St. Mary and Holy Angels at York and then to Ampleforth in North Yorkshire (see Appendix B).[193] Another tax was levied on the clergy of the southern province in 1380. This was to be paid at the rate of 16d in the mark, i.e. one-tenth of the value of benefices already assessed in 1291, and 16d in the mark on two-thirds of the value of benefices not assessed. Those clergy not in possession of a benefice were taxed at 2s each. The tax was to be levied on all persons including the exempt, the privileged and the members of the royal free chapels.[194]

The notorious poll tax of 1381, imposed by royal writ in September 1380, assessed many taxpayers at three times the rate of 1377 and 1379. It was agreed by Simon Sudbury (archbishop of Canterbury), the Convocation of clergy, and Sir Robert Hales (the king's treasurer), who together had determined the rates and were responsible for the scheme, that all clergy should be taxed without exception, at a normal rate of 6s 8d. The only concession was for the lower orders, who would be subject to a payment of 3s 4d. Skirlaw, as dean of St. Martin-le-Grand, was successful in exempting himself and the staff of the church and college from all tenths, fifteenths, or subsidies granted to the king; neither were they to be made collectors or taxers of the poll tax 'during his life'.[195] He argued that St. Martin's had insufficient funds to pay the tax, because its income had declined in the years since the Black Death. In 1383 the king then exempted Skirlaw's successor as dean, John Bacon, and the canons and staff of St. Martin-le-Grand from all similar taxes and subsidies during the thirty years to follow.[196]

The Statute of Labourers of 1351 had been introduced in an to attempt to return wages to the lower pre-Black Death levels after a shortage of agricultural workers had led to higher wages. The resulting depression of wages and the high rate of the 1381 poll tax was enough to spark off what became known as the Peasants' Revolt. During the rebellion, the palace of John of Gaunt was burnt down, the Tower of London surrendered, and Archbishop Simon Sudbury and the treasurer, Sir Robert Hales, were beheaded by the rebels. Foreign traders who operated in the City were hunted out by the mob, and, among those slaughtered were thirty-five Flemings who sought sanctuary in St. Martin-le-Grand.[197] At the same time, Londoners took the opportunity of settling old grudges by violent means. For example, Roger Legett (a questmonger[198]) was dragged out of the sanctuary of St. Martin-le-Grand to Goter Lane end in Cheapside and beheaded by a rebel contingent,[199] and his property burned. Some years previously he had obtained a pardon for placing 'hidden engines of iron' in Fikettesfield (Lincoln's Inn Fields) in order to maim the clerks of Chancery, the apprentices of the king's court and any others who came to play there.[200]

Wat Tyler, the leader of the Peasants' Revolt, and his followers succeeded in persuading the king to stop levying the tax, because it was not related to the incomes of the poorer classes. They also demanded an end to serfdom and feudalism, which the king agreed to at the time but later rescinded. Wat Tyler himself was stabbed to death by William Walworth, the lord mayor of London, but his cause was continued by his followers including John Ball, an English priest. Ball delivered a sermon from the text, 'When Adam delved and Eve span, who was then the gentleman?', with the object of inciting people against the ruling classes, and was later executed in Coventry for his deeds.

During Skirlaw's deanship, the right of sanctuary at St. Martin-le-Grand was much abused. Complaints were made to the king that employees were stealing goods from their employers and living on the proceeds, but no action was taken. Some set up shops in the precinct of the church and sold the goods under the protection of immunity. Many robbers, murderers and forgers found refuge there but could not be brought to justice. The church became well known as the chief sanctuary within the walls of London, and was crowded with criminals and debtors. William, one of the followers of Jack Cade and his rebellion against the tax regime, took refuge here in 1404. Only after incidents like these was action eventually taken to curtail the abuse.[201] Some twenty years later Anne Neville (a relative of archbishop Neville), who became wife of Richard III, was placed in the sanctuary away from his brother George, who objected strongly to the marriage. Neither of Richard's brothers could attempt to control her whilst she was confined there.[202]

From time to time the status of St. Martin-le-Grand was challenged by the bishop of London and others who sought to exercise power over it as they might over other institutions in the diocese. For instance, in 1354, a case brought against the royal free chapel by the Court of Canterbury was dismissed as it had no jurisdiction. Again, when Skirlaw was dean in 1381, the king claimed that the dean had from time immemorial exercised all ordinary jurisdiction within the Tower of London, that the bishop of London had exceeded his powers in placing the Tower under an interdict, debarring it from ecclesiastical functions and privileges.[203]

In 1381, Walter added the posts archdeacon of Northampton and treasurer of Lincoln to his other appointments, and on 8 August 1382 was promoted to the rank of keeper of the privy seal, an office he held until 23 October 1386. The department of the privy seal was based at Westminster and held a key position in the royal administration. It was the third great office of state, ranking after Chancery and the Exchequer. One of the clerks under Skirlaw in 1382 was John Danby, who acted as his personal assistant,[204] and was no doubt his kinsman. Danby had been nominated by signet letter of the king to the canonry of Bosham in the diocese of Chichester in 1379 (see Appendix A).[205]

The privy seal had a part to play in most aspects of government, for its warrants made their way into all offices and to the king's ministers, abroad as well as at home. Most of the letters sent out from Chancery were under the great seal, but all payments other than the regular fees and pensions made by the Exchequer, and all issues relating to money, arms, livery, and other articles from the various royal wardrobes and accounting offices, were authorised by warrants under the privy seal. The authority of the privy seal was widely recognised and respected, and the king's subjects responded to its directions to perform services of all kinds. The king often employed the privy seal, rather than the great seal, for informal diplomatic negotiations with foreign heads of state.

According to the clerk, Thomas Hoccleve, the activities of the privy seal included warrants and writs addressed to the chancellor and various officials of the Exchequer, and writs to all sorts of civil servants operating in the Household as well as elsewhere in the country and abroad. They included the treasurers of Calais, Chester, Wales, Ireland and Gascony, keepers of the wardrobe, mayors, sheriffs, justices, escheators, coroners, clerks of works, the constable and steward of England and 'seneschalx, recevours, fermers et auditors'. Some letters issued by the privy seal were devoted to letters patent and others dealt with the diplomatic correspondence of the king, although many could not be categorised and came under the heading of 'all estates' or were used for summoning councils.[206]

During the reign of Richard II, when Skirlaw was the keeper, the development and growth of the privy seal office had made it a target of critical interest. Opponents of the king tried to make it amenable to their control, while Richard, hampered in the exercise of his prerogative, tried to circumvent this by the wide use of his signet. It has been observed that these circumstances caused the privy seal to go 'out of court'.[207]

At the start of Skirlaw's period of office the signet had been of little importance, and was used only for minor purposes. But when John Bacon became the king's secretary (1381-85), and then Richard Medford (1385-88) there was a dramatic increase in the use of the signet among the chancery warrants. The explanation seems to be the growing officialisation of the privy seal under Skirlaw, and the fact that he was out of the country for long periods. The curialists therefore could exercise little control over the seal. Much of Skirlaw's time as keeper was occupied in conducting negotiations and drafting treaties with foreign countries, in particular France. The privy seal was applied to the documentation of such treaties and agreements. The seal was also applied to other domestic documents, contracts and letters of importance pertaining to the king and his council to signify the authority of the king.[208] The keeper could issue writs and had judicial matters referred to him by the king. Petitions of grace were subject to examination by the keeper, who also had the assistance of assessors in his deliberations.[209] Tout, in his *Administrative History*, shows an example of an impression made by Richard II's privy seal placed on a document in 1378, when Skirlaw was the keeper.[210]

Skirlaw, with his legal background, was in a position to exercise great influence within the government, not only by virtue of the widespread use of the privy seal, but also because of his role as a leading diplomat. The keeper was an *ex officio* member of the king's council, the executive body which, whether or not the king was in attendance, transacted the routine business of government.[211] He became very experienced in matters of the defence of the realm, and saw to it that sufficient funds were appropriated towards keeping the continental forces from invading England.

For a short period following his promotion, from 9 August until 29 September 1382, Skirlaw, together with Sir Hugh Segrave and John Waltham took on the responsibilities of the chancellor's office covering part of the period from the dismissal of Richard Scrope on 11 July, to the appointment of Robert Braybrooke (bishop of London and kinsman of Richard II's mother), on 9 September.[212]

In August 1382 Skirlaw, Robert Braybrooke, Sir Michael de la Pole, Sir John Montagu (steward of the household), John Shillingford and Ralph Tregregio went to hear and decide a suit brought before the constable and marshal of England by Sir Hugh Calveley against Roger Scales relating to a debt of 17,000 crowns.[213] In the same month Skirlaw's servant, Ralph Crust, was granted for life the office of controller of the customs and subsidies of wools, hides, and wool-fells[214] in the port of Kingston upon Hull.[215] Skirlaw was also noted as signatory and witness to a document of the abbey of Whitby with the archbishop of Canterbury, John of Gaunt and others at Westminster on 29 October 1382.[216]

Early in 1383, whilst Skirlaw was lodging at the house of the bishop of Bath and Wells, burglars stole his (Skirlaw's) silver plate including dishes, chargers, saucers, bowls, cups and plates to the value of 600 marks (around £160,000 in current terms). The king's council set up a commission in May 1383 headed by Sir Robert Ashton, with Thomas Saville, Walter Leicester and John Ellingham (sergeants at arms), to locate and arrest the offenders and bring them before the king and council.[217] In July the king issued a licence to Skirlaw authorising him to recover the stolen silver if he located it and treat with the thieves. The king authorised a grant of aid to Skirlaw for this purpose and some twelve months later the culprit was found.[218] William Lucy and three others were authorised to arrest, and deliver to the keeper of Marshalsea prison, William Bridport, who was indicted for breaking into Skirlaw's house and taking the silver.[219] The inn of the bishop of Bath and Wells was later acquired by the Earl of Arundel and renamed Arundel House,[220] hence the modern street name. Other inns (houses) owned by bishops were also situated in the area around the Strand. These include Durham House (in Durham House Place WC2), originally built about 1300 by Bishop Bek[221] and rebuilt by Bishop Hatfield, where Skirlaw resided when, as bishop of Durham, he visited Westminster.

After only six months as chancellor, Robert Braybrooke wished to be relieved of his office, and on Tuesday 10 March 1383 he delivered to the king, in the presence of William Courtenay (archbishop of Canterbury), and other prelates and lords present in the council chamber at Westminster, a bag under his seal which the king passed to the custody of John Waltham (keeper of the rolls of chancery) until provision was made for another chancellor. On the following Friday Skirlaw, Sir Hugh Segrave and Sir John Montagu witnessed the presentation of the bag containing the great seal, various charters, letters patent and writs by John Waltham to the king in the great hall of Westminster. The king then presented them to the newly-appointed chancellor, Sir Michael de la Pole, who had previously indicated he would accept the office.[222]

On 22 March 1383 Skirlaw relinquished his position as treasurer of Lincoln to Peter Dalton for a prebend in the church of St. Martin-le-Grand.[223] He also received the prebend of Gillingham in the diocese of Salisbury, in exchange for relinquishing the position of king's clerk to John Bacon on becoming keeper of the privy seal the previous year.[224] The mandate to induct Bacon as dean of St. Martin-le-Grand was issued on 20 June 1383.[225]

In April 1383 the king's council ordered that the fruits, rents and proventions[226] of the prebend of Erlington in the cathedral church of Chichester were not to be taken by the king, so long as Skirlaw was the king's clerk and the farmer (or steward). The prebendary, John de Bona Aura, had been classed as an alien and was therefore deprived of the revenues from the prebend. Skirlaw, as the farmer, attested that he was a man of truth and a friend to the king, and the council therefore decided that the prebendary was to receive the prebend, valued at £20 per year, instead of the king for as long as Skirlaw was farmer.[227]

In June 1383 Skirlaw, Sir Hugh Segrave (treasurer), Sir Simon Burley (under-chamberlain and Richard II's tutor) Sir Richard Abberbury (queen's chamberlain), Sir Robert Plessington, William Gunthorp, Richard Stokes and Laurence Allerthorp (barons of the Exchequer), and John Appleton and John Gosburn (auditors of the Exchequer) were commissioned to audit the account of the king's clerk, John Bacon, keeper of certain of the king's jewels and gold and silver vessels named in a certificate. This certificate was then sent for and produced before the king in chancery by John Hermersthorp (one of the chamberlains of the Exchequer) and William Sleeford (dean of the king's chapel of St. Stephen within the Palace of Westminster).[228]

On 22 September 1383, Sir Hugh Segrave, the king's treasurer, delivered a royal crown in a coffer to the mayor and people of the City of London as part security for the repayment of a loan of 4,000 marks. The indenture witnessing the delivery was sealed with the seals of Michael de la Pole (chancellor), and Walter Skirlaw. On 20 December 1383 letters patent under the privy seal were delivered acknowledging the return of the royal crown by the mayor.[229] A similar transaction involving Skirlaw and the privy seal took place on 26 June 1385, this time for £5,000, to be repaid the following Easter. The repayment was to be made out of the customs and subsidies on wool, leather, etc. in the Port of London, after deducting 20 shillings on every sack received for the defence of Calais. Again a royal crown was used as security.[230]

Skirlaw was appointed canon of St. Martin-le-Grand in 1384 and prebendary of Good Easter in the following year, as well as becoming canon of Lincoln and prebendary of Milton Ecclesia. Richard Renhold (Ronhale), the former warden of the King's Hall, Cambridge,[231] who like Skirlaw was a doctor of laws, had succeeded him as king's clerk on 8 October 1382.[232]

In January 1385 a special mandate was given to Skirlaw, the bishops of Winchester and Exeter, the earls of Arundel and Oxford, Sir Hugh Segrave, Sir Simon Burley and John Appleby (dean of St. Paul's, London) to hear and determine the cause of the appeal of Sir John Montagu in a suit before Matthew Gournay and John Molton (as constable and marshal of England respectively), between William Montagu (earl of Salisbury) and Sir John Montagu, and, if necessary, to annul and quash the original decision and proceedings in the court relating to them, and to inform the king of their decision.[233]

In June 1385 the king licensed Robert de Vere (earl of Oxford), to enfeoff (as trustees) Skirlaw and nine others of the castle of Hedingham (Essex) and twenty-one manors held in chief.[234] On 28 June 1385, provision was made by the pope for Skirlaw to be elevated to the bishopric of Coventry and Lichfield, taking over his position in January the following year. He continued as keeper of the privy seal until October 1386. In the meantime the pope on 18 August 1386 promoted Skirlaw to the see of Bath and Wells, and in the following November Richard II handed him the temporalities.

As described in Chapter Four, Richard entered Scotland on 6 August 1385 to face Franco-Scottish forces. At Hoselaw Loch near Sprouston (Roxburghshire) he halted his army and announced he was creating a number of new titles. His uncle, Edmund of Langley (John of Gaunt's younger brother, the earl of Cambridge and earl of Buckingham) became duke of York; another uncle, Thomas of Woodstock (John of Gaunt's youngest brother) became duke of Gloucester; Sir Michael de la Pole became earl of Suffolk, and Robert de Vere marquis of Dublin. These creations were witnessed by John of Gaunt who was leading the forces. In October 1385 Skirlaw pronounced an eloquent eulogy in Parliament explaining why Richard had made these awards which, he said, had been given for faithful service to the Crown. The real motive, however, was to appease Gaunt in the hope that it would lessen the possibility that he might try and usurp Richard's position as king. Also, Gaunt was an experienced campaigner in Scotland, who controlled most of the fighting men, and Richard, who was young and inexperienced in war, needed all the help he could muster.[235] Skirlaw was also witness to a charter making the king's favourite, Robert de Vere, duke of Ireland, which gave him vice-regal powers over that country in December 1385.[236]

In 1386 John of Gaunt, who had been at the centre of politics, set off on an expedition to Castile with an army to claim the throne by right of his wife, and did not return to England until 1389. He had left his son, Henry Bolingbroke, to look after his English estates. At this time a new aristocracy was rising in England replacing the feudal barons. It consisted of a few families all connected by blood with the throne, including the Lancasters, the Yorks, the Gloucesters, and the dukes of Cornwall and Clarence. A group of younger nobles led by Robert de Vere backed the court. The accumulation of household and government offices by the clique around the king and his effeminate favourite, de Vere, affronted the feudal party and to some extent the national spirit.

The period from 1386 to 1388 was a time of political crisis. The king and his court were at odds with the magnets and many bishops and other spiritual leaders withdrew from their involvement in secular politics. A few bishops, however, did become embroiled with one or another faction, and two lost their bishoprics as a consequence, while another was demoted. There was always pressure on churchmen at times of crisis to lend their support to one or other point of view. As members of the House of Lords, bishops were involved in debate and were expected to make their contribution. At the same time, some bishops were serving in great offices of state, whilst the archbishops held a special position in the council of the king. By 1388 the episcopate was facing a critical situation where certain bishops had become personally unacceptable to the ascendant political faction.[237]

One of the chief areas of contention was the past policies of the king relating to taxation. Although the magnates accepted that taxes had to be raised to finance the wars with France, there was considerable pressure in the Commons to reduce the burden on the laity, and therefore increase the imposition on the Church. The problem with this course of action was that if the magnates were to mount a *coup* against the government they needed to consider the reactions of the pope and the English Church. William Courtenay was not much involved in governmental affairs other than in steering the Church through the political problems of the day. In contrast, Alexander Neville, the archbishop of York, became one of the king's closest advisers during this period. In 1385, Neville had accompanied the king on his military expedition to Scotland, where they discovered they had many opinions in common. When Neville was appointed to a commission to supervise the king's government in 1386, he virtually deserted his diocese to that purpose.[238]

From the point of view of the barons, the announcement in October 1385 of the four new titles was a most unpopular act, and Skirlaw was immediately considered a zealous supporter of Richard II and the court. The so-called 'Wonderful Parliament' met on 1 October 1386 and Richard

II reluctantly attended. The chancellor, Sir Michael de la Pole, was clearly backing the policies of the Crown, which the magnates found totally unacceptable; the prime task of the session was therefore to remove the officers of state. These were the chancellor, Skirlaw (as keeper of the privy seal), John Fordham (bishop of Durham and treasurer from 17 January 1386, in succession to Sir Hugh Segrave). Some reports include two further officers, the steward of the household and the chamberlain.[239]

De la Pole was removed from office on 23 October 1386. He was accompanied by Bishop Fordham and by Skirlaw (who was by then bishop of Coventry and Lichfield). No recriminations were made against Fordham and Skirlaw and in fact Skirlaw's resignation as keeper of the privy seal had not been demanded by Parliament, although they were clearly too closely associated with the discredited regime.[240] The bishop of Ely, an enemy of the king, was made chancellor in place of de la Pole, and Parliament also substituted John Gilbert (bishop of Hereford) and John Waltham (keeper of the rolls) for Fordham and Skirlaw. De la Pole was only convicted on three of the seven charges made against him and these only on technicalities. Although he was sentenced to forfeiture of his estates and imprisonment in Windsor Castle, he only served a small period and most of his property was safeguarded. His brother Edmund and son Michael recovered most of the landed property, whilst he in due course escaped abroad.[241]

In order to supervise the government following the crisis a commission was established in November 1386, which included the archbishops of Canterbury and York and bishops Brantingham and Wykeham together with other officers. In due course the commissioners put pressure on the king to dismiss his personal friends from high office. Richard countered this by moving out of London to the West Midlands,[242] and sought to marshal his forces for civil war.[243]

The actions and policies of the Crown so incensed the magnates in November 1387 they took up arms against it. Thomas of Woodstock, the youngest and most ambitious brother of John of Gaunt, joined up with his friend Thomas Mowbray of Nottingham, young Henry Bolingbroke, and the earls of Arundel and Warwick, and marched on London. They called themselves the Lords Appellant and accused Richard's closest advisers of treason. One of the accused, de Vere, raised an army in Cheshire and marched to the king's rescue, but he did not get very far. Just before Christmas 1387 troops led by Gloucester and Bolingbroke scattered his army at Radcote Bridge in Oxfordshire. The Lords Appellant were now in command. The king's friends, including Burley, were executed. Some of the bishops and others on the commission endeavoured to mediate between the parties. However, the issue was decided in favour of the magnates and, when they returned to London after defeating de Vere, they set about restoring Parliament. Bishops Gilbert, Arundel and Wykeham, and the duke of York again acted as mediators between them and the Crown.[244]

The warrant of the original commission had expired on 31 December 1387, so a new committee was established by the Lords Appellant on 1 January 1388 'for the continuous government of the king' composed from among those appointed in 1386. Of the original episcopal representatives Wykeham (bishop of Winchester) was the only one who was willing to participate.[245] Skirlaw seems to have survived this crisis with his reputation intact. It appears that he was respected as an able and efficient administrator, and not seen as an active participant in the turmoil. He was appointed to the committee but only served for four months and was replaced by Braybrooke when the committee was reviewed. He had been appointed by papal decree as bishop of Durham on 3 April 1388 and he may have had matters to attend to in Bath and Wells before moving to the north. Also his diplomatic expertise was soon to be employed.

On 3 February 1388 the 'Merciless Parliament' met. All but four of the bishops attended, and the absentees, with the exception of Neville, sent proctors. Bishop Arundel read the cause of the summons concerning the trial of the king's friends and it was decided that their trial should be held by parliamentary form and not by court or common law. The bishops insisted that they were prevented from making judgements of blood and withdrew to the chapter house of Westminster Abbey. The Lords Appellant recognised the canonical obligations of the Lords Spiritual over and above their obligations as Lords in Parliament.[246]

The first act of the Cambridge Parliament of September 1388 was the translation of several bishops (see Chapter Five). Neville was condemned to the Scottish see of St. Andrews, which was in reality a nominal see outside the realm. Fordham was removed, as Tout says, 'from the fleshpots of Durham to the more meagre temporalities of Ely', and Arundel was promoted to York from Ely. Erghum was moved from Salisbury to Bath and Wells and Waltham, the keeper of the privy seal, was promoted to Salisbury. As a separate issue Rushook of Chichester, a supporter of the king, was condemned and exiled to the poor see of Kilmore in Ireland.[247]

It was not until Richard was twenty years of age that he set out to become the complete master of his council and to escape the control of his uncles and the Appellants. In January 1398 he decided to reassert his authority as king and ruler of the country. Arundel and some of his associates were declared traitors and executed following parliamentary sessions at London and Shrewsbury. Skirlaw obtained exemption from the session at Shrewsbury pleading ill health. This may have been genuine or it could have been political expediency.[248] Warwick was exiled to the Isle of Man. Gloucester was arrested and taken to Calais and there murdered by Richard's agents. When Henry Bolingbroke, Richard's cousin, quarrelled with Thomas Mowbray (duke of Norfolk), they decided to settle matters by a duel. However, Richard forbade this and exiled Mowbray for life and Bolingbroke for ten years. In February 1399 John of Gaunt died and, instead of letting Henry inherit his vast estates in England, Richard took them over.

During his nine years in London, Skirlaw spent long periods abroad as the envoy of Richard II with the object of negotiating peace with France and Flanders. He went on missions to try to negotiate a marriage between the king and Marie, daughter of Charles V of France, and to form an alliance with Brittany. In addition he negotiated with the king of the Romans, and German and Italian princes, and conferred at the Roman Curia about measures for combating heresy and for an alliance with the Holy See. Eventually he was successful in negotiating a contract for a marriage between Richard II and Anne, the daughter of Charles IV, the Holy Roman Emperor. Skirlaw's diplomatic missions are dealt with in more detail in Chapter Four.

CHAPTER FOUR
SKIRLAW, THE DIPLOMAT

The kings of England in medieval times were in frequent conflict with other states which threatened the peace of their territories, so an efficient diplomatic service was essential to negotiate on their behalf with the enemy. The Hundred Years War with France started in 1337, when the French king Philip VI confiscated the English-held duchy of Aquitaine. In retaliation Edward III claimed the French throne through his mother, who was sister of the late French king. The war lasted until 1453 and for twenty-five years Skirlaw was frequently appointed by the government to negotiate with the French and other nations on behalf of the king. These duties came on top of the other ecclesiastical and governmental appointments that he held and involved many months at a time out of the country.

Skirlaw's duties as a diplomat commenced in May 1377, soon after he had been appointed dean of St. Martin-le-Grand. As royal clerk to Edward III he was assigned to renegotiate the existing truce with France which was due to expire on 24 June 1377. This truce, negotiated at Bruges in 1375, was originally due to expire on 1 May 1377, but had been extended to 24 June by Charles V of France giving him more time to muster his forces at Harfleur for an attack on England. On that date, just three days after the death of Edward III, the Franco-Castilian fleet was launched against the south coast of England. It turned out to be a series of destructive raids. Skirlaw was away from England in May and June of 1377. He was accompanied by Sir Hugh Segrave, one of the executors of the Black Prince, who took over as steward of Richard II's household, and Sir Guichard d'Angle, who in his youth had served with the king of France, but had been captured at Poitiers and subsequently gave his allegiance to the English, becoming a close friend of the prince. Richard held him in affection and created him earl of Huntingdon at his coronation. Other envoys were Adam Houghton (bishop of St. David's) who was the new chancellor, John Gilbert, William Montagu (earl of Salisbury), Sir Robert Ashton, Sir Aubrey de Vere and John Sheppey.[249]

When he became king, Richard II was a very eligible bachelor and serious consideration was given to finding him a suitable bride, both for political purposes and to preserve the succession. Various possibilities were considered including a match with Marie, the daughter of Charles V of France, or the daughter of King Robert of Scotland. These proposals were received unenthusiastically in London. More seriously considered was a union with Catherine, the daughter of the Visconti Duke of Milan, and Lord Berkeley and his retinue, including Geoffrey Chaucer, were sent to Milan in May 1378 for possible negotiations. However, she became betrothed to the nephew of Duke Bernabo, and so the search continued.[250]

On 16 January 1378, the government gave Skirlaw power to embark on a diplomatic mission to Calais, still in English hands, to treat with the French and also to treat for a marriage between the Richard II and the daughter of the French king. He was accompanied by Sir Guichard d'Angle and Sir Hugh Segrave.[251] The French had been incensed by the collaboration of Charles the Bad (king of Navarre), a vassal of the king of France, with the English. In the spring of 1378 two of his envoys were arrested in France, and papers found on them were said to prove that he was plotting to poison the French king. The English offered to give the king of France military support, but only on the condition he ceded the port of Cherbourg. The departure of the English fleet was delayed, and by the time it arrived in Navarre, it was too late to give assistance. The port of Cherbourg was a valuable defence in shielding the south coast from attack.[252] Negotiations with the French towards peace between the countries made little progress and the marriage proposition appears to have been abandoned.

Skirlaw and his fellow envoys continued on to Flanders to treat with the count and cities of that state.[253] Flanders was England's most important trading partner. The greater part of the English wool clip was sent there every year to be made up into cloth, and much of it was sent back in the form of tapestries and luxury clothing. A regular supply of wool was vital to the economic well-being of both countries. If this was undermined the looms would come to a halt in Flanders, and the livelihood of the English exporters and growers would suffer. The problem for England was that the count of Flanders, Louis of Male, was a vassal of the king of France and looked to the French for protection and leadership, while the cities of Flanders looked to England because of their economic interests. Relationships between the cities of Ypres, Bruges and Ghent were also tense and the envoys' mission was to safeguard English exports and attempt to maintain cordial relationships as far as possible.[254] Skirlaw and the other envoys were away from London from 22 January until 31 May 1378.[255]

On 26 June Skirlaw was despatched to Rome on a royal deputation to offer England's good wishes to Pope Urban VI, who had replaced Pope Gregory XI following his death on 27 March 1378. This was at the beginning of the Great Schism, when England supported the election of Urban, and the French that of the 'antipope' Clement VII. The implications of the Schism to the English throne are discussed later in the chapter. Skirlaw returned to London in January 1379.[256]

The duke of Brittany, John IV, was another vassal of the king of France and lived in the shadow of his powerful neighbour. He sought to preserve his independence by playing the French king off against the king of England. When the Hundred Years War resumed in 1369 John's position became untenable. In 1372 he declared for Edward III and fled to England. The French moved to occupy the duchy and for the next six years Brest was the only town of any importance that held out against the French. In 1378 Charles of France announced that he was annexing the duchy of Brittany. The Bretons were so incensed by this that they invited Duke John to return. However, he was unable to do so unless he obtained funding from England. Unfortunately for him the treasury had no spare cash available. Funds had to be borrowed from individuals and corporations and eventually Parliament had to be recalled and money was then raised by a second poll tax. An agreement was then made with Duke John, promising him a force of two thousand men and as many archers for four and a half months to serve from 1 August 1379. The Duke crossed the channel and landed at St. Malo on 3 August.[257] Skirlaw was sent as an envoy to confirm the alliance with Duke John. The other envoys entrusted with arranging the alliance were the admirals Sir Thomas Percy (earl of Worcester) and Sir Hugh Calveley, and Sir Richard Abberbury.[258] Sir Richard was for a time one of the inner circle of Richard's household responsible for training him in his royal duties. He had fought under the Black Prince in Aquitaine and Castile.[259] The party travelled between Penryn in Cornwall and Brest and was away from 14 July, returning to England on 20 September.[260] The money raised in England from the poll tax was far less than projected, and the force had to be scaled down to 650 men and archers. When the force sailed from Plymouth in December it was caught in a terrible storm. Nineteen vessels transporting horses were wrecked in Mount's Bay off Cornwall and others were blown into the Irish Sea. None of the force reached the shores of Brittany. The House of Commons was furious at the fiasco which ended the careers of some notable members on the council of ministers.[261]

On 29 September 1379, nine days after returning from Brest, Skirlaw was sent from London as envoy to Calais, and then on to Picardy with William Montagu (earl of Salisbury), (John) Lord Cobham, Sir Robert Ashton, and Sir Hugh Segrave to treat with the French, returning to London on 12 November. The same party returned to France on 6 December 1379 to continue their negotiations for peace with the enemy, returning to London on 18 January 1380.[262] Their power to treat with the French had been given by the government on 26 September 1379 together with the power to grant safe conduct to the envoys of the French king during their visit to Calais.[263]

In 1380 Skirlaw again went to Calais to treat with the French government, leaving on 31 March and returning to London on 6 June. On this occasion Skirlaw was accompanied on his mission by Thomas Brinton (bishop of Rochester), and John Lord Cobham, together with Sir John Devereux (captain of Calais), these latter being members of the inner council running the country during Richard's minority. Also attending were Sir Robert Ashton and Sir Brian Stapleton (warden of Calais Castle). They were given powers to grant safe conduct for the French on 1 April 1380.[264]

Richard II was almost constantly at war with Scotland, although since 1369 there had been, in theory at least, a truce between the two countries. Although the Scottish king was prepared to accept peace, he had little control over his subjects. Border families on both sides were to blame for the many acts of aggression and plunder which took place over the years. In the summer of 1380, there was an unusually flagrant breach of the truce when men from Hull and Newcastle captured a Scottish ship with a valuable cargo. The Scots sought revenge by invading the northern counties of England, taking back with them prisoners and loot. In response Richard placed his uncle, John of Gaunt, as lieutenant of the Marches and head of the border commission on 6 September 1380, and four days later sent a letter from Westminster Palace to Richard Scrope (banneret), Thomas Ilderton (chivaler, chamberlain of Berwick), Walter Skirlaw (dean of St. Martin-le-Grand), and John Waltham (canon of York) concerning an assignment to negotiate with the Scots.[265] On this occasion Skirlaw travelled from Beverley, met John of Gaunt at York, and accompanied him to Bamburgh Castle. There they joined up with the others of John of Gaunt's retinue together with a large armed force of two thousand men. On entering the Scottish Marches for a preliminary meeting at Liliot Cross they were prepared for war, Scots but found the Scots in conciliatory spirit. The party then moved to Berwick for their March Day meeting with the Scottish Commissioners of king Robert II (the earl of Douglas, the bishop of Glasgow, and the chancellor), which took place around the end of October, when it was agreed to prolong the truce until 30 November 1381.[266] This mission lasted from 19 September to 10 November.[267]

The Church had been plunged into crisis in 1378 because of a double election to the Papacy. Pope Gregory XI died in April 1378, and two rival candidates were poised to succeed him, the Italian, Urban VI, and Clement VII from Geneva. Urban's backing came chiefly from the Italians, the English and the Germans. Clement's backing came from the French and their allies the Scots and the Castilians. The schism could not be settled until the larger dispute between England and France had been resolved. It took forty years before the Church in Europe was again united under a single pontiff. Urban's supporters were scattered over a large area of Europe and had little in common. It was essential to draw them into a firmer alliance, and Richard's search for a bride provided a means for doing this. To draw his supporters together and thereby consolidate his position, Urban and the Curial diplomats hatched a scheme for a match between Richard and a princess of the imperial house of Luxembourg, which would, as a result, deprive France of an ally.

Towards the end of September 1379, de la Pole and Burley, the two English envoys to Italy, left Rome for Germany to meet with Wenceslas, son of Charles IV (king of the Romans) and the legate. Favourable outcomes were reported to the council in London. They did not return to London until 20 May 1380, being detained *en route* by bandits and held to ransom. At a meeting of council a fortnight later, a decision was made to dispatch a new embassy to negotiate terms for a treaty of marriage. The envoys, Sir Simon Burley, Robert Braybrooke and Sir Bernard van Zetles (a Bohemian-born knight and friend of the Black Prince), left on 18 June for Bohemia where discussions proceeded smoothly. It was agreed that final negotiations should be opened early in the following year in Flanders, each side equipped with full powers to conclude an alliance.[268] During the period from 21 December 1380 to 4 February 1381 Sir Richard Hereford journeyed to Flanders concerning the proposed marriage of Richard II to a member of the royal family of Romania or Bohemia.[269] Skirlaw with Sir Simon Burley, Robert Braybrooke, Sir Hugh Segrave, Sir Richard Abberbury and John Gilbert, under the leadership of Thomas Holland (earl of Kent), followed Sir Richard Hereford on this mission to Flanders, meeting at Bruges with Wenceslas's envoys led by the duke of Teschen, and then went on to Brabant, starting out on 2 January 1381 and returning to London on 28 March.[270] Most of the details were settled during the negotiations and on 28 March, both parties came over to London when they were lavishly received by John of Gaunt, who dined with them at the Savoy Palace on 3 April. On 2 May, in the presence of the king and an assembly of prelates and magnates, the final treaty was sealed in a ceremony of sealing which was accompanied by a lavish distribution of annuities to the duke of Teschen and his fellow envoys.[271] One important result of the treaty was that the Holy Roman Emperor offered his sister Anne to Richard II.

A commission to treat with the pope about proceedings against schismatics and to confirm the alliance with the Holy See was given to Hawkwood, Dagsworth and Skirlaw (then dean of St. Martin's) on 5 May 1381.[272] On 12 May 1381 power was given for Sir Simon Burley, Robert Braybrooke, Sir Bernard van Zetles, Sir Nicholas Dagsworth and Skirlaw to contract a marriage with the emperor's sister.[273] On 16 May 1381 power was also given to Sir John Hawkwood (who had formed a close association with the Visconti family whilst an English mercenary, and who was already in Italy), Dagsworth and Skirlaw to treat with those lords and commonalities of Italy who were not schismatics.[274] On 20 May 1381 Sir Simon Burley, George Felbrigg (member of the royal household), and Walter Skirlaw set off to Prague, in the company of the Bohemians, to negotiate with the king of the Romans and the German and Italian princes and then onwards to confer with the Roman Curia to secure ratification of the treaty (which addressed the formal arrangements for the marriage, the dowry and also broader issues of Anglo-Imperial co-operation and union against schismatics, and to make the arrangements for Anne's passage to London. Dagsworth and Skirlaw went first to the king of the Romans. The long negotiations with the pope necessitated the dispatching from Rome to England of messengers to ask for further instructions; first John Northwood, a yeoman of Hawkwood, then Adam Bamford, an Augustinian friar.[275] The ratification was completed on 1 September 1381. There was widespread criticism of the financial terms of the match in London. The original discussions agreed that the size of Anne's dowry would be negotiated at a later date between the two parties. It gradually became apparent that no dowry would be forthcoming. Gifts of money were lavished on the Bohemian envoys in London, including annuities of several hundred marks to the duke of Teschen. Richard was very aware that an outward show of extravagance was important in confirming his status with the Roman Emperor. Skirlaw returned from further negotiations in Rome on 5 August 1382.[276] The English envoys came back in January and February 1382[277]

Eventually Anne started her journey to England to join Richard II as his wife. After a lengthy interval traversing the continent, she made her crossing to Dover on 18 December 1381, in the company of the earls of Devon and Salisbury. She then travelled on to Leeds Castle where she spent Christmas. On 20 January 1382 the marriage ceremony took place in Westminster Abbey. Skirlaw and Burley failed to agree a dowry with Wenceslas because he was very short of funds.[278] Richard also had a policy of 'marrying some of the queen's countrywomen to (English) men of rank at royal expense'. One such marriage was between Margaret, the duke of Teschen's daughter, to the king's knight Sir Simon Felbrigg, the cousin of Sir George Felbrigg, Skirlaw's companion.[279] On 21 April 1383, Pope Urban VI congratulated the king on his marriage, and commended Skirlaw and Dagsworth.[280]

On 15 April 1382 Sir Nicholas Dagsworth and Skirlaw set off again to treat for an alliance with Charles III, king of Naples.[281] In 1380 Charles had been ordered by Pope Urban VI to dethrone his mother by adoption, Joanna I of Naples, because of her support of the antipope, Clement VII. Charles conquered Naples, imprisoned Joanna, and had her put to death, and was crowned by Urban in 1381.[282] The embassy from England was no doubt sent to secure relations with Charles.

On 11 November 1383 Skirlaw (by now keeper of the privy seal) crossed to France with John of Gaunt to treat with the French.[283] Other envoys included Henry Bolingbroke and Sir John Holland (Richard's half-brother). During 1383 English knights had surrendered French towns, eventually withdrawing to England for want of men-at-arms and food supplies, razing to the ground the town and fortress of Gravelines near Calais. When Parliament opened on 26 October, the king of France sent to Richard and his council a proposal that they should send men of rank and judgement to Calais to conduct negotiations for peace, and that the French king would do likewise. This seemed a surprise move on the part of the French considering that they now held the upper hand. The French envoys who met the English included the duke of Berry (uncle of Charles VI), the duke of Brittany and the count of Flanders and negotiations took place at Leulingham. Other English representatives included the bishop of

Hereford, John Sheppey and Sir William Neville. They reached Calais in November and remained there over the whole of the Christmas season returning on 3 February 1384. Towards the end of their stay the count of Flanders entertained John of Gaunt and his fellows in 'the great tent of Bruges'.[284] Skirlaw was accompanied on the mission by two clerks from his office, Guy Rockcliffe and Roger Elmham.[285]

Between 15 June and 28 September 1384 Skirlaw again visited Calais and Picardy to negotiate with the French.[286] Others who went were John of Gaunt, his brother the earl of Buckingham, Sir Thomas Percy (senechal of the household), John Holland, Raymond Guilhem du Puy, and John Gilbert. The negotiations took place at Leulingham near Boulogne. When the party arrived at Calais (Percy and Skirlaw had set out on 11 and 15 June respectively and the rest on 30 June), they spent a long time waiting for the French. When the French eventually came to Boulogne, it was reported that 'they adopted a consequential tone, continually dwelling on irrelevant subjects, and neglecting entirely, as if they cared little about them, those matters which bore on peace'.[287] The French negotiators were Charles VI's uncles, John of France (duke of Berry) and Philip the Bold (duke of Burgundy). Negotiations went on until 21 September before the conclusion of a truce between the two countries to last until the following May.[288] The reason for the *volte-face* was almost certainly the changed situation in Flanders, where Count Louis had died in 1384 and Duke Philip had succeeded to his inheritance. The French now wanted a free hand to crush the city of Ghent, the remaining centre of opposition in the county, which looked to the English for protection. John of Gaunt and his brother reported back to Richard and his council that the French were more inclined to war than to peace.[289]

John Gilbert, William Beauchamp (captain of Calais), Sir John Clanvow (a chamber knight and favourite of Richard's) and Skirlaw with his two clerks were empowered to treat for a final peace with France. Similar powers were given to Sir Edmond de la Pole (captain of Calais Castle and brother of Sir Michael) and Guy Rockcliffe (canon of Ripon). The embassy visited Calais and Paris for meetings between 23 March and 30 April 1385, which came to no successful conclusion[290]

In 1385 England was threatened by invasion by a combined Franco-Scottish force which had joined together in May. As a consequence, Skirlaw accompanied Richard II and an armed escort of thirty esquires and thirty archers to command an armed force to deal with the enemy. On arriving at Durham, the king joined John of Gaunt and mustered nearly fourteen thousand men-at-arms and archers obtained from the retainers of the great feudatories of the region. On 6 August the king entered Scottish territory, pursuing the retreating enemy to Edinburgh and beyond; there were reports of skirmishes with the Scots as far north as Perth and Dundee. The Franco-Scottish forces counter-attacked on the West Marches and plundered Cumberland. The English retreated to deal with this and the enemy moved back to Scotland.[291] The Scots appear to have been daunted by Richard's expedition and accepted a number of short truces, the last of which ended on 19 June 1388.

Commission was given on 22 January 1386 to Skirlaw, Michael de la Pole, William Beauchamp and four others, to treat for peace or a truce with the king of France and his allies or with France alone, at the request of the king of Armenia, Leo VI (refer to Chapter Five for more background to King Leo VI).[292] Skirlaw was accompanied by Sir Michael de la Pole and Sir John Devereux to Calais to meet the French between 10 February and 28 March 1386.[293] Other envoys were Sir John Clanvow, Richard Ronhale and Roger Elmham (a privy seal clerk).[294] After a brief interval the king of Armenia followed the envoys in the company of Sir Simon Burley. Before leaving England, King Leo VI had obtained a sealed royal patent promising him £1,000 a year if a permanent peace could be achieved and consolidated but if not 1,000 marks only. These payments were to cease if Leo recovered his own kingdom.[295]

In 1386 Skirlaw was a witness to the treaty establishing an alliance with Portugal. In August 1385, a battle had been fought there which was to have far reaching effects on England's relationship with the peninsula. A Portuguese force met a Castilian force and the Portuguese scored a resounding victory. John of Gaunt had a claim to the Castilian throne through his wife, Constance of Castile ('Queen of Castile'), and it seemed an ideal time to launch an offensive on the seriously weakened Castilian kingdom. Preparations were made but at the same time a diplomatic initiative was also taking place. A draft treaty was agreed and the terms recited in Richard's presence at Windsor with Skirlaw as a witness, and ratified at Westminster a week later. John of Gaunt left England in July 1386 for the Iberian Peninsula and was not to set foot in England again until 1389; his continued absence weakened the position of the king. The French were upset with John of Gaunt's tactics as Castile was an ally of theirs. In response, they resumed their military build-up and made plans for a major attack on England, although they were having financial difficulties and were unable to raise sufficient taxation to pay for the offensive. At the same time the weather also conspired against them. In England the government also urgently required a substantial grant of taxation from the Commons to pay for its many commitments. For months the threat of invasion hung over the country; chancellor de la Pole failed to provide a lead and was dismissed and impeached (see Chapter Three).[296]

In 1388 the Scots refused to renew the existing truce with England due for renegotiation on 9 June. At this time Richard was in conflict with the Lords Appellant, and the Scots saw a favourable opportunity to renew hostilities with England. Their armies soon appeared south of the border and on 5 August defeated the English forces at the battle of Otterburn. Because of the turbulence in the north of England, the magnates were inclined to look favourably on proposals for peace with France.

An embassy led by Skirlaw to Calais at the end of 1388 was the first of several which produced a series of truces with France, culminating in 1394 in an agreement to suspend hostilities for four years.[297] Due to the English attacks on Flemish commerce French interest in invading England had waned since in 1388. Philip the Bold had written to the duke of Gloucester saying that, at Leo VI's request, Charles VI was prepared to negotiate a truce of several years. Envoys were appointed on 26 November 1388, including Skirlaw, Sir William Beauchamp, Sir John Devereux (steward of the household), and the royal retainers Sir John Clanvow and Sir Nicholas Dagsworth. John Sheppey and Richard Ronhale were also listed as negotiators. Richard commissioned his delegates to leave England early in December 1388. The conference, first planned to last a few weeks, continued during the whole of the winter and spring. When at last an agreement had almost been reached, the meeting adjourned, and fresh commissions were issued by the two kings in May 1389. The count of St. Pol and the earl of Salisbury were the chief additions to each side. The truces brokered by the duke of Burgundy were formally signed at Leulingham, on 18 June 1389, a little over a month after Richard's recovery of power.[298] The French were afraid to come as far as Calais although a safe-conduct was issued on 16 November, so business was postponed until after Christmas.[299] The initial agreement was for three years but it was extended in 1392, 1393 and 1394; Skirlaw was employed in all these negotiations both in France and in Flanders. Although the earl of Salisbury was back in England on 30 June, Skirlaw was kept busy on the continent for another month sending messengers to publish the truce in Aquitaine, Portugal and Gelders. At first João, the king of Portugal, refused to be included in the Anglo-French truce and continued the armed conflict with Castile, but in December, after a local truce, he ratified it.[300]

On 5 November 1389 Skirlaw, William Beauchamp, Sir John Clanvow, Sir John Say (baron of Wemme), Richard Ronhale, and six others were commissioned to treat for a truce and peace with the count and commonalities of Flanders. Preparatory negotiations had already taken place in October 1389. Skirlaw took part in an embassy in Picardy lasting from 10 November to 18 December. The French king promptly warned against talking peace with the English without his permission and authority if they wished to pass their future in peace and quiet.[301]

On 8 April 1390 to Skirlaw, Henry Percy (earl of Northumberland), Sir John Devereux, and five others were again empowered to agree a truce or final peace for the king and his allies, or for England alone, with France.[302] Skirlaw left London on 13 April and returned on 15 July. The conference opened at Leulingham on 4 July and in the course of the talks a number of demands were put forward by each side. These were put into writing and submitted to the two kings, so that they might consider and dispose of them in consultation with their councils.[303]

During Lent 1392, Skirlaw accompanied John of Gaunt, and his nephew, Edward, the earl of Rutland, into France to the city of Amiens to treat for a final peace with France. There, according to Knighton, 'the king of France, accompanied by the king of Armenia, came to greet the duke with great and saintly honours, placing before him a great number of citizens of that place, all mounted, then many counts and barons, and then the royal dukes, his uncles. Lastly the king himself came to meet him, and greeted him as the pre-eminent and most renowned man of knightly worth in all Christendom, excepting only those anointed to kingly power. And the said lord duke under the terms of his safe-conduct had seventeen days in which to negotiate the peace. The party then returned to England with 1,000 knights, it was said, arrayed in marvellous elegance.'[304] The reality was not a peace but an extension of the existing truce for a further year. On the day after their arrival in Amiens, Charles VI of France held a banquet at which Gaunt and Skirlaw had places of honour. Subsidiary positions were accorded to John Holland (earl of Huntingdon) and Edward (earl of Rutland), paralleled by the dukes of Touraine and Bourbon as Charles VI's supporters. After dinner the king talked affably to the Lancastrian knights and esquires present and rewarded them, the French dukes following suit. Musicians from the courts of the French king and of Gaunt were present at most of the events and processions at the conference.[305] The English party then met for five weeks of fruitless talks with the French at St. Omer, making frequent visits to Calais throughout the period. They returned to England about the beginning of April empty-handed and with no hope of agreement.[306]

In early Skirlaw had also been involved in negotiations to maintain the truce between Richard II and Robert II, king of Scotland, following Scottish complaint that the English 'were preventing the Scotch from buying goods and food in the Marches'.[307] Sir Nicholas Dagsworth headed the ambassadors. A 'March-day' was appointed for the swearing of oaths after much haggling between the parties. Skirlaw, the bishop of Carlisle, the earl of Northumberland, Lord Neville, Baron Graystock, Lord Harrington and Lord Dacre, and the captains of Berwick, Carlisle and Roxburgh were appointed conservators of the truce with Scotland on 22 July 1392.[308]

On 22 February 1393 John of Gaunt and his brother Thomas (duke of Gloucester) were once more commissioned to treat with France. Similar powers were also given to Skirlaw, Thomas Mowbray (Earl Marshal), Sir William Beauchamp, Sir Thomas Percy, Sir Lewis Clifford and Dr Richard Ronhalc.[309] Skirlaw, John of Gaunt and Thomas of Woodstock went to Calais and thence to Leulingham to discuss peace with the French king, and succeeded in prolonging the truce, returning around Easter. In the summer of 1393 they again returned and agreed a truce with the French and the Scots for four years and four months.[310] A provisional treaty was concluded by John of Gaunt, the duke of Gloucester, and the dukes of Berry and Burgundy on 16 June 1393. The outcome was that England would receive Calais, Mark and Guines in northern France and certain parts of Aquitaine. These were the provinces of Saintonge, Angoumois, Limousin, Périgord, Quercy, Agenais and Rouergue, the towns of Montauban and Rodez, and the counties of Tarbes, Bigorre and Gavre. In return Richard II was to renounce Saintonge, north of the river Charente, la Rochelle, Aunis and Poitou, and the county of Ponthieu.

Skirlaw visited Picardy again with Sir John Newton from 11 August to 12 October 1393.[311] As legal experts they were sent to meet the French to work out the proposed restrictions on the exercise of French sovereignty and jurisdiction. The final stage of the treaty was scheduled to take place on 9 February 1394, but this plan was wrecked by the uncertain health of the French king. John of Gaunt and the duke of Burgundy finally met in March 1394, when it appears that discussions must have come to a deadlock and were not pursued further. For John of Gaunt, the sticking point may have been the proposal to divide up his duchy of Aquitaine, which had previously been regarded as a possession of the English Crown and of which he had been made duke in 1390.[312]

The early 1390s was a period of relative calm in English domestic politics. However, on 7 June 1394, Richard II's wife, Anne, to whom he was devoted, died childless. An heir was needed and the council acting on Richard's behalf initiated a search for a suitable bride. John Orewell had already been entrusted with a letter from Richard II to Robert III, king of Scotland, proposing negotiations over possible marriages between some of his kinsfolk and some of the Scottish king's children. Queen Anabella replied from the abbey of Dunfermline on behalf of the king suggesting a date in July, but due to delays in communication 1 October was eventually proposed:. Skirlaw, who took part in the negotiations,[313] was granted the power with Henry Percy, John Redington (prior of St. John of Jerusalem in England), William, Lord Roos of Hamelake and eight others including Sir Ralph Percy, Sir Richard Stury, Gerard Heron, Thomas Stanley (clerk), Alan Newark (advocate) and John Mitford, to treat with Scotland on 27 August 1394,[314] and to explore the possibilities of marriage between the royal families.[315] The Scottish envoys included the bishops of St. Andrews and Glasgow and the earls of Carrick and Douglas.

Other royal brides were considered for Richard by his council. Yolande, daughter of King John of Aragon, was favourite for a while, but the idea caused alarm in France. King Charles of France then offered his own daughter, six-year-old Isabella, whom Richard was happy to take as his wife. Skirlaw does not appear to have been involved with these negotiations. The results were not generally well received in England, as Richard was perceived to have become pro-French and an upholder of French policies in Europe.[316] Isabella was handed over to Richard in 1396 at Ardres, and they were married in Calais on 4 November. Richard appears to have treated Isabella as the child he never had, and indulged her various whims and fancies. At Christmas and other festivals, he showered her with presents; on one occasion, when Skirlaw gave Richard a present of a whistle inlaid with precious stones, he immediately handed it over to Isabella to play with.[317]

On John of Gaunt's death on 3 February 1399, Richard rashly seized the lands belonging to the dukes of Lancaster. The king seemed oblivious of the possible consequences and set off on an expedition to Ireland, leaving his kingdom unguarded. Henry Bolingbroke of Lancaster landed at Ravenser (now covered by the North Sea) at Spurn Point in the East Riding of Yorkshire in late June 1399, declaring he had only come to claim his lawful rights. Henry had hired three vessels from Brittany and was accompanied by a handful of followers, including Thomas Arundel who had been archbishop of Canterbury until banishment by Richard II two years previously.[318] Henry immediately attracted adherents from the Lancaster estates and also among the all-powerful northern lords, led by Henry Percy (earl of Northumberland). It took some time for the news to reach Richard in Ireland. Returning to the mainland he marched through North Wales and eventually submitted to Henry Bolingbroke at Flint Castle. Richard was then imprisoned in the Tower of London, where under duress he resigned his right to the Crown, and Bolingbroke became King Henry IV. Skirlaw attended the Parliament which received Richard's abdication and assented to his imprisonment.[319]

Not everyone believed that Henry had the right to be king. The French in particular, were bound by a secret treaty to come to Richard's aid should he be attacked. Henry needed to bolster his position by gaining the respect of his people. He allowed Parliament to strengthen its power over the realm's finances and tried to deal with what were seen as the excesses of the Lollards by declaring them heretics, and ordering them to be burnt at the stake. Henry was also aware of the need to secure recognition abroad. Even before he was crowned king, he wrote to the king of the Scots suggesting that the truce which was due to expire at Michaelmas be renewed.

When the French king heard the news of Richard's capture it came as a severe blow; he became deeply melancholic and the event hastened the return of his mania. He assumed that Richard was dead or would shortly be put to death. His immediate concern was for his daughter Isabella and he sent messengers across to England to see her in person and report back on her condition.[320] However, Henry remained on good terms with the duke of Berry (the king's uncle), and the duke of Orleans. Some of their retainers were present at Henry's coronation.[321] Skirlaw too was present at Henry IV's coronation feast on St. Edward's Day, 13 October 1399.

Henry ruled with the assistance of a king's council which had its first meeting on 11 November 1399. Those present included Archbishop Arundel, Walter Skirlaw, the earls of Northumberland, Westmorland and Worcester and the chancellor, treasurer, and keeper of the privy seal, together with the Lords Cobham and Lovell, and Sir Matthew Gourney.[322] Skirlaw attended further meetings of the council in November and

December 1399, acting as a witness to several charters signed at that time, indicating that he was one of Henry's leading followers. He attended the session of Parliament which assented to Richard's further imprisonment in Pontefract Castle, where it is said he died of starvation in January 1400.[323]

In 1399 Skirlaw was made chief ambassador in negotiations to continue the truce with France, crossing the channel four times on this business over the next two years. When he was not abroad, Skirlaw continued to attend the king's council until at least August 1401.

On 29 November 1399 he proceeded to France with Sir Thomas Percy (earl of Worcester) to announce to Charles VI that Henry had taken possession of the kingdom of England. He also carried proposals of friendship and even an offer of marriage between Henry's eldest son, Henry, Prince of Wales, or his brothers and sisters, and the children of the king of France. He was also to treat for a confirmation of the truce previously made with Richard II and for a new alliance with France.[324] Neither Charles nor Henry was in a position to make war because of domestic difficulties. The truce was confirmed by Charles VI on 29 January 1400 and by Henry IV on 18 May 1400.

On 9 February 1400, in consequence of letters brought by Sir William Faringdon from Skirlaw and his colleagues in France, and in consequence of the invasions of the Scots, a memorandum was published by the lords of the council which granted certain aids to the king for the maintenance of the war, which avoided the necessity of summoning a parliament.[325]

On 19 February 1400 power was again given to Skirlaw, Sir Thomas Percy, Sir William Heron, Lord Say and Richard Holme (canon of York) to continue to treat for marriages between the families of the kings of England and France, and also to treat for a confirmation of the truce for a new compact between the nations.[326] Also on 10 March 1400 commission was given to Skirlaw and his colleagues to receive the oath of the king of France confirming of the truce originally made with Richard II and to seek an explanation for the ambiguities within it.[327]

On 18 May 1400 powers were granted to Skirlaw, Sir Thomas Percy, Sir William Heron, Lord Say and Richard Holme, to reply to the requests made for the return of Queen Isabella and her property to France.[328] Skirlaw was involved in these negotiations and was dispatched to France on 11 October, only to be recalled after eleven days as meanwhile the French envoys had arrived in England. On his return, Skirlaw met the two French envoys, Hangest and Blanchet, to discuss arrangements and later dined with them at Canterbury.[329]

On 1 April 1401 the same group of envoys was empowered to treat with France for a truce, for a new league, and for the restoration of Queen Isabella, and to grant safe conduct to the French ambassadors.[330] On 21 June 1401 commission was given to Skirlaw and his four colleagues to return Queen Isabella and to treat with France.[331] A plan to marry Isabella to the prince of Wales had been discussed and then abandoned. Once the arrangements were made Isabella began her long journey home.

She set off from London on 28 June 1401 dressed in mourning. She had been very fond of Richard and on leaving had nothing to say to Henry whom she regarded as responsible for her husband's death. She was accompanied by a large number of dignitaries appointed by the council. It was arranged that two French lords were to come over to Dover and accompany the party to Calais. To escort Isabella to France the court thought it necessary to send the duchess of Ireland (widow of Robert de Vere), and the countess of Hereford (the king's mother-in-law), each with one knight, one lady, three damsels, three squires, two yeomen and a groom. There were also Bishops Skirlaw and Hereford, the earl of Worcester and the earl of Somerset (as captain of Calais), four lords, the queen's chamberlain, confessor and secretary, six knights, four ladies, seven damsels and two maids, in all a total of fifty-five persons, some of whom would themselves have had a large number of attendants. The whole operation was expected to last six weeks and cost £1,500. 1,000 marks was to be paid for the services of nine damsels, ten clerks, thirty-three squires, sixty-seven yeomen of the chamber, thirty-one yeomen of the stable, thirty-nine boys and thirty pages; making another two hundred persons together with ninety-four horses.[332] It took a month for the party to travel from London to Calais.[333] A safe-conduct was granted on 21 June for as many as 500 persons, and the total estimated expense for wages, gold and silver vessels, carpets, tents, and other apparatus, amounted to £8,242 0s 10d. Other costs included the acquisition of horses and harnesses for the journey, and the Cinque Ports were to provide three barges and two armed vessels for the crossing from Dover. Isabella crossed to France from Dover on 28 July in a state of deep mourning and tearfulness.[334]

On 3 August 1401 an indenture was to be made between Jean de Montaigu (bishop of Chartres), Jean de Poupaincourt (president of the French Parliament), Jean de Hangest (lord of Heugueville) and Walter Col (secretary of the French king), and Skirlaw, Thomas Percy and his colleagues, for the redress of injuries and the preservation of the truce.[335] With the return of Isabella to France, Henry had given up a valuable bargaining counter. French hostility increased, threats of invasion multiplied, and Henry's hope of a marriage alliance with the French royal House of Valois, which Skirlaw and his colleagues had late in 1399 discussed came to nothing.[336] However, in due course, Henry succeeded in marrying his daughter, Blanche, to Ludvig, the son of the newly elected king of the Romans, Rupert III, although Skirlaw was not involved with these negotiations.[337]

On 16 July 1401 Bishop Skirlaw, the bishops of Hereford and Bangor, Sir Thomas Erpyngham, Sir John Cheyne and four others were commissioned to hear an appeal against the sentence delivered by Henry Percy (earl of Northumberland) against Thomas Stokes (executor) and Sir John Roth (acting for the late Robert Hauley), concerning the ransom of the count of

Denia.[338] The case arose out of the capture of the count of Denia at the battle of Najera during the Black Prince's expedition in 1367. As a pledge for the large ransom demanded, the count gave his son Alphons as a hostage to his captors, Robert Hauley and John Shakell. Hauley died in 1378 and his sister (Maud Hauley), his heir, ceded her rights to John Hoton (citizen of London). Hoton proceeded to sue Shakell, who held the hostage, for the ransom. Shakell denied that Hoton had any interests in this matter and asserted that the whole ransom now belonged to himself as executor and heir of Robert Hauley. The case, which was heard in the Court of Chivalry, lasted from 1390 to 1395 without conclusion following the death of Shakell. Then Hoton petitioned the king concerning the delays in hearing the case and a legal commission was appointed in December 1396 which was renewed and extended in number in 1397. However, the death of the Constable of England and then the events of 1399 caused further delays. The new Constable, Percy (earl of Northumberland), pronounced a sentence by default against the party of John Shakell, which was then appealed by Thomas Stokes, his executor. It was at this point that a strong commission, which included Skirlaw, was appointed by the king, to deal with the appeal. This commission was renewed and increased in number in September 1401 to fourteen members, following which only four members delivered judgement which was made against the party of Shakell. Further appeals were made against the sentence and the dispute continued for some years, although Skirlaw himself was not by then involved.[339]

The treaty with the French in May 1401 was Skirlaw's final success as a diplomat. He wrote a letter later in 1401 to Thomas Arundel (archbishop of Canterbury) to the effect that he had been very busy in the king's service and had leave from the king and the prince to remain now in England. After this he retired permanently to the north, excusing himself from attending Parliament on grounds of infirmity.[340]

CHAPTER FIVE
BISHOP SKIRLAW

Skirlaw was ambitious and had impressed the pope with his dedication to duty and his diplomatic, organisational and legal expertise. His promotion to a bishopric, with its prestige and financial rewards, was the natural reward. The various moves that took him to the bishopric of Durham were influenced by the barons who wished to gain political advantage from them, and these are discussed below. An opportunity for Skirlaw arose in the bishopric of Coventry and Lichfield when the incumbent, Robert Stretton, who had held office from 1360, died on 28 March 1385.[341] The pope provided for Skirlaw's elevation to the bishopric on 28 June. This was not welcomed by Richard II, although he accepted it reluctantly, as it appears that at that time he had some dispute with Skirlaw.

The see of Coventry and Lichfield was sometimes referred to as 'Chester' from the time after the Synod of 1075 when Bishop Peter decided on Chester as his cathedral city, because Lichfield was a very poor place. However, his successor, Robert Limesey, transferred his seat to Coventry.[342] The diocese of Coventry and Lichfield was spread over the counties of Cheshire, Derbyshire, Shropshire, Staffordshire and most of Warwickshire, and was divided into five archdeaconries, Chester, Derby, Shrewsbury, Stafford and Coventry. The chapter at Lichfield continued to be maintained, and work started on rebuilding the earlier Norman cathedral in the present Gothic style in 1195. The cathedral of Lichfield on which the diocese was centred was dedicated to St. Chad, who established his monastery on this site c.669.[343] The three imposing spires of the cathedral, known as the 'Ladies of the Vale', dominate the town. The Lichfield Gospels, beautifully illuminated manuscripts, dating from c.730, still exist as do three wall paintings dating from Skirlaw's lifetime.

Appointment to a bishopric was a lengthy affair. Richard II granted Skirlaw the custody or constableship of Eccleshall Castle in the following October. This was done through Skirlaw's esquire or agent, Peter de la Hay, who continued to serve him until his death in 1406. The constableship covered the residence of the bishops of Coventry and Lichfield at Eccleshall, together with the office of chief forester of the forest or chase of Cannock and its adjacent parks, and lasted for as long as the see of Coventry and Lichfield remained vacant and the temporalities remained in the king's hands.[344] Later in the same month Skirlaw was granted the custody of the bishopric and all its temporalities.[345] Skirlaw then made his profession of obedience at Otford in Kent (one of the archbishop of Canterbury's palaces) on 7 January 1386, having received the temporalities of the bishopric the day before.[346]

Skirlaw was finally consecrated as a bishop in Westminster Abbey on 14 January 1386.[347] The ceremony was officiated by the archbishop of

Canterbury, supported by the archbishop of York and five bishops, in the presence of Richard II and Queen Anne, King Leo of Armenia, John of Gaunt and the duke of Gloucester, as well as a large number of English nobles, and was reported to be a striking occasion.[348] The king of Armenia had for some years been in exile from his kingdom, which had been overthrown by the Mamluks, and had spent his time travelling from court to court in Europe with the object of enlisting aid to recapture his kingdom. This may well have been the reason for his visit to the court of Richard II which happened to coincide with Skirlaw's consecration.[349] It is interesting that in the present day the ancient Church of Armenia (the original Garden of Eden and Mount Ararat are claimed to be situated there) has close relations with the Church of England, one of the youngest churches.

Skirlaw continued as keeper of the privy seal until October 1386. The reason for his resignation is not clear, although it followed after his colleagues, Michael de la Pole and Fordham, had been expelled from Parliament for policies which had sent the country into financial difficulties (see Chapter Three). Skirlaw's move may not have been politically motivated but simply that the post was considered beneath that of a bishop.[350]

At this time, the Lollard Movement was gaining followers and becoming a threat to the established Church. In May 1386 the king, through the archbishop of Canterbury, gave Bishop Skirlaw and his suffragans the power 'to arrest and imprison all maintainers or preachers of conclusions contrary to sound doctrines and subversive of the Catholic faith, which have been condemned by Holy Church, some as heresies, others as errors, after good and mature deliberation by the common council of the archbishop of Canterbury, his suffragans, doctors in theology and clerks learned in the Scriptures. All the king's lieges are prohibited, under pain of forfeiting all they can forfeit, from aiding them, and are to obey the bishop, his suffragans and ministers in the execution hereof, so that due and open proclamation against these conclusions and their maintainers may be without disturbance.'[351]

During his short time Skirlaw as bishop of Coventry and Lichfield little of note took place. In June 1386 James le Boteler, the earl of Ormonde, paid the king for a licence amounting to £10 for him to enfeoff[352] Bishop Skirlaw, John Waltham (archdeacon of Richmond), Sir Robert Plessington, William Dyghton and John Scarle (clerks) of his manor of Aylesbury, Buckinghamshire, so that they might grant the possession to the earl and his wife Anne in tail[353] with the remainder[354] to his rightful heirs.[355] In September royal assent was signified to Skirlaw to the election of Robert Bawkewell (canon of Rochester) to be abbot of Rochester.[356] On 15 September 1386 the king received £100 from tenths and fifteenths or quotas from Skirlaw as bishop of Coventry and Lichfield.[357] Skirlaw's register as bishop is presently stored at the Lichfield Record Office.

Skirlaw was hardly a year in office at Lichfield and was never instituted to the diocese before he secured a better position as bishop of Bath and Wells.[358] The see had become vacant and Richard Medford was elected by the chapter at the request of the king, who was attempting to find him a bishopric. Meanwhile, however, Urban VI, in a bull issued at Genoa on 18 August 1386, had promoted Skirlaw to the position.[359] Unwillingly the king had to yield to the *fait accompli* and in November 1386 returned the temporalities to Skirlaw.[360] This dispute in no way improved the already strained relationship between Skirlaw and Richard, but at the same time Skirlaw's relationship with the opposition was healed. Bishop Jocelyn Trotman of Wells had named the see in 1219, changing it from the previous title of Bath and Glastonbury, although in earlier time it had been called either Wells or Bath.[361] The diocese covers the whole of modern Somerset and the southern part of the present county of Avon, originally part of the old county of Somerset, together with a few parishes in Dorset and Wiltshire. The archdeaconries are Bath, Wells and Taunton.

Skirlaw resided at Wells, the smallest cathedral city in England, within the splendid walled and moated palace situated near the cathedral. The grounds cover an area of some fourteen acres complete with gatehouse with portcullis and drawbridge over the moat. Skirlaw's name is recorded on the wall inside the bishops' chapel, together with others, in the grounds of the palace (dedicated to St. Mark and to the Holy Trinity).

During Skirlaw's time the Great Hall of the palace was in full use for banqueting occasions. The following record of an occasion when two royal commissioners visited the palace some fifty years before Skirlaw became bishop gives some insight into the standard of living they enjoyed there. The bishop's household and that of the commissioners with their retinues as numbered more than 200; there were 37 extra horses to feed and look after. The banquet provided for 268 guests with the following:

Hundreds of candles for lighting
672 loaves
86 pipes of wine
340 pipes of ale
Main course:
Fish – pike, eel, hake, salmon, plaice, bream, pollock and pickerell
Meat – a sheep, half a cow, ducks, chicken and other dishes
Total cost to the bishop = £6.53 (in today's terms at least £2,500)[362]

The Great Hall is now only a picturesque ruin, although other parts of the palace and St. Andrew's Well in the grounds are still functional. The bishop's palace, with some modification, continues in its original function; the present bishop resides in the Bishop's House in the northern part of the walled and moated area with a view of the south side of the Cathedral *(Plate 5 shows the moated entrance to the palace with drawbridge).*

Plate 5. Wells, Bishop's Palace entrance.

Plate 6. Wells Cathedral.

The magnificent Wells cathedral church of St. Andrew with its remarkable west front embellished with hundreds of carved figures, the ornamental medieval clocks, the quaint old Vicars' Close, and the grammar school, all of which survive today, have not changed substantially since Skirlaw's time. Bath Abbey as it now stands, however, was not rebuilt until after his death *(Plate 6 shows the east end of Wells Cathedral).*

On 24 December 1386 Skirlaw as bishop was granted the revenues of the bishopric as from 26 September, and the hay made in the episcopal manors.[363]

On 17 January 1387 Skirlaw, as bishop of Bath and Wells, like other bishops of the province of Canterbury, was required by the king to appoint a trustworthy member of the clergy to levy and collect in his diocese the moiety (half) of a tenth of ecclesiastical benefices for submission to the king's treasurer in the fourteen days after Easter.[364] A similar order was made on 14 March the following year.[365]

Around 1388, Skirlaw became the *custos* or warden of the Priory of Alien Benedictines of Holy Trinity, York, in Micklegate (between Trinity Lane and Priory Street). The previous prior, John Castell, appointed in 1383, may have withdrawn at the time when the Great Schism was having its effect on the position of the cells of priories of France established in England. The French Benedictine priory, which was a cell of the abbey of Marmoutier near Tours, was faced with a dilemma because the English accepted Urban as their pope but France supported Clement. The schism and the Hundred Years War caused many disputes with the French abbey and as a consequence the Benedictine priory at York was suspended for a while. As warden Skirlaw was responsible for paying the king an annual rent, with an additional understanding that 'Divine Service' there should be maintained. Skirlaw continued as warden until 1390 when the king ordered that Jean Coüe, a religious from Marmoutier, should take over as prior on the condition that he would take an oath that he regarded pope Clement as a schismatic and anti-pope. In due course Coüe took the oath and became prior of Holy Trinity, although he may not have had the approbation of the abbot of Marmoutier. The priory did not come within the jurisdiction of the archbishop of York. Parts of the original nave and north-west tower are the only surviving relics of the old priory. They are situated in Holy Trinity Church, together with traces of the choir in the rectory garden and Jacob's Well house nearby.[366]

Early in 1388 a political crisis emerged in the episcopate following the actions taken by the Lords Appellant and their supporters against Richard II, and many bishops became unacceptable to the new regime because of their political leanings. As a result the pope, although considered a supporter of Richard II, was pressed into making changes in the episcopate in 1388.

The first change on 3 April 1388 was complex and involved six moves: the translation of Alexander Neville (archbishop of York) to the Scottish see of St. Andrews, which, owing to Scottish allegiance to pope Clement VII, could only be classed as a titular post; the promotion of Thomas Arundel (bishop of Ely) to be archbishop of York; the translation of John Fordham (bishop of Durham) to Ely; the translation of Walter Skirlaw (bishop of Bath and Wells) to Durham; the translation of Ralph Erghum (bishop of Salisbury) to Bath and Wells; and the promotion of John Waltham (keeper of the privy seal) to be bishop of Salisbury. Then in June 1388 Thomas Rushook (bishop of Chichester) was exiled to Ireland, and in 1389 the pope translated him to the bishopric of Kilmore in Armagh. He was unable to take possession and took refuge in Cork.

Such a sequence of moves at one time is unique in English history and reflects the unscrupulous manipulation of the episcopate for political ends in medieval times. Favent suggests that the translations, apart from that of Neville, were inspired by the pope, who was in urgent need of funds from the clergy to support his wars, but most historians agree that the moves were initiated by the magnates. It is likely they struck a bargain with the pope that only if he accepted the moves they proposed, would he receive his subsidy. All the appointments were formally promulgated on 3 April 1388.[367]

The changes brought about by the Lords Appellant meant that Neville and Rushook were eliminated from power and that Skirlaw, Arundel and John Waltham were promoted. Ralph Erghum, Gaunt's former chancellor, received Wells, and Waltham was left with Salisbury.[368] Skirlaw was given Durham, where Fordham, who was more strongly associated with the court, was degraded to the poorer see of Ely. Additionally, Fordham may have been removed 'from the fleshpots of Durham to the more meagre temporalities of Ely' because, as chronicled by the monk of Westminster, he was blamed for the defeat of the English at the battle of Otterburn.

It has also been suggested that the Appellants had doubts about Fordham's loyalty in this strategic area of the country, in a post with wide secular responsibilities. Although Durham was the more prestigious bishopric with its privileges, wealth and honorial status, it also represented hard work, travel and expense to a bishop who also had major responsibilities to the crown. Ely, which ranked fifth in the order of bishoprics, was smaller and more compact than Durham, was not subject to the problems of violence and disorder found in the borders; and travelling to London from the manor at Hatfield was relatively easy. Fordham, who was also a native of Ely, may have welcomed the move to a diocese with a less demanding regime, but without experiencing a substantial drop in income, particularly when he was approaching old age. However, an old *History of the English Prelates* written in the seventeenth century states that Fordham 'was by Parliament banished the court, as a pernicious instrument and corrupter of King Richard II, a traitor, a flatterer, a whisperer, a slanderer, and a wicked person'. Hutchinson suggests that 'it appears that the barons, by whose influence Fordham was removed, were determined to fill the see of Durham with a prelate who should not interfere in political matters, and that was a mere ecclesiastical character; for [Skirlaw] who was translated hither, is not noted by historians in any public capacity in state affairs, during his whole prelacy; and his life was occupied in works of munificence, not limited to his own province only, but extended to other parts of the kingdom.'[369]

Skirlaw's translation to Durham also went against the wishes of the king, who wanted John Fordham to continue in the position. On a previous occasion, Richard II had wanted Richard Medford to become bishop of Durham following the death of Bishop Hatfield in 1386, but eventually gained for him the see of Chichester in 1390.[370] Medford was the king's secretary and as a reward for his services Richard wrote to the seneschal of Aquitaine inquiring how many vacant benefices there were in the duchy and especially in Bordeaux Cathedral. When he was told that none were available at the time, Richard ordered that Medford be given the best of them as soon as it became available. In November 1386 the king appointed him Dean of St. Martin-le-Grand by signet letter and later obtained for him the archdeaconry of Norfolk and numerous prebends. Richard finally tried to procure a bishopric for him. When Bishop Harewell of Bath died in July 1386 Richard sent a signet letter, to the chapter recommending Medford's election, and sent one of his clerks, Richard Ronhale, to Rome to sue for confirmation of Medford's election. Richard's attempts were unsuccessful and the royal nomination and diplomacy at the Curia were of no avail against the canonical election and papal provision of Skirlaw.[371]

A number of views concerning Skirlaw's move to Durham have been put forward. Tout suggests that it was partly because the king had backed Medford in opposition to him for Bath and Wells, and partly because, ambitiously seeking an even richer see, Skirlaw saw which way the wind was blowing politically, shifted his allegiance to the Appellants and duly had his reward.[372] Although Skirlaw had been a valuable link between Richard and the papacy, he was never one of his intimates like Medford. However, Davies considers that Skirlaw was taken on by the Appellants more for his skills as an administrator and diplomat than for any political aspirations. He points out that Skirlaw had no evident history of political activity. He did not, for instance, attract recriminations on resigning his position as keeper of the privy seal in October 1386, and was not attacked, as were de la Pole and Fordham, in the Wonderful Parliament. Davies also argues that Skirlaw was the logical choice for Durham partly because of his track record and partly because there were few other possible contenders.[373] Other commentators have added that conviction might have induced Skirlaw to support the Lords Appellant. It could also be said that, from the point of view of the Appellants, who represented conservative inclinations for visible order and stability, Skirlaw was the obvious choice for Durham.[374] Finally, his promotion to Durham may simply have reflected the favour of the pope.

When Alexander Neville was translated to the see of St. Andrews, the temporalities of the archbishopric of York fell into the king's hands until such time as they were translated to Thomas Arundel. The forfeiture took place on 11 July 1388 and custody of the temporalities was granted to Walter Skirlaw, William Courtenay, Thomas of Woodstock, Robert Braybrooke (bishop of London), Richard Fitzalan (earl of Arundel), Sir Henry Percy (earl of Northumberland), Sir John Neville, Sir John Devereux (steward of the household), John Waltham (archdeacon of Richmond), Henry Percy junior, Lord Cobham, Sir Richard Scrope, Sir Robert Swillington and Sir Brian Stapleton, William Gunthorp, Richard Thorne and John Hermesthorp (clerks), Robert Morton, Walter Frost, Robert Garton (clerk), John Berle and Andrew Loby. As long as the temporalities remained in the king's hands, the issues and revenues of the see of York (apart from knight's fees and advowsons which were payable in full to the king) could be taken by these men to be applied towards the repair and improvement of its manors, houses and other possessions and implements, with power to appoint officers and ministers towards that purpose. This was in consideration of the great labour and expense of Thomas Arundel, then bishop of Ely, in his office of chancellor, and of the dilapidations and waste in the possessions of his new archbishopric.[375]

Pope Urban VI issued a bull for the translation of Bishop Skirlaw, then of Bath and Wells, to the see of Durham on 3 April 1388;[376] followed a week later by a mandate (from Perugia) to the chapter of Durham Priory to receive Skirlaw as their new bishop.[377] Restitution of the temporalities of Durham to Skirlaw was made on 13 September 1388.[378] Skirlaw's installation as bishop of Durham took place on 2 October 1390, in the choir and chapter house of Durham Cathedral, and was conducted by Robert Walworth, prior of Durham. The appropriate declaration was made and the oath sworn in the presence of witnesses, John Fishburn and William Thrislington, clerks, and the proceedings were recorded by William Barton, notary public.[379] In 1390 Skirlaw's jurisdiction as bishop of Durham was extended by Pope Boniface IX over the subjects of the English king within the diocese of St. Andrews, Scotland, as the bishop of this diocese was then an adherent of the antipope Clement VII.[380]

The area round Durham had long been an important centre of Christianity in Britain. A community of St. Cuthbert was established in 635 in Lindisfarne, and its leader, St. Aidan was the area, In 883, the community settled in Chester-le-Street. Support from Bishop Eadulf, its then leader, had enabled the Danish king, Guthred, to occupy the vacant throne in York following the death of the previous king in battle in the north of Ireland around 877. In return for this support, king Guthred granted him extensive lands between the Tyne and the Wear. These were extended by purchase and gifts from king and nobles, so that the bishop and his followers soon owned the whole Tyne-Tees region excluding the wapentake of Sadberge. In 995 Bishop Aldhun led his followers to

Durham, where the diocese was finally established. His main reason for choosing the Durham site was its strategic position, much easier to defend against the frequent attacks of the Scots.[381] The area of the Durham diocese extended to 1,075 square miles and became known as the Palatinate of Durham. It comprised Durham county as it was before 1974 and those parts of Northumberland known as North Durham, i.e. Northamshire, Islandshire and Bedlingtonshire. In 1189 the wapentake of Sadberge was sold by Richard I to Bishop Hugh le Puiset of Durham and thus became a separate part of the palatinate.[382]

In Norman England the Durham area became a frontier county under constant threat of invasion by the Scots. The bishop became the king's trusted representative looking after the area on his behalf. In the early Middle Ages Bishop Hugh de Puiset (1153-1193) was a close friend of Richard the Lionheart and was created regent of all England north of the Humber whilst Richard was away on the Crusades. Another bishop, Anthony Bek (1284-1310), increased the powers held by his predecessors. He was also known as Lord of the Isle of Man and Patriarch of Jerusalem. In 1292 Edward I's attorney admitted that the bishop of Durham had a double status, i.e. the status of *bishop* as to his spiritualities and the status of *earl palatine* as to his temporal holdings.

As bishops held the same status as earls, they like other noblemen and royalty had coats of arms. The coat of arms adopted by Skirlaw was described by some authorities as 'Argent, six osier wands interlaced in saltire', poetically described "in true love".[383] However, the arms were recorded in the Heralds' College as: Argent (silver), three pallets (slim vertical bands) interlacing three barrulets (slim horizontal bars)[384] *(an example of the arms is on Plate 7)*. Skirlaw's coat of arms, like those of other Durham bishops, denotes his princely status; the shield is set against a crosier and a sword, instead of the usual two crosiers for a bishop, and the mitre above the coat of arms is encircled with a coronet. The arms of the see of Durham are also surmounted by a mitre with a peer's coronet around its base as a symbol of this dual capacity.

The powers of the bishop were given by the king but could also be taken away by royal authority. The bishop had no power to make laws or alter them. He was an agent charged with enforcing the law of England and the requirements of

Plate 7. Bishop Skirlaw's coat of arms.

its statutes. The bishop had no power in the field of foreign policy, although he would often be used by the Crown in an ambassadorial capacity, particularly in dealings with the Scots. However, the rule of this northern county was politically and militarily delicate, and there were several occasions when power was seized back by the king. Extended vacancies of the see did occur, when the revenues of the palatinate went to the Crown, but successive kings recognized the importance of a strong independent governor of the area, and the powers of the bishop were restored with each new appointee.[385]

Although the early bishops were named by the king, the Durham monks were sometimes successful in securing the appointment of a member of their own house. However, from the installation of Richard de Bury (1333-1345) all bishops were appointed by the pope, and from the thirteenth century onwards many were university graduates like Bishop Skirlaw. The majority of those who became bishop had also enjoyed successful careers in the service of the king prior to their appointment.

Fifteen bishops covered the period from the time of S Aidan until the move to Chester-le-Street, and a further eight bishops held the diocese until the move to Durham. By the time Skirlaw became the bishop of Durham there had been twenty-four previous incumbents.

In the next two chapters Skirlaw's dual role as prince bishop of Durham will be examined. Meanwhile, his diplomatic career continued; his various missions to other countries have been described in Chapter Four.

CHAPTER SIX:
SKIRLAW AND THE DIOCESE OF DURHAM

The bishop of Durham, as a man of high standing aristocratic rank, owned a number of important residences and extensive estates in the diocese and beyond. He also had a household to match his position with well over a hundred servants and officials. His staff included several concerned with diocesan government; his spiritual chancellor and registrar and their clerks, the dean and clerks of his household chapel, the treasurer of the household, the keeper of the wardrobe, the clerk to the kitchen, the chamberlain (a layman who was the chief officer of the household), and various esquires, yeomen, grooms and pages. Most of the staff positions in his household were repeated at each of his many residences. Skirlaw's will gives some insight into many of those he remembered for their service and loyalty during his years as bishop of Durham (see Chapter Twelve). The annual cost of the bishop's household and the upkeep of his residences was estimated to account for around half his yearly revenue.

An elaborate system of diocesan administration had gradually evolved over the Middle Ages. Canon law was becoming more complex and needed a growing network of courts and court officials to implement it. Skirlaw made sure of good organisation by appointing reliable men with sound ability. They understood the bishop and were happy to co-operate with him. Some, like Peter de la Hay, had been associated with or employed by Skirlaw well before he became bishop of Durham. Others had been in the service of the previous incumbent.

Bishop Skirlaw had his own seals, of which two were oval or almond-shaped and were similar to those used by other bishops. The earlier seal, 83 mm x 51 mm, bore the inscription '*sigillum : walteri : dei : gracia : dunolmensis : episcop.*' The seal depicted in the centre a richly decorated niche, and beneath a canopy of elaborate tabernacle work was the figure of St. Cuthbert vested in alb, dalmatic, chasuble, apparelled amice and jewelled mitre. His right hand blessed, while his left hand held, in front of his breast, the crowned head of St. Oswald. His crosier rested in the crook of his left arm. In a smaller niche to his right was the robed figure of St. Peter holding a key in his right hand and a book in his left hand. On the left of St. Cuthbert was the robed figure of St. Andrew, holding his cross in his right hand and a book in his left. Below St. Cuthbert was Skirlaw's coat of arms *(Plate 8)*. The later seal, described as '*ad causas*' (or business seal), was 67 mm x 41 mm in size, and carried the inscription '*fac : pia : walterum : causarum : noscere : verum.*' In the central niche, Our Lady was seen robed, with the child Christ robed and standing on her right knee. On each side were niches in two tiers, in the upper were busts and in the lower a demi-angel looking out of a window. Below, bishop Skirlaw was depicted in mass vestments, holding a crosier, praying. On each side was his shield *(Plate 9)*.

Plate 8. Bishop Skirlaw's episcopal seal.

Plate 9. Bishop Skirlaw's 'ad causas' seal.

A principal officer of the bishop's household on its diocesan side was the spiritual chancellor. In Skirlaw's time Richard Holme took this role. He, like many others under Skirlaw, came from the bishop's own county of Yorkshire. He was well-qualified for the office, and, having obtained a bachelor's degree at Cambridge, was an abbreviator of letters at the Roman Curia. He had also been chancellor to John Waltham (bishop of Salisbury), a royal clerk and diplomat during Skirlaw's time as bishop of Durham (see Chapter Four), and also rector of Wearmouth and canon and prebendary at York. After Skirlaw's death he continued as chancellor to his successor, Thomas Langley.[386] The chancellor's duties were to act mainly as the bishop's chief legal counsel and as his permanent adviser on legal matters, in particular when the bishop acted as judge.[387]

The other senior officer was the registrar, whose duties included preparing the official diocesan commissions and letters for the bishop. Skirlaw appointed Robert Blundell to this position and he also became his personal chaplain, notary and scribe for some years before the bishop's death. Blundell had been a notary of the diocese of Chichester, and became rector of Wearmouth in 1400 for a short time, before exchanging the benefice for Bishopsbourne (Kent?).[388] The registrar advised on the correct form of documents and on their preparation, and employed a staff who wrote the actual documents to which he appended his sign and subscription. The registrar was also the custodian of the bishop's archives, filed and preserved letters and reports received, and maintained copies of records and letters going out in the bishop's name. The bishop's register was maintained by him as a final record of this correspondence. His chaplains were responsible for supervising documents sent out in the name of the bishop, and were also leading figures in the household which travelled with him.[389] Skirlaw's register as bishop has not survived, which means that information on some aspects of his work is drawn from other sources and may be incomplete.

Because the bishop was frequently involved in state business requiring his absence from the diocese for long periods, so capable administration which could function in his absence was vital. During these times the diocesan administration was presided over by the official principal, otherwise known as the vicar general. When the bishop was absent the vicar general was empowered to hold diocesan synods, institute benefices, issue dispensations for nonresidence of clergy, and collect and receive money due to the bishop. His commission lapsed whenever the bishop was in the diocese.[390]

The official principal's normal duties included presiding over the consistory court which was the centre of the local organisation of the diocese, and for Durham was held in the Galilee Chapel of the cathedral. He dispensed justice according to canon law and was assisted by the court registrar, who supervised the making of records kept separately by the court. Any appeal of the official was heard by the bishop's court and would then be recorded in the bishop's register. The consistory court was where the rural deans and parish priests, officers around the diocese, and other individuals reported alleged wrong-doings and other matters concerning the laity and clergy.

So that Skirlaw could act as bishop of Durham whilst absent in London, he was granted a licence by Robert Braybrooke (bishop of London) to conduct Durham business matters within the diocese of London. Braybrooke consecrated the altars in the chapel of Skirlaw's residence, Durham House, so that divine services might be celebrated by Skirlaw and his household. Skirlaw had the power to prove wills and deal with the administration of the goods of deceased subjects of the bishopric of Durham, to confirm elections to dignities[391] in the diocese of Durham, and to deal with any other matters concerning episcopal jurisdiction. The grant was made on 1 March 1389 at the bishop of London's manor of Stepney,[392] and was followed on 11 March by a similar licence giving Skirlaw power to exercise his jurisdiction as bishop of Durham during his residences within the diocese of London.[393]

To assist in the performance of his sacerdotal duties, Skirlaw used the services of a suffragan bishop, who was often called upon to deal with such duties as the ordination of clergy and the confirmation of laity in the Durham diocese. His other tasks included the consecration of churches and graveyards, and the bestowal of episcopal benediction on newly elected heads of religious houses.[394] Skirlaw appointed Oswald, the bishop of Whithorn (Galloway), to carry out these duties on his behalf.[395]

Two archdeacons were appointed by the bishop; the senior of the two covered the county of Durham and was supported by revenues from Easington (Durham) church, while the other covered Northumberland and financed by Howick church.[396] Hugh Herle was archdeacon of Durham from 1388 to 1393.[397] He was succeeded by Thomas Weston who held the position until Skirlaw's death and continued to serve Bishop Langley until 1408. During his time with Skirlaw, Weston held a number of appointments in the bishopric. He was a canon of Howden, holding a prebend at Barnby, spiritual chancellor of bishop Skirlaw, master of Greatham Hospital, rector of Easington, canon of York with the prebend of Grindale, and rector of Sedgefield. His seal bore the inscription 'sigillum : thome : weston : archdiac : dunolmensis.' On each side of Thomas, portrayed in a cassock and almuce, were two shields: on his right was that of Bishop Skirlaw and on his left his own shield identical to Skirlaw's except that the six interlacing bastons formed a saltire (crossing diagonally) instead of a cross. It would seem that he had adopted Skirlaw's shield with this difference. A comparison with the 'ad causas' seal of Skirlaw shows that the design was virtually identical. Weston may well have been quite close to Skirlaw, as he was named an executor of Skirlaw's will (Plate 10).[398] Thomas Weston's private seal also incorporated his shield of diagonal bastons. (Plate 11) [399] Before his appointment as archdeacon of Durham, Weston had

Plate 10. Thomas Weston's archidiaconal seal.

Plate 11. Thomas Weston's private seal.

also been appointed to deputise as prior of Durham during the vacancy which followed the resignation of Prior Robert Wallworth in 1391.[400] The Northumberland archdeacons during Skirlaw's time as bishop were John Derby (1370-?), Louis de Fieschi (1400), John Repham (1400), John Dalton (?-1405) (licentiate in laws, bachelor of decretals and canon of Darlington, later an official under bishop Langley[401]), and William Morwyk (1405-1409).[402]

The bishop appointed a sequester-general for each of the two archdeaconries who also kept a close watch on the behaviour of clergy and people. He had the power to grant probate of wills, and deal with other testamentary jurisdiction in respect of all apart from the nobility. He would also take over any benefices which became vacant and collect pensions due to the bishop from churches in his archdeaconry. Because the archdeacons were often absent for long periods from their archdeaconries, the sequester-generals also undertook further responsibilities on their behalf during those times.[403]

Apart from catering for the personal needs of the bishop, the household managed the administration of the palatinate and the diocese. The bishop had a palatinate council presided over by the Steward of Durham, who could deputise on many matters during his absence, and a council for diocesan affairs. The bishop issued warrants under his own privy seal.[404]

Around Skirlaw's time the bishopric and convent of Durham were said to be worth 20,000 marks a year, equal in value to the combined revenues of the archbishopric of Canterbury, Christ Church of St. Augustine, Canterbury, and three other houses, plus the see of Lincoln and the convents of Ramsey and Peterborough. It is estimated that the bishop of Durham was one of the five richest landowners in England behind the bishop of Winchester.

Most of the bishop's income came from his ownership of large estates in the north of England, known as the patrimony of St. Cuthbert, and much of it comprised rents as feudal dues and from farms. In fact the bishop had two states, that of temporal ruler of the palatinate and as ordinary of the diocese, in other words he was the secular lord of his tenants but also their father-in-God.[405] At one time the bishop owned fourteen residences in the form of six castles and eight manor houses.

During Skirlaw's time the stewards (seneschals) responsible for the management of the bishop's estate were listed by Hutchinson as follows:

Hugh Westwick, occurred 13 October 1388, again 25 March 1389
Sir Thomas Gray, appointed 'during pleasure' 1388/89
Sir Ralph Eure, appointed 'during pleasure' 20 January 1394, annual fee £40, occurred again 1403 (Ralph Eure and William Gastan, justices 20 September 1392)[406]

The tenants-in-chief held their land in return for various services rendered, including contributions to the Durham exchequer, and hereditary tenants were normally persons of some social standing in the community. Coroners, who were recruited from the tenants-in-chief, were responsible for the collection of rents and employed around ten collectors in each of the four wards of Darlington, Chester, Easington and Stockton, and in the Sadberge wapentake. The bishop also owned estates in Norhamshire in Northumberland, and Howdenshire, Allertonshire and the manor of Crayke in Yorkshire, which had their own officers for overseeing and rent collection, and also contributed income to the exchequer.

Another important source of revenue came from profits generated by the forests and parks which the bishop owned or claimed rights over. The forests, which included the vast forest of Weardale, were at first used mainly for hunting, but by Skirlaw's time they were largely given over to grazing. Another major contribution to the bishop's wealth came from the leasing of mines and other mineral deposits, as Durham was particularly rich in valuable resources including iron, lead, silver, salt and coal. The bishop also received pensions from various churches. Although most of his income came from his position as bishop, part of it was generated from his lordship of the palatinate.

Bishop Skirlaw's official residence was Durham Castle in the City of Durham, a vice-regal residence built by the bishops, which dates from 1072. It lies just across the green from the cathedral, situated on a promontory high above the River Wear which surrounds three sides of the site. The cathedral and castle stand in a very commanding position over the city and surrounding countryside. Durham Castle was founded soon after the Norman Conquest as a key fortress in the defence of the border with Scotland, but in time became the chief residence of the medieval bishops. Following the establishment of the University of Durham, the castle buildings became the centre of University College and they were adapted for teaching purposes and residential accommodation for students.[407]

Apart from Durham Castle, the bishop's residences in the diocese during Skirlaw's time included Norham Castle, Auckland Castle and deer park, and the manors at Stockton, Gateshead and Darlington. The bishop owned property in Yorkshire, including the castles at Crayke and Northallerton, and manors at Wheel Hall and Howden. He also owned Durham House in London.

Norham Castle held a strategic position on a picturesque promontory above a main crossing point on the River Tweed, on what was then the border between Scotland and England. It was founded by Bishop Ranulph Flambard of Durham in 1121 as an administrative centre for his most northern territory and was a wooden motte and bailey construction. It was soon destroyed by the Scots, and in 1157 Henry II ordered Bishop Hugh de Puiset to rebuild it in stone. The new castle, extended in the fifteenth century, which now stands in ruins, was capable of withstanding invasion for long periods. Skirlaw continued to use the castle as an administrative centre for the northern parts of the diocese.

Auckland Castle, situated at Bishop Auckland, is at present the chief residence of the bishops of Durham, but in Skirlaw's time it was used by him as a country retreat with its extensive deer park. Skirlaw spent a lot of time at Auckland; whilst bishop of Durham he was there in October 1390, May 1391, April, June, October and November 1394, January 1395, January and February 1397, October and December 1398, February and May 1399, April 1402, January to May, September and December 1403, and January to April 1404.

The bishop's manor of Wheel Hall was situated near the village of Riccall, on the east bank of the River Ouse, some nine miles south of York, only two miles from the fortified residence of the archbishop of York at Cawood and eleven miles north of Howden.[408] Riccall was famous as the landing place in 1066 of the Norwegian and Danish forces prior to the battle of Stamford Bridge some fourteen miles north-east. The bishops of Durham built the palace then called La Wel Hall, which stood at the head of a 'wheel' or sharp turn in the river about half-a-mile above the village. It was protected on one side by the river and on the other by three broad moats. The hall was pulled down around 200 years ago and only some foundations and traces of one moat remain.[409] Wheel Hall was one of Skirlaw's main residences and he certainly spent time there in January 1391, January 1393, January and August 1394, March and September 1395, March, June and July 1396, May and June 1397, March 1398, September 1399, February and December 1402, May, June, September, November and September 1404, and March, April, May and June 1405.

The estates of the diocese of Durham in Yorkshire consisted of rectories and vicarages, some of them situated within York. The bishops possessed a manor situated adjacent to Howden Minster, which was a collegiate church with six parishes around Howden. They claimed the rights to fishing on the rivers Ouse and Humber from Cawood to Melton, some thirty miles in distance. It is claimed that in 1342 two whales and two sturgeons were caught on the shores of the manor of Howden. The buildings of the manor, which was used as one of the bishop's residences were extensive in Skirlaw's time, but only the hall which he built (see Chapter Nine) still exists and is now used for commercial purposes. The manor was also maintained as a stopping place for bishops on their travels to London. This was said to be Skirlaw's favourite residence and he spent much of his time there. He was at Howden in August 1394, May and August 1402, May to September 1404, July and August 1405, and January, February and March 1406 when he died.

The strongly fortified and moated bishop's palace at Northallerton was often used by kings as a stopping place on their journeys to and from Scotland. It eventually became neglected and was pulled down in the 1660's. The old castle at Crayke and the extensive lands surrounding the village had been in the ownership of the bishops of Durham since 685. All that now stands of what had once been an important fortress is the four-storey tower house built after Skirlaw's death by Bishop Neville around 1450, and the ruins of an early tower.[410] There is no record that Skirlaw stayed at either of these residences.

Skirlaw's London residence, which had been rebuilt by Bishop Thomas Hatfield, was Durham House with its chapel and garden, located between the Strand and the River Thames, not far from Charing Cross. Skirlaw made a considerable number of visits there when attending Parliament and the king's council, and he also used it as a base for his diplomatic missions to the continent. The London houses of the bishops of other dioceses were mainly located in the same area.

His many commitments required Skirlaw to travel extensively and the following illustrates the extent of some of his movements early in his episcopate. In 1389 he spent time in France, returning to London and Westminster in July and going back to France in November. He was in London during the first half of 1390 but visited Calais in June, returning the following month. In October he was installed as bishop of Durham, and then spent some time at Auckland before going to Parliament in November. In early 1391 Skirlaw was at Wheel Hall but returned to Durham before going to Auckland in May; he then travelled to London in August to deal with the vacancy caused by the resignation of Robert Walworth as prior of Durham, straight after his visitation, and he was in London and Windsor in September.

The Public Records Office and Durham Archives include the proceedings of the halmote court of Skirlaw's Durham estates during the time of his episcopy. Many relate to coal transactions at Ryton, Whickham and Newcastle, and to turf at Ryton. The halmote court dealt with the copyhold land and the tenants on the estates belonging to the bishopric of Durham. Copyhold refers to the lands held by title written into the halmote court rolls which on the death of a tenant reverted to the bishopric as lord of the manor, being the bishopric. The conditions of copyhold were a payment of some kind, or a service to the lord of the manor such as a few days' work or the provision of fowl. With a copyhold, possession was more complete than with a leasehold, but less complete than with a freehold.[411] The bishop also held various other courts at Howden: a manorial court; a forester's court in right of the bishop's possessions in the Forest of Ouse and Derwent; and a criminal court, which may have been held in the precincts of the manor.[412]

The muniments of the Durham dean and chapter include a file of over fifty indentures made between Robert Wycliffe and the collectors of dues of various townships and other officials of Bishop Skirlaw. Wycliffe had his own seal which was based on his coat of arms and was described as: round, armorial, a chevron between three crosses crosslet with the inscription '*sigillum roberti de wycliffe*'.[413] The indentures state both the name of the collector and the name of the township concerned. Skirlaw appointed Wycliffe constable of Durham Castle from 1390 to 1405. He also appointed him temporal chancellor and receiver-general of the bishopric, rector of Hutton Rudby, Kirby Ravensworth and Romaldkirk, and keeper of Kepier hospital. He was one of Skirlaw's executors, and died at Kepier in 1423.[414]

The file of indentures records that Robert Wycliffe, as constable of Durham, paid money to John Dolfanby, who was master coal miner to the bishop, at Gateshead on 31 December 1394 and at various dates thereafter.[415] An undated petition was made by John Dolfanby for payment and compensation. He was employed to mine and carry coal from the bishop's mine at Gateshead to the Tyne. Six keels[416] had sunk and he had spent extra money in saving the mine from flooding. He was given £6 for his trouble and allowance was to be made for the keels in his next account.[417] Wycliffe also paid sums to John Thodhowe, who was supervisor of works to the bishop, on 10 February 1395 and thereafter.[418]

John Cockin, who was deacon of the collegiate church of Lanchester[419] and sequestrator of Durham, paid amounts to Peter de la Hay, Skirlaw's chamberlain, on 5 April and 29 April 1395 at Wheel Hall.[420] Various letters from Bishop Skirlaw gave authority to the collectors to deal with special cases within their townships in accordance with his instructions. These included appropriating dues from a farm to repairing its gale damaged fences, extending payment date for dues, pardoning payment of rent from poor tenants, and pardoning a fine for cutting down trees in a park. Various accounts of expenses relate to the bishop's estates and their activities. There are details of herbage in the new park at Auckland with lists of graziers, beasts, charges made and maintenance expenses. There is a memorandum of expenses relating to the building of Norton Mill and the repair of Stockton Mill. Another list relates to the expenses and repairs of John Pottowe (bailiff of Darlington), and concerns the carriage of fish, timber, repairs to stables, a pinfold, roofing, ditching, etc., at Auckland, Allerton, Darlington, Feetham and Besmond. Other lists of expenses concerned the bishop's South Mill and tollbooth at Durham.[421]

There are files of letters sent by Skirlaw to the auditor of the bishop's estate records, Wilkin Brafferton, in response to questions raised by him. From Auckland Castle he wrote on 3 November 1394 informed him that Julianne Gray, a tenant at Whitburn, had until next Whitsuntide to pay what she owed, and that William Marnhull (parson of Whitburn) was her guarantor.[422] On 23 November Skirlaw informed him that Robin Clerk of Stanhope had been pardoned 30s he owed.[423] Another letter dated 1 December 1394 informed Brafferton that a tenant at Heighington had been given until the following Easter to pay what he owed, on the surety of John Gylle (vicar of Heighington), and that his impounded beasts could therefore be returned to him.[424] Two further letters dated 12 December 1394 told him that Henry Freend (collector of Lynesack), had been given respite from paying certain sums and that he was pardoned for his trespass,[425] and that the tenants of Middridge had been given until Candlemas (2 February) to pay what they owed.[426]

One November Skirlaw wrote from Auckland Palace to the collector of Bondgate in Darlington informing him that a chaplain, John Houton, had been pardoned the amount for which he was amerced (fined) in the halmote court at Darlington,[427] and told Roger Blerthorn and Robert Bell (collectors at Wolsingham) that two poor tenants of Wolsingham had been pardoned, John Fisher (rent) and Lawrence Robinson (amercement)[428] at the halmote court.[429] From Wheel Hall Skirlaw wrote to the constable on 23 March 1395 that John Lewyn had been pardoned his fine for cutting down three ash trees in the park at Coudon.[430] In 1402/03 Lewyn's son, Walter, and Peter Dryng entered into a recognizance with bishop Skirlaw to deliver John Kellowe, described as a late farmer of the vill of Durham, to the gaol there, and was also a party to several other recognizances in the same year.[431] John Lewyn was the mason who worked with Peter Dryng in the reconstruction of Finchale Priory from 1364 onwards.

In 1403 Skirlaw issue a mandate to Ralph Eure and others to hold an assize of novel disseisin[432] brought by John Wyndelston junior and Cecilia his wife against John Wyndelston (his father?) and others over tenements in Windlestone, Shelom and Kirk Merrington.[433] An application made by Thomas Gretham, the rector of Ryton, for the construction of an aqueduct and pipes from the Strotewell spring, was confirmed by Skirlaw after John Burgh became rector in 1403.[434] The first known commissions of conservatorship of the Wear and other rivers were first granted during Skirlaw's time in 1390.[435] At some time during his episcopacy Skirlaw also granted a commission of survey of the river Wear.[436]

The diocese of Durham was within the northern province of York, and the bishop of Durham was its senior bishop. Despite his special position in the bishopric of Durham as the king's tenant-in-chief, the bishop still came within the northern province, and under the spiritual jurisdiction of the archbishop of York. He was suffragan to the archbishop and was expected to attend provincial synods and give him the same respect and obedience as other bishops in the province.[437] Although some bishops of Durham had considered themselves immune from the influence of York, Skirlaw did recognise the relationship and accepted the archbishop's authority. An important duty of the archbishop was to call a convocation of the northern province from time to time for the purpose of granting subsidies to the king and related matters. Other meetings were called to deal with matters of Church policy and to discuss other ecclesiastical affairs.[438] Skirlaw or his representative attended these occasions.

As senior bishop in the province of York, Skirlaw stood second to the archbishop and was able to sit in the House of Lords as of right. In accordance with custom already established in 1386, it was his duty together with the bishop of Bath and Wells to escort the sovereign at a coronation,[439] and this no doubt happened when Henry Bolingbroke was crowned in 1399. By convention the bishop of Durham was and is allowed to describe himself in formal documents as being bishop '*by divine providence*', whereas most bishops reserve this courtesy for addressing fellow bishops but style themselves '*by divine permission*'.[440]

On the 28 February 1390 a joint session took place in Richard II's Parliamentary (Jerusalem) Chamber at Westminster. To this came both the archbishops of Canterbury and York and their suffragans, including Skirlaw, in the presence of William Wykeham (chancellor of England) and others, lords temporal and spiritual, to consult on the Lollard movement, and to protest in strong language against any statute which might be passed by Parliament against the authority of the pope, or against the ecclesiastical liberties. A protest was read by the clerk of the Parliament on their behalf which was duly inserted in the Rolls of Parliament.

The numbers of the Northern Convocation were small; from three to five bishops, a considerable company of *ex-officio* members, and proctors for the archdeaconries. In order to elect proctors for convocation Skirlaw's official produced a writ. For instance, in 1396, in accordance with a mandate issued by the official of Skirlaw, William Esshe (the rural dean or *decanus Christianitatis* of the diocese) was instructed to summon the prior and chapter of Durham, the archdeacon of Durham, and the clergy (including all deans of collegiate churches, rectors, vicars, and masters of hospitals) to meet in St. Nicholas' church in the Market Place of Durham to elect a proctor for the archdeaconry of Durham. The elected proctor would undoubtedly be a rural dean, who fulfilled convocational and other duties.[441]

In general York refrained from exercising any influence over the see of Durham. The main cause of friction between the bishop of Durham and the archbishop concerned the peculiars each held in the diocese of the other. In the case of York the only peculiar was centred on Hexham, but Durham's possessions in York were more complex, consisting of eighteen churches in Howdenshire and Allertonshire and three churches in York itself.[442]

York's only serious attempt to interfere was Archbishop Alexander Neville's metropolitan visitation in 1376, which was almost immediately subjected to royal inhibition. When Durham was without a bishop, the prior and chapter usually, if reluctantly, conceded the archiepiscopal right to jurisdiction in their diocese. A more insoluble problem arose after Skirlaw's death, when York was also without an archbishop following the beheading of archbishop Scrope in 1405 and before the appointment, in 1407, of Henry Bowet. Durham Priory delegated two of its members as keepers of the Durham spiritualities, although York's dean and chapter protested that they themselves were the lawful custodians. This led to an appeal to Rome followed by apparently ineffective arbitration before the bishop of Exeter.[443]

In the early 1390's under Archbishop Thomas Arundel the choir of York

Minster was demolished, and during the decades that saw the building of the new choir the drama surrounding the throne of England had its repercussions in the see of York. Richard II had close connections with Archbishop Arundel and gave money for the work at the Minster. In 1396 he translated Arundel to Canterbury and York received an Austin friar, Robert Waldby, for its archbishop, although in the two years before his death it is believed he never actually visited the Minster. The chapter elected Bishop Skirlaw as Waldby's successor in 1398, but was immediately overruled by the now desperate Richard II, who installed another aristocratic friend, Richard Scrope. A brave and learned man, Scrope nevertheless betrayed two kings and died a traitor's death. Only a year after Richard II had personally secured him the archbishopric, he was in the Tower of London with other lords to hear the king's statement of abdication. In 1405 he led several thousand men in revolt against the new king, Henry IV. Tricked into surrender, he was executed under the walls of York amid a huge crowd on the feast of St. William. After this disaster the see of York was vacant for two and a half years whilst Skirlaw, ousted by Richard II's appointment of Scrope, attempted to gain office. He never succeeded and died with the matter still unresolved. In 1405 Skirlaw commissioned and paid for the glazing of the great east window, which ensured his immortality.[444]

In his role as bishop, Skirlaw was also elected a member of the king's council during the reign of Richard II and later of Henry IV. His attendance at many meetings is well recorded for the period 1392-93. During that time he attended at least twenty-four meetings. Many of the matters discussed were concerned less with great issues of policy than with innumerable details of administration and jurisdiction.[445] Royal charters were witnessed by members of the king's council, although in some instances other leading men of the realm added their names at the king's request. Skirlaw witnessed many of these charters as a member of the council under both kings.[446]

In 1391 memoranda from the king's council recorded the delivery to Sir Richard Scrope of a commission to Bishop Skirlaw and others to receive the final 24,000 marks due for the ransom of David II, king of Scotland, and their return to the chancery on 9 May.[447] David II had been captured by the English forces at the battle of Neville's Cross on 17 October 1346. On 13 July 1354 a treaty was concluded offering to free him in return for the payment of £60,000 in nine years by the four principal burghs of Aberdeen, Perth, Dundee and Edinburgh and the giving of twenty hostages. This appears never to have been ratified, and a further treaty was eventually concluded in Berwick on 3 October 1357. David was liberated for a ransom of 100,000 marks, payable in ten years by equal instalments each midsummer, together with the return of hostages. He had difficulties raising the necessary funds and died in 1371 with part of the ransom still owing. No payment had been received since 1377 soon after Edward III's death leaving 24,000 marks outstanding. This was the debt which Skirlaw and his colleagues were charged with recovering in 1391.[448]

In 1394 Richard II was in Dublin with an armed force to secure the punishment of rebels there and to establish good government and just rule over his faithful lieges.[449] On 8 January 1395 he sent messages to Skirlaw, the duke of Gloucester, and Walden among others to inform them that the Irish clan of O'Neill had surrendered. This was a major coup for Richard and he was clearly hoping to pacify the whole country, but it is unclear why Skirlaw was singled out for a personal message.[450]

John of Gaunt's wife, the Duchess Constance, died in 1394 on the 24 or 25 March whilst he was in France. In the previous July it is recorded that she had gone to Bishop Robert Braybrooke of London's house at Much Hadham (Herts) for a hunting party. Three of the king's minstrels and one of Bishop Skirlaw's had provided the entertainment. Skirlaw, himself, was away in France at the time.[451]

The grant of customs revenue for the life of the king was sufficient in times of peace to cover his expenses, but during periods of conflict Richard required extra funds to raise armies. In spring 1399 the king needed to raise funds to mount another expedition to Ireland and he fell back upon the well-tried device of the forced loan. Royal serjeants-at-arms were sent round the country with letters under the privy seal. The king asked for a 'notable' sum and, when the loan was negotiated, an indenture was sealed between the serjeant-at-arms and the lender. This method proved very effective and met little opposition. Those offering excuses were accepted, but others who refused were required to appear before the council and explain themselves. There is some evidence, however, that resistance to the loan was higher in the north of England than elsewhere. The earl of Northumberland and bishop Skirlaw both asked to make their excuses before the council. Others including Sir William FitzWilliam, Lord Greystoke, Thomas Ughtred, John Savill, Sir John Hotham, Sir William Melton, Sir Stephen Scrope and Sir Henry FitzHugh of Ravensworth lent nothing. These men formed a sizeable proportion of those approached in Yorkshire and the north-eastern counties, implying that Richard's government was widely unpopular in the north, particularly in Yorkshire. Henry Bolingbroke owned extensive duchy estates in the county as well as a number of powerful duchy castles.[452] On 23 October 1399, the archbishop of Canterbury acting on Henry's behalf required all the lords spiritual and temporal to sign their allegiance to the new king in place of Richard, and to assent to the latter's imprisonment. Skirlaw was one of many who did so.[453]

The first recorded meeting of the new king's council took place on 11 November 1399 and included Bishop Skirlaw, Archbishop Arundel, the earls of Northumberland, Westmorland and Worcester, the chancellor, treasurer, keeper of the privy seal and king's chamberlain, the Lords Cobham and Lovell and Sir Matthew Gourney. At a later meeting on 4 December the number of council members was increased by the addition of the bishops of London, Exeter, Hereford and others.[454]

At the beginning of his reign Henry IV was very short of cash and to avoid the time-consuming task of summoning Parliament to vote taxes he used the more informal route through his council. Henry needed funds to keep the Scots and the French at bay. A number of wealthy men made loans and the clerics paid their tenths, although they were slow to do so.[455] In 1403 to demonstrate their support for Henry when there was a threat to the king and to the temporal goods of the Church from the barons of Parliament, Skirlaw lent him 1,800 marks and Archbishop Arundel 1,000 marks. The knights of the shires were reluctant to give their own money to the king and the idea of confiscating the wealth of the clergy had appeal, under the influence of Lollard ideas.[456] However, the proposal to seize the riches of the Church was abandoned and its goods were safe for a time.[457]

According to Wylie, in 1403 Skirlaw was implicated indirectly with other bishops in a plot to depose the king in favour of Sir Edmund Mortimer (earl of March), and to create Wales as a separate principality under the Welsh activist Owen Glendower. Mortimer was Richard II's nearest male relative and had a legitimate claim to the throne as he was descended in the female line from Edward III's second son, whereas Henry IV was descended from the third. The earl of Northumberland entered into a secret alliance with Glendower and Mortimer towards achieving this aim with the support of many English lords and clergy including Richard Scrope (archbishop of York). At the battle of Shrewsbury on 21 July 1403 the revolt was crushed, when the forces led by the earl were defeated by Henry IV's men. Skirlaw is said to have fled to France and was offered safe asylum by Charles VI 'if he feared to return to England'.[458] Whether this is true is doubtful as Skirlaw was not in good health by this time.

The devastation wrought by the Scots in the North had left the people of the border counties too poor to be taxed, and so there was no imposition in Northumberland, Westmorland and Cumberland. When the Convocation of Canterbury met at St. Paul's on 21 April 1404 it sanctioned the unusual grant of a tax amounting to two shillings in the pound upon all ecclesiastical offices or benefices which had until then escaped, half to be payable at 11 November 1404 and the rest on 1 May 1405. The tax was unpopular with holders of small livings and chantries, some of whom refused to pay. Some high-ranking Church functionaries, having met to vote the tax, were willing to make loans in advance. These included Skirlaw who lent 2,000 marks, covered by substantial guarantees, which was repaid on 3 November 1405.[459]

CHAPTER SEVEN

SKIRLAW AND THE RELIGIOUS ACTIVITIES OF DURHAM

On taking up his appointment as bishop of Durham, Skirlaw had three chief concerns: his relationship with the chapter and the cathedral priory of Durham; his relationship with the archbishop of York who was ecclesiastically superior to the bishop; and the proper discharge of his episcopal duties in the diocese, a volatile area bordering Scotland. Various records give some insight into Skirlaw's activities relating to the diocese during his term of office. Some of these are outlined below, while those relating to the prior and chapter of the priory of Durham are summarised separately.

The politics of the border area were of relevance to the bishop because the English town of Berwick-upon-Tweed, the castle of Roxburgh, and the Durham cell of Coldingham (Berwickshire) lay in the diocese of St. Andrews. Like other Scottish sees, St. Andrews came under the jurisdiction of a supporter of the antipope Clement VII of Avignon during the time of the Great Schism, and on 3 June 1390 Pope Boniface IX granted Skirlaw jurisdiction over the subjects of the king of England in the diocese (see Chapter Five).[460] Then on 20 October 1390 Skirlaw at Auckland Castle sent a letter to Robert Claxton (prior of Coldingham), repeating the contents of the papal bull he had received and appointing the prior to investigate and correct the state of affairs there.[461]

In 1395 Skirlaw was asked by Edmund Stafford, dean of York, to lend him a sum of money to meet costs incurred at the Roman court in securing his elevation to the bishopric of Exeter. His request followed the death of Bishop Thomas Brantingham, when Stafford had been informed by the king and chapter of their eagerness for him to become bishop.[462] Whether Skirlaw obliged the dean is not recorded.

The church of St. Hilda, Hartlepool in the Durham diocese established several chantries before the Reformation. Bishop Skirlaw, on the 3 April 1396, granted a licence to the mayor and commonality of Hartlepool to found two chantries, one in honour of St. Helen, for one chaplain, to pray for the 'good estate of the bishop whilst living, of Maude, wife of Roger Clifford, and their heirs'. The chaplain and his successors were to be subject to the rules and orders of the corporation, which was also permitted to grant lands and property for the perpetual maintenance of the chantry. Another chantry was also granted in honour of the Blessed Virgin for two chaplains. Around the same period Skirlaw granted a further licence 'to refound to the honour of St. Nicholas a third chantry, of one chaplain, to pray at the altar of that saint.'[463]

Around 1403 a number of Lollard priests were found to be preaching heretical doctrines in the diocese of Durham and were mandated to appear before Bishop Skirlaw. The account of one, Richard Wyche, has survived. He was summoned to Auckland Castle and travelled from Northumberland on foot. Due to the pains of a rupture he could only make Chester-le-Street, where he left his cloak, purse and cases in pledge at the inn and hired a hackney to take him the remaining miles. On 7 December 1402 Wyche was brought into the presence of Skirlaw, who required an oath from him that he would obey the law of the Church. Wyche refused to comply and was placed in prison until he changed his mind. Some time later Skirlaw again summoned him and asked him by whose authority he was preaching in his diocese. When he could not produce one, the bishop told him that he suspected that he was one of the sect of Lollards who did not believe the truth about the Eucharist. As Skirlaw was not satisfied with his replies he was again sent to prison. A master was sent to him from Newcastle to try to reason with him and offer him some promotion if he conformed, but without success.

After a period of three weeks Wyche was again brought before Skirlaw, but nothing could be made of him and so he was placed in prison again. Ten days later a knight visited Wyche in his cell and together with the bishop's chancellor and notary they managed to get Wyche to agree to take the oath of obedience to the Church. The next day he kneeled before Skirlaw, kissed the Book and thought he had finished the matter. However, he was required to swear a further oath which he declined and was then sent back to the cells. The next time he came before Skirlaw the bishop read to him the recantation of Purvey (a follower of Wycliffe) made in London on 6 March 1401, but this meant nothing to him. Back in prison Wyche was given paper and ink to write down his views on transubstantiation but he declined. On 7 February 1403 a Franciscan and a Carmelite friar attempted to instruct him on the Eucharist, but he would not be moved, so they told him that the bishop now had legal power to judge him a heretic. Wyche accepted the possible consequences if this were to be the case.

Skirlaw, who had not been well, had recovered sufficiently to participate in a further meeting with Wyche in March 1403, where he was pronounced excommunicate and condemned to be imprisoned until his degradation was finalized and all his possessions confiscated. He asked to appeal to the pope, but the court said he was too late and sent him back to his cell. Whilst in prison Wyche wrote a letter to his friends in Newcastle urging them to pray for him that he might persevere to the end, and to send him some sheets containing the Gospels in red ink by a local priest. This secret letter was only brought to light some 500 years after it was written when it was discovered in Prague. He also wrote a letter to John Hus (who led the Hussites in Bohemia with a similar doctrine based on Wycliffe and the Lollards) and his comrade Jacob of Mies (who was one of the four masters who had undertaken the defence of Wycliffe's Decalogue at Prague) encouraging them to persevere with their beliefs. Later Wyche withdrew his heretical position and became vicar of Deptford near Greenwich. Eventually, on 2 August 1439 he was burnt on Tower Hill because of his beliefs and many Londoners made pilgrimages to his tomb, as they considered him to be a good, just and holy man.[464]

Other priests were certainly brought before Skirlaw for various offences against the Church around the time of the trial of Richard Wyche. These included James Nottingham, John Roxburgh, John Whitby and Robert York, although nothing is known of the outcome of these trials. There is evidence that the Lollard activities of these men were centred on Newcastle. Snape suggests, in the light of Wyche's account, that in bishop Skirlaw they met a man who was anxious to persuade rather than condemn.[465] This approach may well be a reflection of his vast experience as a diplomat.

In May 1404 Skirlaw travelled to Bridlington in the East Riding of Yorkshire, where he was present with Archbishop Scrope and the bishop of Carlisle at the translation of the ashes of John of Bridlington. St. John Twenge (or Thwing as he is sometimes known) was the prior of St. Mary's Bridlington. He came from the Wolds village of Thwing situated eight miles west of Bridlington and may have been related to the well-known family of that name. He was canonised because of his reputation for great holiness and miraculous powers.[466]

The diocese of Durham was divided into five deaneries, and one hundred and thirty parishes, sixty-five of them situated in the county of Durham. In this county the advowsons of over twenty-five churches were in the hands of the bishop, while a further eighteen were held at the prior and convent of Durham – a concentration of patronage which originated with the patrimony of St. Cuthbert. Another six churches were under the control of the masters of the hospitals of Sherburn, Greatham and Kepier, who were themselves appointed by the bishop. There were six collegiate churches situated at Auckland, Chester-le-Street, Lanchester, Darlington, Norton and Staindrop, and nearly forty prebends also in the bishop's gift in Northumberland. Of the sixty-two parishes in Northumberland the prior and convent of Durham were the greatest largest patrons with eight churches, of which two were held by the bishop; with the others were spread amongst twelve other lay patrons. Some of the vicarages were held by religious orders; the Premonstratensians of Alnwick and Blanchland held eight churches and the Augustinians of Hexham and Brinkburn five.[467] Cistercians and Premonstratensians were established at Newminster and Blanchland respectively.

Skirlaw, like other bishops, had a great deal of freedom in exercising patronage, placing livings with friends and their kinsmen and with the leading diocesan administrators, and many wealthy livings became additional sources of income for these men. As the duties of the administrators usually precluded them from taking an active role in these churches, they employed chaplains to carry out the day-to-day parish duties.[468]

Beneficed clergy often neglected their parishes and failed to reside in their livings. One John Burgeys was accused by Skirlaw in 1403 of maladministration and failure to reside in his parish. He had been Bishop Fordham's treasurer in 1386, and had become the dean of Lanchester and master of Sherburn probably in 1388 (and certainly before 1392). He later exchanged the deanery for that of Auckland. Skirlaw deprived him of the custody of Sherburn Hospital and ordered him to resume residence in Auckland under threat of further deprival. However, it transpired that Burgeys had obtained a papal licence in 1403 to be absent for the duration of his life, although in fact he returned to Durham in 1408. Skirlaw appointed Alan Newark to succeed Burgeys as master of Sherburn hospital on 2 January 1403. Church buildings were often not properly maintained and clergy were frequently reprimanded by the bishop following reports of dilapidations. Many clergy found it too much of a burden to keep the chancel, rectory and other buildings in order. Some new building and renewals did take place, but these were mainly financed by rich benefactors including Skirlaw himself.[469]

Parishes generated income from offerings and dues, and also from the tithes imposed on every parishioner. Some parish clergy received the benefit of endowments attached to the living known as glebes. The rector had to maintain the chancel of his church from his income together with service-books and vestments, whereas the parishioners were responsible for the upkeep of the nave and, using income often from pew rents.[470]

Some disputes, because of their nature, were brought before the king and council rather than the courts of the bishop. However, Skirlaw was still involved in these cases in carrying out the requirements of the king's letters patent.

Thomas Cotham, for example, who had held the prebend of the late John Kyngeston in St. Cuthbert's church, Darlington, petitioned in the king's courts to gain possession, as he claimed it had been wrongly collated to Robert Dalton, chaplain, by the Crown. The prebend had recently been held by William Lynton, clerk, but had become vacant. A warrant to consider the petition was dated 1389 and, as many objections to the Crown's action had been received, an order was issued on 5 July 1390 for Skirlaw to arrest Dalton. On 15 October 1390 Richard II 'ratified' Dalton's possession of the prebend and Cotham lost his case. Dalton is listed as being a canon of Darlington between 1390 and 1403.[471]

During the time when Urban VI was pope and John Fordham was bishop of Durham, John Kyllome, clerk, was provided with two benefices worth twenty-five marks and eighteen marks, respectively, the first with and the second without cure of souls. He also had a claim on a portion of Norton parish church worth only nine marks, without cure of souls, in the patronage of the bishop of Durham. The previous incumbent, Robert Scampston, died some time before 29 January 1390, significant in that this was the date of limitation fixed in the re-enactment of the Statute of

Provisors 1391, when the portion became void. Kyllome took possession of it in accordance with papal provision until William Ryall, clerk, intimated to the king that it was in the royal gift. Ryall was then awarded collation by royal letters patent, and Skirlaw duly put him in corporal possession and ejected Kyllome. Kyllome petitioned the king to order the chancellor to summon Ryall to chancery to show the royal title and subsequently a warrant was issued in 1391. Records show Ryall as portioner of Norton in 1390 and Kyllome as vicar of Billingham (Norton is in the vicinity) in 1396, so it may be that Kyllome won his case.[472]

In 1393/94, a case similar to that of to Thomas Cotham concerned John Herl, clerk, who petitioned the king regarding the provision made by the late Pope Urban VI for the prebend of Lamesley, under the patronage of the bishop of Durham, in the collegiate church of St. Mary in Chester-le-Street in the franchise of Durham. John Fordham, late bishop of Durham, had placed Robert Scampston, clerk, in corporate possession of the prebend. Following Scampston's death, it became void and Herl, by virtue of this provision, took possession and continued peaceably until he was ejected by a royal nominee, Thomas Westminster. Herl requested a Chancery writ of *scire facias* to warn Westminster to appear before the king and chancellor to show why the royal letters patent appointing him to the prebend should not be repealed and annulled and the plaintiff restored. Herl was made canon of York in 1387, in 1388 was confirmed canon of Chester-le-Street, Norton and Lanchester, and was eventually confirmed to the prebend of Chester in 1398.[473]

Cases brought before the Court of York include one relating to a dispute in 1395/96 between John Derby (dean of the collegiate church of Chester-le-Street), Thomas Smyth, William Melotte, Thomas Belton, John Gray, and other parishioners, and Bishop Skirlaw. An appeal was made to York relating to the tithes of the Plawsworth and Walridge parishes of Chester-le-Street. Another case involved a dispute between William Lampton (squire) and Bishop Skirlaw in 1397. Appeal was made to the Apostolic See and for the tuition of the Court of York but the nature of the charge is unknown.[474]

The most important religious foundation in the medieval diocese of Durham was the Benedictine Priory of the Cathedral Church of St. Cuthbert of Durham; and the bishop of Durham as its titular head was involved with many aspects of the institution. The prior of Durham Cathedral held a position of great importance and his rank was equal to that of the border lords. He was the source of all authority within the monastery and presided over all the chapter meetings. When he visited the outlying houses of the order he went with a train of attendants and took with him his own furniture. The Durham monks endeavoured to maintain their independence from the bishop of Durham and resisted his encroachment into their affairs. Over the centuries there had been a history of friction between the bishop and the priory. For instance, during the twelfth century when Hugh de Puiset was bishop, the monks had continually struggled against him in an effort to maintain their revenues and their privileges, only obtaining the right to these on de Puiset's deathbed. Similar conflicts occurred with de Puiset's two successors; indeed one of the priors was excommunicated by the bishop.[475]

The priory of Durham was very wealthy and owned extensive lands and magnificent buildings. The Benedictines who held Durham Priory also had dependent priories in the diocese at Jarrow, Wearmouth and Finchale, and cells at Holy Island and Farne. Although the wealth of Durham Priory was greater than the total of the nine other monastic houses of the diocese, Durham also ranked as one of the greatest foundations in the country. At the Dissolution, only six houses — Christ Church, Canterbury, Bury St. Edmonds, St. Albans, Glastonbury, Westminster, and St. Mary's, York — had larger incomes.[476]

There were nine convents and other religious houses situated in the diocese, outside the jurisdiction of the bishop of Durham, of which eight lay in Northumberland. Ranking next to Durham Priory in wealth was Tynemouth Priory, a cell of St. Albans, a house of considerable proportions, said to be worth around £400 a year. The abbey of the Premonstratensian canons at Alnwick followed with an annual value of less than £200 a year, and then the poorer house at Blanchland, both ruled by the father-abbot of Newhouse, in Lincolnshire. There were also houses of Cistercian monks at Newminster and Austin canons at Brinkburn. Hexham Priory, another Augustinian house, also lay outside the bishop's jurisdiction in the archbishop of York's temporal and ecclesiastical franchise of Hexhamshire. The four nunneries in the diocese were situated at Newcastle-upon-Tyne (St. Bartholomew's, the wealthiest), Holystone in Redesdale (near the Scottish border), Lamley on the South Tyne, and Neasham in County Durham (on the north bank of the Tees, close to the bishop's manor of Darlington).

Skirlaw, as bishop, was concerned with the conduct of life at the priory of Durham. In accordance with the constitution of Boniface VIII, his duties included the conducting of visitations to the priory and the other priories and cells dependent in the diocese.[477] Although honorary and titular head of the Durham Priory, the bishop concerned himself very little with monastic affairs. The estates of the bishop and those of the priory of Durham were separate. The prior was the working head of the house; he held the same rank as an abbot, lived in a palace which was nearly as grand as that of the bishop, and also had a number of manors in the county, in which he sojourned.[478] During his episcopate Skirlaw participated in at least three visitations (in 1391, 1394 and 1397) and caused offence by attempting to introduce Benedictine monks from other houses in the inspection process. One reason for a visitation was to ascertain that accounts had been produced for audit by the convent's annual chapter. Skirlaw commented during one visitation that, despite the complicated system of accounting used, it did not appear too difficult for a reasonably conscientious Durham monk to keep his obedience (accounting responsibility) in a fairly competent state.[479]

During Richard Poore's episcopate in the early thirteenth century an agreement was made between him and the prior (Ralph Kerneth) and the chapter of Durham regarding the relative position of the two parties on many matters which had previously been in dispute. The terms of the agreement were manifold and its principal clauses are given below:

> The monks had the right of free election of their prior, the election being subject to examination and confirmation by the bishop. The prior was to do canonical obedience to the bishop and was ranked as the first person in the bishopric after the bishop with the same position as an abbot.
>
> The prior was to have an abbot's stall on the left side of the choir (but without pastoral staff), and the right hand of the bishop, and full powers, with the chapter, of governing the priory in all its internal and external affairs.
>
> In the absence of the bishop, the prior, with the bishop's official and the archdeacons, could take action in synod on spiritual matters on behalf of the bishop.
>
> Monks who had made profession in chapter in the presence of the prior were to repeat their profession at mass in the presence of the bishop, who would then solemnly bless them.
>
> The prior and chapter were to present vicars for their appropriated churches to the bishop of Durham, to whom, when instituted by him, the vicars would be responsible for the cure of souls.
>
> The monks, by the authority of the bishop, were thrice a year solemnly to excommunicate those who within the bishopric of Durham knowingly disturbed the rights, privileges or possessions of the bishop and the church of Durham.
>
> When the bishop visited the priory once or, if necessary, twice a year, he was to correct faults with the agreement of the prior and chapter.
>
> With regard to pleas of the crown, all attachments were to be made by the bishop's bailiff, through the prior's bailiff. Prisoners were to be kept in the bishop's prison until tried in the bishop's court or released on bail. The bishop's bailiff was to carry out sentences involving forfeiture, mutilation or death. If any free man from the prior's land or fee was convicted of felony and as a result forfeited his land then the bishop was to hold the forfeited land for a year and a day, and the bishop and prior were to share the issue of the land equally. After that period the prior and chapter were to have the land as their escheat. All fines and incomes from pleas of the crown and others related to the prior's land or fee were to be divided equally between the bishop and the prior.

Wrecks of the sea found on the prior's land were to be shared equally by the prior and the bishop, but all customs on the Tees (except the ferry at Billingham which belonged to the prior and monks) were to belong to the bishop.

In the appropriate circumstances of cases brought before the prior's court use could be made of the bishop's gallows, pillory or tumbrel.

The custody and sequestration of vacant churches, in the gift of the monks and in the bishopric of Durham, were to remain with the bishop.

The monks were to have free watercourse *(aquae ductum)* through the bishop's lands.

The bishop was to retain the woods of Brackenholm and Woodhall, while the monks retained their wood at Hemingbrough.

The bishop's forest was reserved to himself, the prior and monks being forbidden to take firewood or timber from it without permission.[480]

Despite the terms of this agreement a number of disputes arose during Skirlaw's episcopate. The prior and chapter list injuries suffered at the hands of Skirlaw's officials for which they sought remedy. Their complaints concern: their right to free ingress and egress to and from the monastery for themselves and their goods; the destruction of the prior's pillory and therefore of his jurisdiction in the Old Borough and Elvet; the prior's half-share of income from the ferry at Monkwearmouth; the seizure by the bishop of the wardship of a minor heir to which the prior had a right; their fear that the improper manner in which the bishop had forced them to meet him at his installation might be taken as a precedent; the seizure by the bishop of their jurisdiction in Allertonshire; and the infringement by their liberties concerning the vill at Hemingbrough.[481]

Another case (undated), concerned the right of the prior and chapter to twenty named churches in the diocese of Durham. The proctor argued that the prior and chapter, when required by Bishop Louis Beaumont to prove their title to these churches, had appeared before the bishop's commissaries, Richard Eryholme, canon of York, and William Whickham, rector of Staindrop, and produced evidence which satisfied them. The bishop had confirmed this judgement, as had his successor, Richard Bury.[482]

A mandate was issued from Durham on 29 March 1390, by Thomas Gretham, rector of Ryton and vicar-general of Bishop Skirlaw, to the official of the archdeaconry overseeing the churches appropriated by the prior and chapter of Durham, to induct Ds [Dominus] William Wardall, chaplain, to the vicarage of Ellingham, made vacant by the resignation of Ds Henry Leyng, chaplain.[483] A similar letter dated 9 January 1390 was sent by Gretham to the archdeacon to induct Ds William Crayk, chaplain, on the presentation of the prior and chapter, to the vicarage of Edlingham.[484]

A document dated 26 April 1391 confirms the appropriation by Bishop Skirlaw of the church of Longhorsley to the priory of Brinkburn. Thomas de Wytton, prior of Brinkburn, had presented a petition for the appropriation on the grounds that the priory's income had been so diminished by pestilence and invasion that it could not, without help, support the various burdens upon it. After consulting the prior and chapter of Durham, the bishop granted the appropriation, stipulating that the priory of Brinkburn paid an annual pension of 6s 8d to the bishop and 3s 4d to the prior and chapter of Durham. There was to be a perpetual vicar of Longhorsley and canon of Brinkburn, presented by the prior and chapter of Brinkburn to the bishop. Robert Wallworth, prior of Durham, and the chapter added their approval and appended their seal. The witnesses were Master Thomas Gretham (bishop's official) and Master Thomas Weston (Licentiate in Law, canon of Wells), with the notarial certificate of John Cockin (clerk, scribe to the bishop).[485] In 1391 Skirlaw also granted an indulgence in favour of Kepier Hospital, where Robert Wycliffe was appointed master.[486]

The church of St. Oswald in Elvet, City of Durham, was a peculiar belonging to the dean and chapter of Durham. Application was made for a chantry to be dedicated to St. Mary the Virgin with an annual value of £4. Skirlaw granted his licence on 20 September 1392 to John Sharp and William Middleton, chaplains, to give two messuages with their appurtenances in Elvet of a annual value of 12s to Alan Hayden, chaplain, *custos* of the chantry, to be held by him and his successors for ever, for their better support and maintenance. On 5 June 1402 Skirlaw issued to them another licence to erect a chantry of one chaplain at the altar of St. John the Baptist and St. John the Evangelist, so that they and their ancestors and heirs might be prayed for, with authority that lands and rents of ten marks each year might be given to the chaplain and his successors for ever. To this end the manor of Edderacres with its appurtenances, a messuage in Fleshewergate in the borough of Durham, two messuages in the borough of Elvet, and one messuage in Old Elvet near the cemetery of St. Oswald, with a total annual value of £6 10s, were permanently conveyed to the chaplain and his successors. The bishop gave his consent on the 26 April 1403.[487]

In a letter dated 7 January 1394/95 Skirlaw confirmed the freedom of the prior and chapter of Durham from procurations for their appropriated churches. Skirlaw's grant, like those of his predecessors, was valid only for the duration of his own episcopate.[488]

Certification was given by the official of the prior of Durham, at Pittington, to the official of Bishop Skirlaw that on 24 April 1402 he received the following: "mandate of the official of the bishop of Durham to the official of the prior of Durham, archdeacon, to his own churches, in accordance with the bishop's mandate containing the tenor of the king's writ for summoning Parliament at Westminster for 7 May 1402 to summon the prior in person, the chapter by one proctor and the clergy of the archdeaconry by another proctor."[489]

Other drafts of letters from Skirlaw to his justices, Richard Norton and John Conyers, relate that the prior and chapter of Durham had protested to him about the injustices they were suffering in respect of half-shares in amercements levied on their tenants in the bishop's court. The bishop asked Norton and Conyers to investigate, taking into consideration the evidence put forward by the prior and chapter and that put forward on behalf of the bishop by Sir Ralph Eure, Dr Robert Wycliffe and Sir Peter de la Hay, and to inform him of their opinion.[490] Norton and Conyers suggested that the prior and chapter should have half the profits of justice levied in the bishop's court from tenants within their fee, and that the bishop should have the wardship of heirs within their fee who were minors, and half the lands of such heirs, provided that they held some land of the bishop by military service.[491]

Although provision was made for a bishop's visitation on an annual basis, only three visitations to Durham Priory are recorded during Skirlaw's episcopate. Documentary evidence on these and other visits is summarised below. The first visitation took place in 1391 when Wallworth was prior.

> On 22 February 1391 John Hemingbrough, prior of St. Leonard's near Stamford, sent a letter to Robert Walworth, prior of Durham, acknowledging and reciting a mandate from Walworth (dated 13 February 1391) ordering John to be present himself and to cite his fellows to be present in the chapter house at Durham on 6 March, when Skirlaw intended to visit the priory. Prior Hemingbrough said that he had done as instructed, and had attached a list of twelve monks who would be present with him.[492]
>
> A notarial instrument records most of the preliminaries — the sermon and the reading of certificates of citation and of protestations — to the visitation of Durham Priory by Skirlaw on that date. Apart from the prior and sub-prior fifty-five monks were present at the visitation. Witnesses to the document included: John Southwell (advocate of the court of York), Thomas Gretham (vicar general), Robert Ashburn (lawyer), William Barton (clerk and notary), and the notary was John Stanton (clerk of the diocese of York).[493]
>
> On 21 March 1391 an appointment of proctors was made to represent the prior and chapter in respect of their appropriated churches in the diocese at synods, visitations of Bishop Skirlaw, and other occasions.[494]

In August 1391 Robert Walworth, prior of Durham, resigned from that office and a public instrument was issued to that effect.[495] The reason for his resignation is not known, although it seems likely that it came about as the result of Skirlaw's visitation. Skirlaw may have been critical of the state of affairs at the priory and Walworth, who had been prior for 16 years, may in any case have been ready for retirement. On 14 August 1391 Skirlaw wrote from his manor in London, informing the sub-prior and convent of Durham that he had received from John Hemingbrough and Robert Lanchester, monks of the convent, notification of Walworth's resignation, together with a petition for a licence to elect another prior. The bishop accepted the resignation and granted a licence to elect a new prior.[496] On 1 September 1391 Skirlaw handed over the care of the priory to his chancellor, Thomas Weston, during the vacancy. He also sent letters from his manor in London informing the sub-prior and convent of his appointment.[497] In due course Hemingbrough was instituted as prior, following consent given by the compromissaries (arbitrators), which was then confirmed.[498]

Skirlaw's next recorded visitation took place in 1394.

> A copy of a notarial instrument records that on 12 May 1394, in the parish church of Jarrow, there appeared before Skirlaw, who was visiting the church, John Hagthorp (clerk, proctor of the prior and chapter of Durham). Hagthorp exhibited letters of the prior and chapter reciting a mandate from the bishop to his archdeacon to summon all beneficed clerks to be present at the bishop's forthcoming visitation, and appointed Thomas Legate and Thomas Launcelles (monks of Durham), and Robert Ashburn and John Hagthorp (clerks), as their proctors to represent them before the bishop at his visitation of their appropriated churches. Hagthorp, at the bishop's command, swore on his own behalf and that of the prior and chapter an oath of obedience to the bishop and his successors, and then read a protestation claiming that the prior and chapter, as a result of grants made by earlier bishops and by popes, were not bound to comply with the bishop's request for procurations[499] on the occasion of a visitation of their appropriate churches. The bishop accepted the claim and agreed not to exact the procurations. The witnesses were: Ds William Billingham (chaplain) and John (clerk of the parochial chapel of St. Hilda).
>
> Then on 14 May 1394, in the parish church of Monkwearmouth, there appeared before Skirlaw, who was visiting the church, either Thomas Legate or Thomas Launcelles (acting as proctor of the prior and chapter of Durham). The proctor read a protestation similar to that read by Hagthorp two days before, and again the bishop accepted the claim and agreed not to exact procurations. The witnesses were: Ds John Stayngreene (chaplain), Nicholas Barton and William Wearmouth (clerks of the dioceses of York and Durham).[500]
>
> Another notarial instrument states that on 19 May 1394 John Hemingbrough (prior of Durham) instructed Uthred of Boldon DD (a monk of Durham), to go to Skirlaw, who was about to visit the prior

and chapter's appropriated church of Pittington, and invite him to stay at their manor at Pittington, on condition that it was accepted that the bishop had no right to require such hospitality. Later on the same day, at Sherburn Hospital, Uthred conveyed the invitation to the bishop, who accepted it and acknowledged that he had no such right. The prior's instructions to Uthred were witnessed by Robert Ashburn (clerk of the diocese of Lichfield) and John Hagthorp (clerk of the diocese of Durham). The bishop's acceptance of the invitation was witnessed by Robert Hemingbrough (clerk of the diocese of York) and Richard Ripon (clerk of the diocese of Durham). The notary in both instances was William Thrislington (clerk of the diocese of Durham).[501]

Then again, on 16 March 1396 a letter was sent by Robert Ripon (prior of Finchale), to John Hemingbrough (prior of Durham), acknowledging and reciting a mandate from Hemingbrough (dated 4 March 1396) ordering Robert to present himself and to cite his fellows to be present in the chapter house at Durham on the Monday after *Laetare Jerusalem*[502] (2 April), when Skirlaw intended to visit the priory. Prior Ripon said that he had done as instructed, and attached a list of his monks.[503]

Skirlaw planned to conduct another visitation of the prior and chapter of Durham in 1397. In response to his request, Pope Boniface IX, in May 1396, issued a bull declaring that Skirlaw could be accompanied by a monk of that chapter or of any other house of the Benedictine order.[504] On 24 November 1396 William Thrislington (proctor of the prior and chapter of Durham) sent letters to John Hemingbrough (prior of Durham), enclosing the bull and the legal opinion of Ds Hubert Navaia on the best method of defence against its contents. The proctor reported that Ds Hubert particularly urged a gentle approach to Bishop Walter Skirlaw, and that he himself recommended secrecy in the matter.[505] Skirlaw then issued a mandate to the prior and chapter of Durham to attend his visitation in their chapter house on 2 April 1397, which he later adjourned until 10 October 1397.[506] However, the prior and chapter of Durham declared it was unreasonable to change time-honoured practices, and appealed to the pope, petitioning for the revocation of the bull issued in favour of Skirlaw. On 20 April 1397 Boniface IX revoked the bull in favour of Skirlaw. Henceforth, the bishop could be accompanied only by a member of the Durham chapter on his visits to the community.[507]

Skirlaw issued various licences to the prior and chapter of Durham and examples of these are given below.

> A licence was granted by Skirlaw on 10 June 1392 to the prior and chapter of Durham to acquire in mortmain[508] lands and incomes to the annual value of £20.[509]
>
> Another licence was given by Skirlaw on 1 September 1392 to the

prior and chapter of Durham to acquire in mortmain from William Cowton (chaplain), and John Appleby (chaplain):

in Durham seven messuages in Elvet held for life by Matilda widow of William Alman of the inheritance of William and John and reverting to them on her death;

one messuage in Elvet held for life by the above Matilda and then by Agnes Langley for life of the inheritance of the above William and John and reverting to them after Matilda's and Agnes' death to remain in the priory;

one messuage twenty acres in Jarrow once held by William son of William;

eleven messuages ten acres in Ferryhill once held by William Yut;

three messuages seven acres in Cocken, ten acres in East Merrington once held by William Haswell former vicar there by Durham;

one croft in Smiddyhaugh once held by Alice Birkby;

one messuage in Elvet, one waste messuage in Rattenrow in Elvet once held by William Haswell;

one messuage in Rattenrow once held by Richard Stanley and Robert Draper;

one messuage in Old Elvet once held by Thomas;

one messuage in Elvet borough once held by William Drayton;

one capital messuage with one croft two acres of meadow in 'vicus' of Mary Magdalene once held by Hugh Chilton;

one messuage in Crossgate, one messuage in South Street and one acre at end of garden 'le Orchard' once held by Thomas Claxton;

one messuage in Old Elvet once held by William Langley; and

two parts of the manor of Preston and two parts of the vill of Simonside once held by Sir Ralph Lumley and Eleanor his wife and held by the prior.[510]

On 29 August 1394 Skirlaw issued a licence for the marriage in Brancepeth church by the prior of Durham of John Neville (son of Lord Raby) and the earl of Kent's daughter.[511]

On 5 May 1404 the prior and convent of Durham confirmed to Ralph, earl of Westmorland, the lease of a lead mine in the Forest of Weardale, granted to him by Skirlaw as bishop of Durham.[512]

Durham College, Oxford, had been founded for the benefit of the monks through a legacy of £3,000 given by Bishop Hatfield. It was established after his death in 1381, and becoming a seat of learning for the majority of monks at Durham and its dependent institutions, but it soon ran into financial difficulties. Four churches (Bossall, Ruddington, Fishlake and Frampton) were allocated by the convent to provide income, but the costs of dispossessing the incumbents, including legal costs and pensions, meant that in early years there was very little in the way of funds to provide for the statutory complement of eight monks and eight secular scholars.

In 1404 the chancellor and masters of the University of Oxford began proceedings against the prior of Durham for failing to maintain numbers. When Skirlaw became aware of this he successfully defended the prior, pleading monastic poverty and thus saving the college from annihilation and destruction. Such university intervention in the affairs of a college was unparalleled at this period. In 1405 articles were drawn up justifying a reduction in the numbers of monks and secular scholars studying at Durham College, and a sentence was pronounced by Ralph Stele (commissary), freeing the prior and chapter from any penalty which might arise from this.[513]

From 1405 the fortunes of Durham College improved rapidly. The monks were able to maintain seven or eight fellows there without much difficulty and in that same year work began on a new chapel.[514] The college, which was dedicated to the Holy Trinity, the Blessed Virgin Mary and St. Cuthbert, continued as Durham College until the foundation of the present Trinity College on the same site in 1555.[515]

The cathedral at Durham was the centre of worship for the monks of the priory. It would be difficult to compile a daily timetable for the monastic day, as the hours of devotion varied between summer and winter, and on the different feast days. Around 1396 the Durham monk, Richard Segbroke, compiled a summary of the *horarium* (book of hours) which gives some guidance, together with evidence in the *Rites of Durham*. The *horarium* uses clock hours as its basis, which would be appropriate as the priory possessed a mechanical clock (which needed frequent repair) towards the latter part of the fourteenth century. The monk's daily routine commenced with matins which started at midnight and lasted an hour. This was followed at 6 or 6.30 by prime (the second daily period of prayer) lasting half an hour. At 9 o'clock mass was sung, followed an hour later by the chapter meeting, with high mass at 11 o'clock. Dinner was served about noon followed by a rest period until the bell sounded for nones (the fifth hour of prayer) at 2 o'clock. At 4 o'clock vespers commenced, followed around 6 or 7 o'clock with collation (a light supper usually with a reading). Compline (the seventh and final hour of prayer) and the *salve regina* (an antiphon sung after compline) ended the day.

Masses were sung in the choir of the cathedral, apart from the Mass of Our Lady which was sung in the Galilee Chapel. During the day monks were also required to serve the chantry foundations in the cathedral and celebrate mass at numerous side-altars including the Chapel of the Nine Altars.[516] The perpetual chantries, five after Skirlaw's death, and particular altars were served by the monks by intablying.[517] Drawing up the rota was the responsibility of the sub-prior, precentor and succentor. It is likely that a monthly rota system was employed and with at least thirty-five monks on the list, each monk would be responsible for a particular chantry duty around one every three years. The monks involved included those with special duties, such as the bursar and chancellor, but not the prior or sub-prior.[518]

Skirlaw donated a vestment of cloth-of-gold with precious ophreys to Durham Priory some time before his death. A memorandum of his generosity includes a reference to a vestment of this nature.[519] It is likely that it remained in use until the dissolution and that it was the cope included in an inventory of the cathedral's vestry ornaments in 1546 recorded as a gift from the bishop of Durham. The royal commissioners had been instructed to send all gold vessels and vestments of cloth-of-gold to the jewel house at the Tower of London, and this document ends with a summary of the few objects sent to the king from County Durham, including the cope. Perhaps Skirlaw donated the cope in response to the particular needs of the church. A splendid cope was essential for the great processions of Ascension Day, Pentecost, Trinity and Corpus Christi and it is likely that the gift was specially commissioned for use at these Durham ceremonies. Nine scenes were depicted on the cope which would be made in a workshop, probably in London.[520]

CHAPTER EIGHT
SKIRLAW AND THE PALATINATE OF DURHAM

Chapter Seven outlined the privileges, powers and responsibilities which Skirlaw enjoyed as the religious leader of the Durham diocese, but these were extended considerably in his role as civil leader over the palatinate of Durham. The title of "Prince Bishop" bestowed on the bishops of Durham reflects the fact that they had considerable civic powers conferred upon them by the king over his subjects in this northern area.

The palatinate of Durham, often referred to as 'the Bishopric', was the secular franchise of the bishops of Durham and consisted of the county of Durham and the wapentake of Sadberge as its core with the addition of lands in Northumberland, the 'shires' of Norham, Island and Bedlington, and a few other townships including two on the south bank of the River Tees. Both in size and in the extent of its jurisdiction, the palatinate represented the greatest of English liberties. In most respects the bishop of Durham wielded an authority over the palatinate equal to that which the king exercised elsewhere in the realm. The common law of England was observed in the palatinate but was administered by the bishop's justices, and only the bishop, not the king, could issue writs. The statutes enacted by Parliament covered the palatinate in the same way as they did the rest of the country, although ordinances made by the king in council were not considered binding there and parliamentary taxation was not imposed on it.

The palatinate was therefore equivalent to an independent state and ordered its own financial affairs. Various charters were obtained from the king to safeguard the liberties of the see. The bishop could not, however, make treaties with foreign powers, although attempts had been known at procuring secret treaties with Scotland. In a way the palatinate became a buffer state between Scotland and England, and in effect possessed a large franchise or immunity, both against the sovereign power of the king of England but also against the earl of Northumberland. This independence meant that the bishop was also responsible for repelling the frequent Scottish invasions and he had to muster his own forces at his own expense for this purpose.

The bishop's headquarters for the administration of both the palatinate and diocese were centred at Durham Castle, which guarded the entrance to Cathedral and Priory, with various offices round the Palace Green. Here the bishop had his own chancery, exchequer and courts. Apart from the offices used by the chancery and exchequer, the buildings round Palace Green also housed the mint, where he had the right to produce his own coins. There was also the hall where the justices sat, and the residences of various ministers. The bishop's gaol was situated in Saddler Street and the town houses of the tenants-in-chief were in the bailey.

The bishop also had an administrative centre at Norham Castle to cover the distant lands at Norhamshire and Islandshire, although they were still subject to the chancery at Durham. Sadberge wapentake, being a separate lordship, also had its own justices, sheriff and escheator who were based at Durham, as was its chancery. The administrative organisation of the palatinate, though on a relatively small scale, reflected the features of the royal administration of which Skirlaw had first hand experience. The bishop shared with the sheriff of Norham ransoms paid for the release of Scottish prisoners.

During the fourteenth century when Skirlaw was bishop the powers of the bishop over the palatinate were at their greatest. He was immediate or mediate lord of thirteen boroughs. He was immediate lord of six Durham boroughs – Bishop Auckland, Darlington, Durham, Gateshead, Stockton and Sunderland, and four other boroughs outside the county – Holy Island, Norham, Northallerton and Barnard Castle. The mediate lordships were the boroughs of Hartlepool, Elvet and St. Giles. These boroughs were the source of substantial income for the bishopric. The chief officer of each borough was the bailiff or provost who was appointed by the bishop's property was held on burgage tenure,[521] and courts all burgesses were required to attend, were held three times a year, coinciding with the halmote courts of the manor where all burgesses were required to attend. Charters of murage were sometimes granted to burgesses giving them the right to levy tolls on goods brought into the borough, the proceeds being devoted to the repair of the walls and streets of the town.[522]

Within his liberty the bishop could claim the full range of royal prerogatives including:

> the rights of pre-emption (to purchase provisions before they were offered to anyone else and at specially advantageous rates);
> the pardon of outlaws;
> the exemption of lands or buildings from the statute of mortmain (those otherwise held inalienably by ecclesiastical or other corporations);
> the granting of free warren (the use of land for breeding small animals or game birds for hunting).
> the claiming of the proceeds of all shipwrecks and treasure trove washed up on the coast, as well as any whales and sturgeon found there;
> the taking of all forfeitures relating to the disposal of the lands of traitors against the Crown following acts of rebellion or treason.

Although this last prerogative had been established in 1327 it did not stop Edward I seizing the baronies of Robert the Brus and John de Balliol in 1306. However, when in 1400 Henry IV seized the lands of Ralph Lumley, including those in Durham, following his rebellion, Skirlaw made no protest against the action. Likewise he made no objection when the king seized and forfeited the Durham lands of Henry Percy.[523] Richard II also made an attempt to interrupt the palatine rights of Skirlaw, when he took possession of lands forfeited by Michael de la Pole lying within the jurisdiction. To pacify the bishop he granted him custody of the land for a period of twenty years at a small rent. The properties involved were the manors of the Isle, the vill of Bradbury, and lands in Bolam, Great Chilton, Fishburn, Foxdon, Styllington, and Preston upon Skerne.[524] However, when his successor, Bishop Langley, met with a similar royal threat, he succeeded in seizing the lands of Henry, Lord Scrope and Thomas Grey. Skirlaw might not have had the strength of character to insist in upholding his rights, but equally may have had good reason to act as he did.

Because the bishop had within his palatinate most of the rights of a king in his country, he was the head of the civil government, and had his own council or assembly which appointed his civil officers. The bishop's council had developed under the feudal system with members chosen by him from among his own followers and trusted officials. The judicial courts grew out of this council as did the administrative and financial bodies together with the bishop's advisers. The bishop was personally responsible for administering civil and criminal law I the palatinate, and therefore appointed chancellors, sheriffs, judges and coroners. Law breakers were tried and punished in the bishop's court rather than in the king's court.

The palatinate was administered by the sheriff (bailiff) who held separate offices for Durham and Sadberge. He presided over the county court and was responsible for matters of 'policing', the arrest and detention of suspects, the collection of monies due to the bishop arising from convictions, and the extradition of accused men from neighbouring counties or franchises. He also supervised the estates of minors in the bishop's wardship, and also collected market and port dues. The sheriff was assisted by coroners, one each for the wards of Durham and one each for the wapentakes of Sadberge and North Durham. The palatine coroners were responsible for investigating cases of sudden death, holding inquests into other matters and collecting certain revenues.

Under criminal law trials took place in the episcopal courts, and the bishop had the right to hang felons and to enjoy all the profits of justice. Breaches of the peace were breaches of the bishop's peace. The arrangements for keeping the peace were similar to with those adopted in the rest of the kingdom, with the appointment of keepers (or justices) of the peace. Equally in administering civil law the bishop was responsible for issuing writs to ensure that his subjects had the same quality of justice as elsewhere. The extensive powers of the bishop appear to have been generally accepted by the inhabitants of Durham in the Middle Ages. The majority of those appointed to the see had previously enjoyed successful careers in the service of the king. From the thirteenth century onwards many, like Skirlaw, were university graduates.

The sheriffs and escheators were linked to the chancery and exercised powers relating to land seizure and law enforcement. The bishop's coroners were financial officers who also participated in administering the law including the viewing of dead bodies. The bishop appointed stewards to deal with all kinds of legal action. The judiciary consisted of palatine ministers and professional lawyers, and an attorney-general also appointed by the bishop. The bishop's justices of assizes were held three to five times a year.[525]

During the time Skirlaw was bishop of Durham the high sheriffs and escheators were listed by Hutchinson as:

> Sir William Bowes, *1388*
> Sir Thomas Umfraville, *occurred?*
> Sir Marmaduke Lumley, *appointed 10 October 1390*
> Sir Thomas Boynton, *appointed 30 November 1391, occurred escheator 10 December*
> William Elmeden, *occurred escheator 27 November*
> Sir Robert Laton, *occurred escheator 15 May*
> Thomas Claxton, *occurred escheator 8 October 1400*
> Sir Robert Conyers, *appointed 18 January 1400, occurred 10 May 1405, appointed escheator 15 January 1400, again 1 October 1401, and 1405*[526]

On 3 July 1405 a number of justices were sworn in before Skirlaw as chancellor at his house in London. These were William Thirning (chief justice of Commune Bank), John Cockin (chief baron of the exchequer and justice of Commune Bank, dean of Lanchester, who later became an official of Bishop Langley[527]), John Hull, Hugh Huls, William Rikhill, William Hankeford and John Markham.[528]

The financial affairs of the bishopric came under the control of the chancellor who headed the palatine chancery. He also controlled secretarial business and the appointment of administrative staff. The bishop's great seal of chancery and rolls were housed in the chancery under the keeping of the chancellor and the keeper of the rolls respectively. The bishop's council was able to authorise the use of the seal on appropriate letters, although the chancellor often used his discretion. The great seal was attached to certain documents including land orders, warrants, and judicial writs. The chancery court of the County Palatine of Durham was only abolished in 1975, although by this time it was a purely secular jurisdiction no longer associated with the bishops.

Skirlaw's seal was large and round, and 79 mm in diameter. It depicted him seated administering justice on one side and on the other armed and mounted on horseback, and on his shield his coat of arms. Green and Blair describe it in the following manner:

> '*Obverse:* round, the bishop, seated on a throne panelled in perpendicular tracery and with a canopy of rich tabernacle work,

Plate 12.
Bishop Skirlaw's great seal (obverse).

Plate 13. Bishop Skirlaw's great seat (reverse).

vested in alb, tunic, chasuble, apparelled amice and jewelled mitre, his right hand wearing the episcopal ring, is blessing, his left holding his crosier. In a smaller niche of similar size to the dexter is the figure of St. Michael the archangel depicted spearing the dragon, and carrying on his left arm a shield of arms charged with a plain cross. [On his right a shield of the arms of Skirlaw.] On the sinister in a like niche is the armed figure of St. George, his sword by his side and holding a spear with which he transfixes the dragon. On his left is a shield of the arms of Skirlaw. On each side of the pediment of the throne is a sitting lion.
Inscription: *walterus : dei : gra : eps : dunolmensis. (Plate 12).*

Reverse: equestrian, the bishop as knight in armour and tight fitting jupon. From the coronet round his helmet rises, as crest, a demi-angel who holds a shield of the bishop's armorials. He carries a sword in his right hand and on his left arm a shield of arms. The horse is fully caparisoned and wears a plume of feathers as crest. His shield and horse trappings are emblazoned with a cross of six interlaced bastons. The field of the seal is strewn with roses.
Inscription: *walterus : dei : gracia : episcopus : dunolmensis (Plate 13).*[529]

The Great Seal of Chancery was very much a copy of the king's seal *(sigillum regis)* or the seal of majesty *(sigillum majestatis)*. The obverse of the king's seal depicted the king robed and crowned seated in majesty upon his throne, and the reverse he was on horseback, fully armed as leader of his army.[530] Skirlaw had a privy seal as bishop of Durham, a round seal of much smaller size than the great seal, only 29 mm in diameter, which was used in a similar way to the king's privy seal as a seal of an administrative office.[531] Skirlaw also used a bishop's seal for his spiritual role (see Chapter Six).

According to Hutchinson, the temporal chancellors of the bishopric during Skirlaw's episcopate were:

Hugh Westwick, *occurred 9 November 1388, again 5 November 1390*
Robert Wycliffe, *occurred 3 February 1390, again 30 November 1391* [532]

The bishop's mint produced coins which were similar to the ordinary coins of the realm but which bore incumbent the initials of the bishop imprinted on the reverse side. The bishop's minting rights can be traced back to the seventh century at the time of St. Cuthbert, although the earliest record of the privilege found in the Boldon Book in 1183. In the reign of Henry II around 1154 the mint of Durham was suppressed in favour of one at Newcastle, but was restored to Durham by Richard I around 1196 in the time of Bishop Philip de Poitou. The mint was taken away again in 1211, when the bishopric was in the king's hands, and was not restored until 1252[533] probably in return for help rendered to the king during the Barons' Revolt in the thirteenth century.[534] No coins were minted during the reigns of Richard II and Henry IV when Skirlaw was bishop.[535]

The bishop also had the power to raise his own taxes, which usually took the form of customs duties and road and bridge tolls, which were used to finance the administration of the palatinate and defend it against the Scots. The income from passage tolls over bridges and entrances to the cities was partly used towards the repair of the bridges. Skirlaw built or rebuilt at least six bridges during his episcopy from which tolls were collected from the pilgrims and goods passing to Durham and the cathedral. The palatinate was exempt from the parliamentary taxation which applied to the rest of the kingdom, and taxation in other forms had only a small effect on the palatinate. If the Crown wanted help from Durham in the fourteenth century it had to apply to the bishop who consulted the County Assembly. In 1388 Durham agreed to grant half of its wool to the Crown following the example of the rest of the kingdom.[536]

The bishop also obtained income from the rights and privileges of his regality; the issue of writs, charters and respites of homage; fines before the justices of the assize and of the peace; offences against the Statute of Labourers; receipts for land taken 'into the bishop's hand' on the death of tenants and others, waifs and strays; and from wrecks. The bishop could create corporations and grant charters for fairs and markets in the County and City of Durham. As a source of additional income he had the power to sell the privilege of holding a market or fair to an individual.[537] All this revenue was received by the bishop's exchequer, and the income of the palatinate was summarised in an account produced by the receiver each Michaelmas, which was subject to audit.

The income of the bishop was used for various purposes, first and foremost for the payment of the expenses of the government of the bishopric, fees paid to his various officers, justices, constable and steward, and salaries to his chaplains. He also paid towards the repair and maintenance of buildings and the erection of new ones. The bishop's domestic expenses came out of the fund as did occasional loans, including those made to the king.[538]

Maintaining good personal relations with tenants, particularly those with power and influence in the land, was essential for the benefit of the bishopric. Among the tenants-in-chief who had gained their lands through 'military service', i.e. homage, fealty and suit of court, were such families as the Hiltons, Lumleys, Eures, Nevilles, Umfravilles and Ogles. In Skirlaw's time there was no professional police force and maintenance of law and order rested on the partnership between such families and the bishop's government. Fines and imprisonment were used to maintain law and order, and an ultimate punishment for wrongdoing sometimes exercised by the bishop was excommunication with papal sanction.[539]

The English Parliament frequently negotiated short-term truces with the Scots. These did not stop the inhabitants of the borders from continuing the predatory activities which prevented the existence of a real state of peace in the area.[540] The border between England and Scotland was an area where raids by inhabitants of both countries into 'enemy' land often took place. The temptation to make a livelihood out of plunder, which would usually carry no legal penalty, was always present. In Cumberland and Northumberland, houses were often fortified and there were over a hundred pele-towers and castles in Northumberland alone in Skirlaw's time. Over the border in Scotland the houses were similarly defended against the English. The Hundred Years War with France when Scotland sided with the enemy did nothing to improve cross-border relations.[541]

The bishop had to give his permission for castles to be crenellated (fortified). Skirlaw's arms appear across the front of Hilton (Hylton) Castle near Sunderland, together with the arms of other notables including Neville, Percy, Lumley, Conyers and Washington. The castle was built during the reign of Richard II,[542] and the presence of Skirlaw's arms indicates that he granted the Hiltons the right to crenellate.[543] Sir Ralph Lumley of Lumley Castle, a huge, handsome building above the River Wear near Chester-le-Street, received a licence for re-edifying and embattling from Bishop Skirlaw on 10 November 1389.[544] The bishop could also create barons of the bishopric.

The district on the English side of the border with Scotland was divided into the East and the West Marches. The East March was formed by the county of Northumberland and the West March by parts of Cumberland and Westmorland. As Northumberland was within the palatinate of Durham, the bishop of Durham was involved in maintaining the border with the Scots. The defence was in the charge of a warden, who was a military officer also commissioned to preserve the truces with the Scots. He was based at the castle at Berwick-upon-Tweed, and received an annual sum which varied depending on whether the two countries were at open war. The warden maintained a permanent armed force which he recruited from the area. The Percy family obtained the wardenship of both marches in 1391, an appointment influenced by the fact that they owned extensive lands in both Cumberland and Northumberland. In 1403 the wardenship of the West March was awarded to Ralph Neville, the earl of Westmorland, and the East March was given to John, the son of Henry IV. The office was granted by means of an indenture, a contract with the king setting out the conditions of service, and a commission which set out what truces, if any, were in operation and the powers of the warden to fine or imprison English truce breakers, to defend the March, summon forces and set watches against invasion. Despite all these attempts to safeguard the border, Northumberland had the reputation of being the most lawless of English counties.[545]

The king of England, based in southern England had always had real difficulties in administering the north, so the bishops of Durham from early times were given semi-regal powers to use all measures necessary to quell threats of invasion by the Scots. The effect was that the bishop of Durham became a 'Prince Bishop' who ruled over a palatinate or kingdom within a kingdom. In return for their support, the bishops of Durham were given extensive privileges, provided that they remained loyal to the king and committed to keeping the peace with the Scots. The bishop was empowered to raise his own army to defend the palatinate and some of the earlier bishops went into battle at the head of their troops. Bishop Bek, for example, led, 140 knights, 1,000 infantrymen and 500 cavalry under the banner of St. Cuthbert I support of Edward I. The relative stability of England in face of the ever-present threat of Scottish invasion was to a large extent due to the strategic role played by the bishopric of Durham. The clergy and laymen of the diocese under the command of the bishop were occasionally mobilised to augment the border forces to defend the area from Scots invasion.

On 12 August 1388, just a month before Skirlaw obtained the temporalities to the see of Durham, the battle of Otterburn, some thirty miles north-west of Newcastle (on the A696 road towards Jedburgh), was fought. The Scots defeated the English and Sir Henry Percy, who led the English forces, was killed together with 500 men. The defeat was attributed to three factors: Percy was accused of excessive boldness in taking his troops into battle so late in the day (they were attending Vespers which would commence at 4 p.m. when the call came); the oncoming darkness played tricks with the English who found themselves killing each other rather than the enemy (everyone spoke the same language); and Bishop Fordham, one of the commanders, failed to deploy his large force of troops to provide the help and support previously been arranged with Percy. Another commander, Sir Matthew Redmayne, and his troops eventually chased the Scots back to the border, where many men were killed or taken prisoner.[546]

Skirlaw was fortunate; he was not called upon to exercise his military skills during almost twenty years as bishop. However, a threat occurred in January 1400 when Henry IV, fearing Charles VI of France would retaliate on behalf of his deposed son-in-law, Richard II, issued a writ to bishop Skirlaw ordering him to array all the clergy in his diocese with the quota of forces they were bound to render in such circumstances.[547] Skirlaw instructed the archdeacon of Durham, Thomas Weston, to issue a mandate with Skirlaw's seal attached, to the prior of Durham, John Hemingbrough, and other clergy of the diocese of Durham to arm and array themselves against the enemies of the kingdom on 17 March 1400. The array assembled on St. Giles' Moor (or St. Gilesgatemoor) on the outskirts of Durham, on 24 March 1400. A list of the clergy present was compiled by the commissioners, who included the prior of Durham and Wycliffe, the constable of Durham. The records show the quota each beneficed clerk was required to provide. For instance, the rector of Sedgefield brought five men-at-arms and ten bowmen, while others provided smaller numbers.

Chapter Nine
Skirlaw, his Buildings and Bridges

Although Skirlaw had financed some projects when archdeacon of the East Riding, it was not until he became bishop of Durham and had large funds at his disposal that he decided on an extensive programme of building. During his career he had travelled widely in England and across Europe, and had no doubt acquired knowledge of contemporary styles of ecclesiastical and other buildings. He used his experiences to give advice on the many projects he financed during the latter part of his life, and his buildings reflected the very latest architectural designs. There is evidence that he employed the same masons on different buildings. The dates of Skirlaw's projects are not always known but many of them incorporate his coat of arms. The various buildings and other structures he created were located in Durham and Yorkshire, and most of them are still fulfilling their original function today.

Durham
Apart from constructing a memorial to himself in the form of a tomb, chantry and bedesmen's benches in Durham Cathedral (see Chapter Eleven), Skirlaw also spent large sums on providing stained glass, some of which depicted Skirlaw himself and his coat of arms. All this glass has now vanished, mainly because the cathedral was used some time after his death to imprison Scots soldiers who smashed windows and many ornaments.

During Skirlaw's time many of the windows of the church were glazed with coloured glass. Rawlinson's manuscript of 1603 records that the sixth window from the Galilee door (at the west end of the cathedral), along the north aisle of the nave, has two long lights and depicts Skirlaw's arms at the top of four turret lights. Below the turrets in the long windows there was, in the first, a picture of St. Oswald and under him St. Paul, and, in the second, St. Peter and underneath him St. James, all in fine coloured glass. Skirlaw's arms could also be found in the top turret light of a window with two lights divided by stonework, at the west end near the north Galilee door, which depicted the Blessed Lady with Christ in her arms and a sceptre in her hands.[548]

Below the great rose window above the Nine Altars at the east end of the cathedral there are three long windows. The central window was situated above the altar of St. Cuthbert and St. Bede. The altars to the south of it, moving outwards were dedicated to St. Oswald and St. Lawrence, St. Thomas of Canterbury and St. Catharine, St. John the Baptist and St. Margaret, and St. Andrew and St. Mary Magdalene. On the north side the altars were dedicated to St. Martin and St. Edmund, St. Peter and St. Paul, St. Aidan and St. Helen, and the holy archangel St. Michael. The glass, which no longer survives, depicted in the centre window St. Cuthbert (with

St. Oswald's head in his right hand and his crosier staff in the other, robed as for mass in alb covered by a red vestment) with St. Bede (in a blue habit). Under their feet were the figures of Bishops Skirlaw and Langley, with crosier staves in their hands, kneeling and looking upwards. Both their coats of arms were recorded in the lower half of the window. Beneath St. Oswald and St. Lawrence in the window to the south was a donor portrait of Langley together with his arms, and in the north window a donor portrait of Skirlaw, along with his shield supported by three angels, beneath portraits of St. Martin and St. Edmond. These windows were executed some time during Langley's episcopate and it has been suggested that a payment made in 1416/17 for new stonework, iron and glass for a window in the Nine Altars would have been towards that purpose. It is also likely that John Thornton, who executed the glazing of the great east window in York Minster donated by Skirlaw, was also contracted to glaze the Durham window. Skirlaw was linked to both churches, and a comparison of the glazing in the two indicates marked similarities of technique and style.[549]

Following the lead given by Bishop Hugh du Puiset in the late twelfth century, Bishop Langley also spent large sums of money on stained glass. When the donations made by Skirlaw and Langley to Durham and its dependencies are placed alongside their great gifts to York Minster, they rank amongst the greatest patrons of glass-painting in the north of England. The other great benefactors to Durham Cathedral were the priors John Fossor, John Wessington and Thomas Castell, who were between them responsible for most of the major windows in the church.[550]

It is generally thought that the cloisters at Durham Cathedral were erected partly at the expense of Skirlaw and partly of his successor Langley, although one source states that they were begun in 1386, two years before Skirlaw became bishop and were not completed until 1498.[551] Skirlaw contributed £600. £200 was paid during his time as bishop, and £400 was provided for the completion of the work by the executors of his will although he had made no formal bequest.[552] Langley then paid a further £238 17s 6d to finish off the fourth walk (*Plate 14 shows part of the west cloisters above which can be seen Skirlaw's dormitory and the twin west towers*).

No accounts for this undertaking survive from before 1409. By then the cloisters were said to be almost complete, with the exception of the glazing, much of the cost of which was borne by Skirlaw's executors. The present tracery is the result of extensive remodelling in the eighteenth century, although there is a very full description in the *Rites* of the cloister as it appeared at the Reformation, with window tracery filled with stained glass, and carrels for the monks in the north alley. Stone came from quarries at Baxter Wood and West Burn, both near the River Browney, a short distance to the west and south-west of Durham. They used timber from the priory manors of Shincliffe and Bearpark just outside the city, with imported

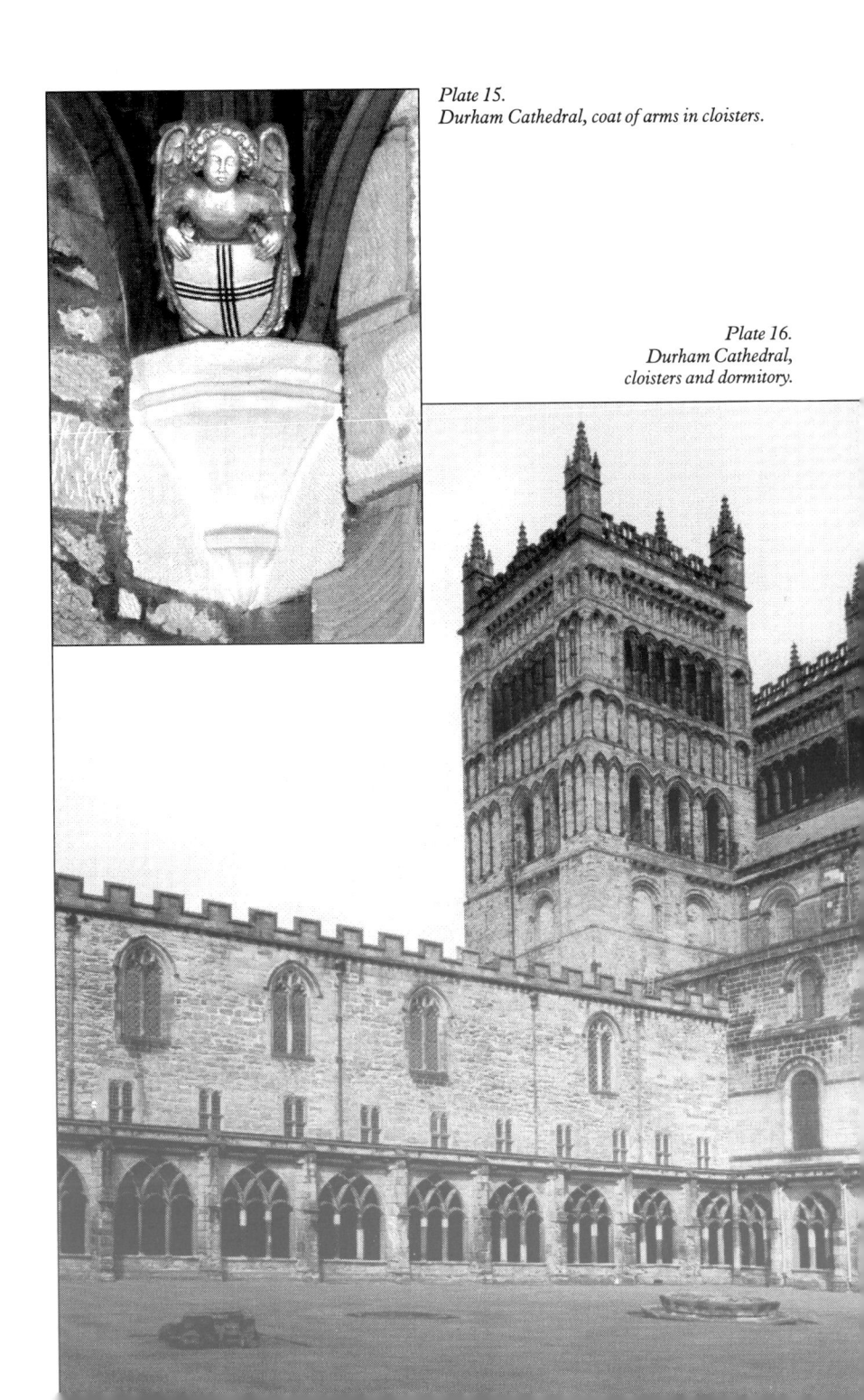

Plate 15.
Durham Cathedral, coat of arms in cloisters.

Plate 16.
Durham Cathedral,
cloisters and dormitory.

planks purchased at Newcastle and Hartlepool, and seven loads of Kendal boards from beyond the Pennines. Iron, lead and nails were all purchased in quantity, while incidental items of expenditure included the cost of cleaning the mason's lodge, and compensation to the paviours of the town for damage done to the pavement by the carriage of stone.[553]

Thomas Mapilton was the chief mason in charge of the building work from 1408. In this, his first important post, he received a yearly fee of £5 6s 8d and a robe of a value of 13s 4d.[554] From the end of September 1416, Thomas Hyndley, who first worked under Mapilton, took over as chief mason. His contract stated that he and four sureties were bound in the sum of £200 that he should complete the work of one-fourth part of the cloisters (the fourth walk) by Michaelmas 1418. Again in 1433 he received £2 'by agreement' as well as payment for the Egliston marble needed for the new octagonal lavatory in the centre of the cloister.[555] Master carpenters, John Rasyn (in charge from 1409 to 1414) and then John Wadley (from 1414 until its completion[556]) constructed the low pitched roofs and flat oak panelled ceilings. The cloisters were described at one time as 'ceiled in pannels with Irish oak, ornamented, particularly in the east walk, with shields of the arms of various personages, patrons of the church, blazoned in colours, most of which, from being exposed to the air, are now greatly defaced.'[557] The arms still remain in the ceiling, the majority of them those of Skirlaw. They were much restored in 1828, when many new shields were introduced, and despite other restorations undertaken in the nineteenth and early twentieth centuries, they remain substantially as completed. The cloisters as they are today have diagonally flagged pavements in the alleys which are of eighteenth century origin *(Plate 15 shows Skirlaw's coat of arms in the south-east corner of the cloisters)*.

Included in the cost of the cloisters borne by the two bishops were painted glass windows depicting the whole story and miracles of St. Cuthbert, starting from the cloister door and ending at the door of the church. There is evidence to suggest that the glass painters were the same as those who painted the St. Cuthbert window in York Minster, and that Langley was responsible for employing them at Durham.[558] One source states that the painted glass windows, which no longer exist, were taken down and destroyed by Dean Horne during the reign of Edward VI,[559] although another indicates that the glass was taken out during the restoration of 1764-1769, when the present 'uninteresting' mullions and uncusped tracery were substituted.[560]

Skirlaw funded a new monks' dormitory between 1398 and 1404 costing 330 marks,[561] and following his death in 1406 a further £100 was contributed towards its completion by his executors.[562] The building was erected on the west wall of the cloisters and above the undercroft, and provided accommodation for thirty to forty monks. This new structure replaced a dormitory already standing on the earlier thirteenth century sub-vault, or monks' common-house, moved there from its more usual

Plate 16. Durham Cathedral, dormitory interior.

position on the eastern side of the cloister soon after the completion of the chapter house during the time of Bishop Geoffrey Rufus (1133-1140) *(Plate 16 shows the interior of the Dormitory).* [563]

The dormitory had a wide stone-flagged passage which ran down the centre of the building. Along each side of the passage were the monks' sleeping chambers, each with half a window, a desk for books, and a bed on a wooden floor. At the south end farthest from the entrance, and adjoining the monk's chambers, were the novices' cubicles, eight on each side of the passage. These had no individual windows, although light was obtained from some large windows situated high above the monks' windows along the hall. The sub-prior slept at the north end near the entrance, although the prior himself slept in private lodgings elsewhere. The principal feature of the dormitory was the timbered roof made from twenty-one oak trees, the main beams being over forty feet long, fashioned by a team of carpenters led by Ellis Harper. At the north end, near the entrance ('day stairs'), 'night stairs' were used by the monks and novices to enter the cathedral for prayers during the night. At night-time and to assist them in the dark a square stone held twelve 12 cressets (metal vessels filled with oil on poles) which were used for lighting their way. On the west wall there was also an entrance to a reredorter (lavatory), whose floor rested on two large pillars. There were separate wood-panelled cubicles for each seat and all the waste was channelled to the river below. After the dissolution in

1539 part of the dormitory provided accommodation for a canon. After 1848 it was turned into a library, and it is now also used as an exhibition hall.[564]

The masons responsible for building the dormitory were John Middleton and later Peter Dryng, with John Dinsdale in overall charge of the work. The documents relating to the two contracts made with successive masons for its building are still in the possession of the treasury. An indenture, dated 22 September 1398, was drawn up between the prior and convent of Durham and John Middleton, mason.[565] Under its terms he was to build the walls on the pattern of the tower in Brancepeth Castle called 'Constabiltour'. He was to build a wall on the west side of the dormitory ninty feet high with any necessary battlements. The outside was to be of ashlar, plainly dressed, and the inside of broken stone. The foundation was to be two ells (ninety inches) in breadth with four or more set-offs. There were to be nine good windows, one for every two beds, so that the monks might have light for their studies. The mason guaranteed to maintain the existing sub-vault in its then current condition. He was to supply all the materials, and other requirements including cartage, burnt lime, iron and wooden implements and other utensils, scaffolding, centring and flakes. However quarries for stone and lime, and timber and boughs for the scaffolding, centrings and flakes, were to be assigned by the prior within a distance of three miles from Durham. The prior and convent, with the mason's advice, were to take down the ancient walls and clean out the foundations. For each of the three years of work, Middleton was to receive a garment of the kind worn by the prior's esquires. He and his boy were also to be given meat and drink, and ten marks of silver for every rood of work containing 6½ ells square. He was to receive £40 at the beginning, and then for every six roods completed, £40 more, until the work was finished.

For some reason John Middleton failed to complete the contract, and after eighteen months he disappears from the accounts. He was replaced by Peter Dryng in 1401, and a further indenture was drawn up between him and the prior and chapter, for the completion of the remaining work.[566] Dryng was a local mason who had worked on the priory kitchen thirty years earlier and was also contracted to build Skirlaw's chantry. At the time of the new indenture only the southern part of the dormitory had been completed. At first he was merely paid a retainer, but on 2 February 1402 he entered into a contract on virtually the same terms as Middleton, except that he was also to receive every day a white loaf, a flagon of beer and a dish of meat from the kitchen, 'as the prior's esquires receive'.[567] The evidence of the accounts is that the work was accomplished by the required date of the Feast of All Saints (1 November) 1404, although Peter Dryng died some months before it was complete.[568]

The chapter house is entered from the east aisle of the cloisters and was originally built by Bishop Rufus about 1136. In later years it was vaulted and embellished by various bishops and in particular Skirlaw to whom the improvements have been ascribed. His coat of arms is placed over the doorway to the cloisters. Many of the earlier bishops were interred in the chapter house, although Skirlaw obtained the consent of the priory to be laid to rest in the cathedral itself (see Chapter Eleven).[569]

Just before Skirlaw became bishop of Durham, there had been trouble in the gaol, then situated on the west side of Palace Green, when a number of men broke out. This no doubt led Skirlaw to initiate the building of a new county prison, to be incorporated in a much reconstructed and strengthened gateway to the cathedral and castle, standing at the head of Saddler Street, which was later completed by Bishop Langley.[570] Richardson's drawing of the Castle Gateway (North Front, Saddler Street) and gaol is the frontispiece to volume III of the *Victoria History of the County of Durham*.[571]

Saddler Street (Saddlergate), which leads to the cathedral and castle, has been considerably raised and levelled since medieval times, but below the present foundations there are remains of three 'land arches' of the old bridge rising to the Gateway, and one or two of these are still visible in the lower basements of premises on the east side of the street. At its southern end the street was spanned by the Castle Gateway (Great North Gate). According to Laurence, the Norman gateway here was 'stately and threatening,' with a tower and barbican. Skirlaw and Langley were instrumental in turning a part of it into the new prison for 'criminals' and 'captives'. Two cells of the prison can still be seen under the western land arch of Elvet Bridge. There were three gates, the outer, the main and the inner gate. The outer defensive portion consisted of a short barbican with walls of great thickness containing defensive passages, and outer turret towers square at the base and octagonal above the gate. Apparently the drawbridge was within the barbican. The main gate had two large turrets, square at base and octagonal above; it is described as possessing 'salliports and upper galleries for the annoyance of assailants', and there was a portcullis. The gaol continued to be the ordinary gaol of the City of Durham until 1820 when the whole structure was demolished (although the title of Richardson's drawing indicates that this occurred in 1818)and a new prison was built at the top of Old Elvet. Skirlaw produced a *valor* (evaluation) of his first year in office which, apart from information about the prison, described the condition of the castle and immediate neighbourhood.[572] Mention of the "jauell yaitts" at Durham in a court case concerning a John Oliver around 1569 refers to the gaol gates of the gateway built by bishops Skirlaw and Langley.[573]

Framwellgate bridge, or the Old Bridge as it was called in medieval times, which spans the Wear at the western side of the Durham peninsula, was originally built by Flambard in 1120, but it was severely damaged by a flood in 1400 and was rebuilt by Skirlaw in 1401 (*Plate 17 shows Framwellgate bridge with Durham Castle and Durham Cathedral towers*).

However, another source suggests that after damage from flooding the crossing was maintained for a time by a ferry and that the present bridge was reconstructed by Bishop Langley. It has since been widened in the nineteenth century and in 1975 was pedestrianised.[574] According to Leland, Skirlaw also built a bridge over the Wear of two arches (or rather one arch with a pillar in the middle) at Finkley (Finchale Priory). The bridge did not survive; Leland reports around 1540 that it was thrown down due to lack of repair two or three years before his visit.[575] The priory was used as a rest home for the Durham monks until the dissolution. Both bridges would ease travel between Durham Priory and Finchale Priory, as well as to Framwellgate Moor which at one time was used as a hunting ground for the Durham bishops.[576]

SHINCLIFFE

Skirlaw is said to have built or rebuilt a bridge over the Wear at Shincliffe, a picturesque village just south of the city of Durham, during his time as bishop. There is some evidence of an ancient bridge over the river at Shincliffe, which had fallen into disrepair when Fordham was bishop of Durham. Funds had been collected to repair it, but the money had been embezzled or misapplied, and so work had not taken place. However,

Plate 17. Durham, Framwellgate Bridge, Cathedral and Castle.

Skirlaw provided the money necessary to replace it and also provided towards its future maintenance through the purchase of lands.[577] Skirlaw's investment in the bridge improved communications with Bishop Auckland and the south. On 7 February 1752 Skirlaw's bridge suffered the effects of a violent flood when a pier and two arches collapsed and were carried away. The bridge was restored at public expense during the following summer.[578] The road to the city passed over Skirlaw's bridge until it was replaced in 1824-1826 by a bridge constructed 100 yards downstream which now carries the A177.[579]

BISHOP AUCKLAND

The prince bishops of Durham have had a residence at Auckland Castle since it was established by Bishop Bek around 1283. It was one of a number of country retreats owned by the bishops, and had its own deer park where the English army camped before the battle of Neville's Cross in 1346. The estate was originally used for hunting and the castle was used by the bishops to entertain their great hunting parties. Over the years the bishops carried out improvements to the estate and Skirlaw made his contribution. He built an imposing gatehouse, as an entrance from the town to the grounds of the castle. This was later replaced by Bishop Trevor between 1752-71.[580] As Leland put it:

> 'Skerlaw, Bisshop of Duresme, made the goodly gate house at entering ynto the castelle of Akeland. There is a fair park by the castelle having falow dere, wild bulles and kin.'[581]

Skirlaw also built the Scotland Wing at Auckland Castle, with a view to housing Scottish prisoners captured during raids into English territory. The Scotland Wing is a two-storey building, where the prisoners were confined to the lower storey in cells which were very cold and damp. Those imprisoned were often high ranking-officers, whose release was subject to the payment of a ransom; if none was forthcoming they would remain until their death. The first floor above the prison cells was designed as a walkway for the ladies of visiting dignitaries, so that they could take a stroll under cover during inclement weather or after dark. Entertainment was provided by the prisoners whose cries and moans could be heard, and who could be seen below through strategically placed peepholes *(Plate 18)*. The Scotland Wing now houses offices for the diocese. The present bishops of Durham have their offices elsewhere in the Castle, and its many other rooms are available for conferences and other events. The coats of arms of Skirlaw and other bishops adorn the chapel walls.[582]

Bishop Auckland is situated on high ground at the confluence of two rivers, the Wear and the Gaunless. Until recently the main road bridge over the Wear to the City of Durham carrying the A689 was that built by Skirlaw in the late fourteenth century. It remained unaltered until around 1900, when the road was widened by constructing footpaths on cantilevered

Plate 18. Auckland Castle, Scotland Wing.

Plate 19. Bishop Auckland, Skirlaw's Bridge.

girders, leaving the original parapets. There are two unequal arches, one pointed, of 91 feet span and one round, of 101 feet *(Plate 19)*. The bridge once had a gateway at the southern end, and in the eastern parapet a stile leads down to the river. On the southern approach is a row of terrace houses leading down to the bridge. Near to Skirlaw bridge is a railway viaduct which has eleven arches and stands 105 feet above the river. It originally carried the Bishop Auckland branch line of the York, Newcastle and Berwick Railway, but became redundant and was converted to a road bridge in 1994-95. The A689 was then diverted from Skirlaw Bridge to the viaduct, although even now at times of strong winds high-sided vehicles drive across the lower, more sheltered Skirlaw Bridge.[583]

CROFT-ON-TEES

Crossing the river Tees there is a seven-arched stone bridge which is said to have been built by Skirlaw *(Plate 20)*. This bridge is still used today and carries traffic on the Great North Road (A167) from Northallerton to Darlington and on to the City of Durham. From medieval times until the early nineteenth century an important ceremony took place on the bridge when a new bishop of Durham was consecrated. This ceremony was revived in recent times, when David Jenkins crossed the bridge into County Durham to take up his position as bishop of Durham in 1984. On

Plate 20. Croft-on-Tees Bridge.

traversing he was presented with a medieval sword called the Conyers Falchion. In the past a member of the Conyers family is said to have used a falchion, a type of broadsword, to kill the infamous Sockburn Worm, a large dragon-like creature. At the ceremony the lords of Sockburn presented the falchion with these words:

> 'My Lord Bishop I here present you with the falchion wherewith the champion Conyers slew the worm, dragon or fiery serpent which destroyed man, woman and child; in memory of which the King then reigning gave him the manor of Sockburn, to hold by his tenure, that upon the first entrance of every Bishop into the county this falchion should be presented.'

The bishop then returned the falchion with his best wishes for the lord's health, long life and prosperity. The last prince bishop, William Van Mildert, received the falchion in 1826. Since the revival of the ceremony, the sword has been presented by the mayor of Darlington. The falchion is now kept on view to the public at the Durham Cathedral treasury. The legend of the falchion appears to date back either to the time of the Viking invaders or to the Harrying of the North by William the Conqueror.[584] The last time the ceremony took place was in 1994 when Michael Turnbull was instituted. It is reported that, following his retirement on 30 April 2003, Turnbull's successor, Dr Tom Wright chose to continue the custom and receive the sword on Croft Bridge from the Area Dean and the mayor of Darlington. The ceremony took place on 4 July 2003.

With his concern to maintain access to strategic routes which crossed rivers it is also noted that in 1394 Skirlaw asked the local people to 'lend a hand' in repairing Chollerford (Chesters) Bridge at the George Hotel on the River North Tyne near Hadrian's Wall. The hotel was a strategic watering hole on the old Roman road (now the B6318) from Newcastle-upon-Tyne and Durham (via Dere Street) to Carlisle.[585]

YARM

The small town of Yarm is situated on the southern bank of the River Tees some three miles west of Stockton and twelve miles from the east coast. In medieval times, and until the first Stockton bridge was built in 1771, Yarm was the nearest crossing point to the North Sea, at first by ford and then by bridge. Yarm was then the most important town and port on the River Tees, Its wealth was so great that it was frequently a target of Scottish raiders, who sacked the town five times in the fourteenth century under the leadership of Robert the Bruce. It was and still is an important crossing point between the north of Yorkshire and County Durham. The road between the City of York and the City of Durham passed through Yarm until relatively recent years. Evidently a timber bridge existed around 1200 which was able to handle the large volume of trade and shipping. In 1305 Edward I granted William Latimer (lord of

Plate 21. Yarm Bridge.

Yarm) pontage (tolls) of the bridge to help to maintain it on the king's highway over the Tees. [586]

The timber bridge became too decrepit by the end of the fourteenth century and about 1400 Skirlaw set about replacing it with one built of stone, having purchased lands towards this purpose. For nearly 400 years Skirlaw's bridge was the only one between Cleveland and Durham. During that period it has been altered, widened and repaired many times. As originally built it was half its present width and had five gothic arches. Three of these original arches with some interesting mason's marks have survived to the present day and can be seen on the west side of the structure (Plate 21 shows the west side of Yarm bridge).

Skirlaw's bridge at Yarm was an important battleground during the Civil War when there was a fight for control of this strategic crossing of the Tees. On 1 February 1643 a Royalist force under the command of General King and General Goring was on its way south to assist troops at York, when they were set upon by 400 Parliamentarian troops as they attempted to cross the bridge. The Parliamentarians were defeated but the Royalists soon recognised the importance of this crossing point. A drawbridge had been incorporated into the northern arch of the bridge to restrict movements, and on 14 February 1643 the commander of the Royalist force at Stockton ordered the rector of Egglescliffe, Isaac Basire, to close the bridge every night. The drawbridge was removed in 1785 when the northern arch was rebuilt in semicircular form with a greater span to reduce the risk of flooding.[587]

Towards the end of the eighteenth century the towns of Newcastle, Shields, Sunderland and Stockton had been connected by the newly introduced turnpike roads, and the Wear at Sunderland had been spanned by a cast iron bridge. Skirlaw's bridge at Yarm was now considered too narrow to deal with the volume of traffic between Thirsk, Yarm and Stockton and so the people of Stockton called for an improved bridge at Yarm. In 1802 the people of Yarm petitioned Parliament to improve and shorten the road from Thirsk, and the subsequent act also gave power to make alterations to the bridge. At a later meeting, in January 1803, the townsfolk argued that the facility to alter the bridge did not go far enough and they demanded a new bridge. They claimed that the stone bridge, being only twelve feet between parapets, was too narrow to allow carriages to pass one another with safety and was very dangerous for pedestrians and that the position would worsen following the road improvements. They also argued that the bridge piers impeded the flow of the river causing sand beds to form which could obstruct the passage of boats, and that in times of flooding there was a threat to Yarm and district. They petitioned to pull down the old bridge of five arches and to build on or near the site a single-span, arched cast-iron bridge of adequate width.

After considering surveyor's estimates for widening the present bridge (£7,000), and building a new stone bridge (over £14,000), or a cast-iron bridge similar to that at Sunderland (£8,000), the joint committee of justices of County Durham and the North Riding recommended the substitution of an iron bridge for the existing one. By the 26 September 1805 the new bridge had been completed on a site adjacent to Skirlaw's bridge, where the east side parapet had been removed. The new bridge was unofficially opened by the mayor of Stockton on that date, although the road on the Yarm side had not yet been diverted and so it was not yet open to traffic. During the night of the 13 January 1806, before the new bridge could be used for traffic, it fell into the river with a tremendous crash owing to the collapse of the south abutment. Fortunately for the public Skirlaw's old bridge was still standing and the magistrates decided to widen and repair it. All signs of the iron bridge were removed, and Skirlaw's bridge continues to carry the traffic on the A67 over the Tees, linking Yarm with Egglescliffe on the north side and onwards in County Durham.[588] A plaque on the west side of the bridge states:

'STONEWORK OF THE BRIDGE BUILT BY BISHOP SKIRLAW IN 1400 SHOWS ON THIS SIDE'

Plate 22. Yarm Bridge, plaque.

(Plate 22 shows the plaque on the lower part of the west side of Yarm bridge).

Another plaque above the footpath on the east side states:

'YARM BRIDGE WAS WIDENED IN 1806 AFTER THE CAST IRON BRIDGE BUILT 1805 COLLAPSED'

YORK
York always held a special place in Skirlaw's heart, and his interest in buildings and architecture went back to the time when he was archdeacon of the East Riding of Yorkshire. Archbishop Thoresby decided that the old choir of the Minster was out of place and did not correspond with the recently erected west end of the church. To finance the new choir project, materials and labour were needed and Thoresby himself contributed £1,810. Efforts were made to raise further funds from the public, and the clergy were threatened with excommunication if they did not produce cash out of their own income and that of their wealthy parishioners. In addition an apostolic bull was issued by Pope Urban VI imposing a tax of five per cent on ecclesiastical benefices for three years for the necessary repairs and re-edification. The old hall and chambers of the archbishop's manor of

Sherburn were demolished to provide stone and other materials for the building of it. The first stone was laid on 29 July 1361. A large sum had been collected but still more funds were necessary. It was only through the generosity of Archdeacon Skirlaw when in 1370 he stepped in with a contribution of further funds to cover the costs of completing the work of rebuilding the choir, as well as taking down the old lantern steeple and erecting a new one, that the work was completed.[589]

Archdeacon Skirlaw is also said to have been the major contributor toward the construction of the central tower (or lantern) of York Minster with a gift of £52, which is assumed to have been used to this purpose.

Plate 23   York Minster, central tower (exterior).

According to Wood's *History of the University of Oxford*, Skirlaw was referred to as an eminent architect, as the central tower which took nearly eight years to complete was built under his superintendence. At that time the wages of a master mason or carpenter were 3d a day and of their "knaves" or journeymen 1½d a day.[590] It appears that additional work was undertaken in later years, and the structure as it now stands was completed around 1430, although the internal vaulting was not finished until about 1470.[591]

The central tower *(Plate 23)* stands 210 feet high and is open from the floor to the timber vault 190 feet above. Four massive columns support four elegant arches which in turn support the lantern. Above the arches and below the windows of the tower, a gallery stretches round the four sides, designed to closely resemble the stall work in the aisles of the nave. Two great windows in each face are nearly 40 feet high and over 10 feet wide and form a great lantern to light the central part of the cathedral. The groined ceiling of wood harmonises with the nave, the centre boss containing small statues of St. Peter and St. Paul with a church between them. On four knots round about are cherubims with their wings, as mentioned in one of Ezekiel's visions, bearing the face of a man, a lion, an ox and an eagle *(Plate 24)*.[592] Skirlaw's coat of arms is on the spandrel of the central tower on the right-hand side of the south side, with the arms of St. Peter on the left side of the arch *(Plate 25)*. On the west arches are the arms of Edward the Confessor and those of Henry IV (who sent his master mason to help build the tower), on the north the arms assigned to the Saxon kings Edwin of Northumbria (founder of York Minster) and Oswald (who finished the first stone Minster), and on the east the See of York Ancient, and the arms of St. Wilfrid.[593] Sheehan and Whellan comment that 'nothing finer than the interior of the lantern can be imagined; the windows are of a size to fill the whole interior with light, and it may be added, that the immense height of the vaulting fills the mind with a feeling of vastness not easily forgotten. The tower forms a magnificent vestibule to the choir.'[594]

In January 1398 the chapter elected Skirlaw as archbishop of York, a position which would fulfil the ultimate aim of the ambitious bishop, but to his great dismay the election was dismissed a month later by Richard II in favour of Richard Scrope. When Scrope was executed in 1405 a vacancy was created, and it seems likely that Skirlaw was tempted to press his candidature once more. For some time the dean and chapter had been looking for a donor for the east window. As none had yet been found, Skirlaw came forward and offered to commission and pay for its glazing. But, despite his generosity, the archbishopric did not come his way. Perhaps his face did not fit or he was just too old and infirm. Indeed Skirlaw died before the next archbishop, Henry Bowet, was appointed in 1407, and in the meantime the contract for the window had been signed and work had begun.[595]

The principal glass-painter at the end of the fourteenth and beginning of the fifteenth centuries in York was John Burgh. But when the choice of

Plate 24.
York Minster,
central tower (interior).

Plate 25.
York Minster, central
tower, Skirlaw's shield.

glazier for the great east window was made, a new man, John Thornton, the master glazier of Coventry, was appointed, perhaps because his ideas and techniques were considered more up to date.[596] Preparations were made to glaze the east end of the church in 1399 for the glass-painter's shop contained:

Clear glass bought for the great window	£18 8s 6d
Coloured glass	£3 10s 0d
Kiln or furnace	4s 0d
Soldering irons, clamps and tongs	

Thornton's task was to design and draw the window panels with all the subjects, figures and other features, and to paint only as necessary. The size of the task was such that he engaged his own workmen to carry out most of the other work. His contract was for the hire of his professional services at a weekly wage. According to the agreement he would receive more than £46 in wages and gratuities (4s a week plus £5 a year[597]), plus £10 as a reward provided he completed the work in the three years allowed and to the satisfaction of his employers. Proof that Thornton completed the glazing on time is found at the top of the window tracery where his signature and date (1408) are written. In fact Thornton received a total of £56 4s, which excluded the cost of materials used and craftsmen employed, provided at the expense of the chapter.

The window is said to be the largest expanse of medieval glass to survive anywhere in the world. It is a masterpiece of narrative design, comparing with some of the great Italian fresco cycles; it covers an area 72 feet high by 32 feet wide, about the size of a tennis court, and in all is supported by a fine internal screen. Two galleries cross the window, one below the bottom row of panels and the other on the second transom, both fronted by a parapet.

Starting with the top central light the window depicts the story of God as alpha and omega, of those who praised him (shown in the tracery lights as angels, patriarchs, prophets, and saints), of the beginning of the world (in twenty-seven scenes showing the book of Genesis, and the story of Israel to the death of Absalom), and the end (eighty-one scenes of the Apocalypse). The bottom row of panels depicts historical and legendary figures from York's past, with Skirlaw in a place of honour in the central panel kneeling at his altar fronted with his coat of arms. On panels to the left of Skirlaw are depicted twelve kings and on his right twelve ecclesiastics, all relating in some way to the history of the minster. Skirlaw's coat of arms appears on three of these panels (from the left of the window: first panel [left]; sixth panel [centre] and eighth panel [centre][598]). The whole window has been described as 'a serene celebration of God and his creation which adds to ancient belief a fresh delight in the natural order and in the infinitely varied individual men who inhabit both heaven and earth' (Plate 26). [599]

In the panel depicting Bishop Skirlaw there is a scroll near Skirlaw's

Plate 26. York Minster, great east window.

head which reads according to Browne the words '*Singe Deus offero sume benigne*.'[600] Rushworth's notes on the inscription are as follows:

> 'Browne's transcription is evidently only the latter part of a metrical [hexameter] line, with the rhyming termination in middle and end, as was usual in such medieval compositions. Here it was *igne*, as we see from the certain last word *benigne*. Browne probably copied the fragment of the first word inaccurately, *singe* for *signe*. *Signe* should be completed as *insigne*, corresponding to *benigne*; and the missing words in front of it would be the common ones of dedication — *hoc opus* — thus making a complete and satisfactory line:
> "*Hoc opus insigne Deus offero. Sum benigne.*"
> ("O God, I offer to thee this noble work. Receive it graciously")' *(Plate 27).* [601]

The glass-painters probably started their work on the bottom row as the work at the top of the window shows considerable advance in design compared with that of the bottom row. It is also likely that the glazing of the bottom row incorporating Skirlaw's portrait and shields was completed before his death, as there was sufficient time in the three months between the signing of the contract on 10 December 1405 and the date of his death. Also there is no indication on the portrait inscription such as '*Orate pro anima*'

Plate 27.
York Minster, great east window, detail of Skirlaw's panel.

to indicate that he was no longer alive.⁶⁰² A question arises as to whether this portrait of Skirlaw represents an actual likeness as sketched by Thornton from a sitting in his studio (or at Howden manor), or whether it is the portrayal of Thornton's vision of the bishop. However, it may be that the part of the panel which includes his face is a replacement of the original made at a much later date. Presumably the original had become damaged at some time. Certainly Skirlaw's mitre and collar are a deeper in hue than elsewhere in the panel and in adjacent panels. It is known that a small amount of the medieval glass has had to be replaced over the years. Sheehan and Whellan name the figure in the central panel on the bottom row as archbishop Aldred at prayer⁶⁰³ rather than to Skirlaw although most other authorities consider it to be that of the donor.

BEVERLEY

Skirlaw, as archdeacon of the East Riding of Yorkshire, was party to an agreement to found a chantry at the altar of St. Michael at Beverley Minster in 1378.⁶⁰⁴ In consequence on 20 October 1380 a licence costing 40s was granted to Skirlaw and Richard Ravenser (archdeacon of Lincoln) to endow certain lands in Beverley and Garton to the Minster in order to pay a chaplain to celebrate divine service daily at the altar.⁶⁰⁵ A return made around 1550 records that:

> 'Robert Webster, clerk and incumbent of the chantry, of the age of 61 years, [was] of honest conversation, qualities, and learning, having no other promotion but only the revenues of the said chantry; and no lands [had been] sold or alienated within past five years. The yearly value of the lands belonging to the said chantry, as appeareth by the particular rental thereof, £13 8s 10d.
> Whereof
> In reprises yearly going out of the same 60s
> And so remaineth clear £10 8s 9d.⁶⁰⁶
> Goods, nil. Plate, nil.'⁶⁰⁷

HOWDEN

The collegiate church of Howden had a close connection with the bishops of Durham from the eleventh century until the nineteenth century, and the town benefited from the market and fairs they established as well as the magnificent minster and the Bishop's Manor House. Skirlaw is renowned for the five buildings he constructed during his episcopy. His banqueting hall is the only building that remains of the bishop's manor. Whilst still owned by the bishops of Durham, it was transformed in the eighteenth to nineteenth centuries from a single-story open medieval hall to a two-storey private house with an attic. In 1836 the manor house, together with the manor, passed to the newly-created bishopric of Ripon. In the 1850s the lessee, the Rev. J. Dunnington-Jefferson of Thicket Priory, removed the manorial buildings which stood on the north and west sides of the courtyard but left the hall intact *(Plate 28)*. A vicarage was built in 1863 in that part of the grounds where the kitchen of the banqueting hall once stood. The doorways from the hall to the kitchen, pantry and buttery can still be seen on its west side although now bricked up. A Mr. Kettlewell then lived in the hall for some time and used the porch as a dairy. In 1927 the surviving building was presented to the people of Howden by Charles Briggs and became a private residence. There is an inscription on the inside of the wall of the porch which states:

'THIS PORCH TO THE PALACE OF THE BISHOPS OF DURHAM
WAS BUILT BY WALTER SKIRLAW, BISHOP 1388–1405
AND RESTORED BY MR CHARLES BRIGGS 1938
ARCH^T ERNEST WALKER, YORK.'

Some twenty-five years ago the building, which had been unoccupied for some time and was in a neglected state, caught fire and the eastern end including the roof was substantially damaged. Despite pressure to pull down the building, local people vigorously opposed this action and in 1977 it was scheduled as an ancient monument.[608] Evidence of Skirlaw's work can be seen on top of the battlemented canopy above the outside entrance to the porch on the north side of the hall, where his arms held by an angel are carved in stone in the middle of the parapet with two beasts *(Plate 29 shows the porch with the coat-of-arms of Bishop Skirlaw on the canopy)*. Inside the porch the vaulted roofing also incorporates Skirlaw's arms held by two little angels as a key, and there are other stone carvings of his arms on the stone benches against the inside walls on each side of the porch. These arms may not have originated there but may have come instead from above an arch over the west wing of the manor. The strategic positioning of his arms would indicate that Skirlaw had built the kitchens and some living quarters attached to the west end of the hall, which were part of the manorial buildings pulled down in the nineteenth century by Dunnington-Jefferson.[609] William de Chambre, the early historian, relates that '[Skirlaw] built the *whole* hall and expended large sums of money moreover in edifices of the same manor house'.[610] Hutchinson states that Skirlaw most probably erected the hall which:

> 'occupied the extreme eastern portion of the south side [of the quadrangle of the manor-house whose inner dimensions were 186 feet from east to west and 126 feet from north to south]. It was 62 feet long with a width of 24 feet. It was built wholly of freestone, having seven fair clerestory windows, above which arose a battlemented parapet. At the western extremity of the hall a porch projected 14 feet square. In a line continuing westward with the front were a pantry and other offices, leading to a spacious kitchen, and this was followed by three living rooms; the whole of this western part was of the same height as the hall, but, forming a pleasing variety, its

Plate 28.
Howden Manor Hall.

Plate 29.
Howden Manor Hall, porch.

material was brick, finished above with the stone battlement. To break the line of the parapet, two elevations, described as louvres by the surveyor, were raised, one of very curious workmanship, and both roofed with lead. It was a lofty building and must have presented an imposing appearance to people coming from the town, to whom access could be given without entering the courtyard. It was intended, no doubt, as the bishop's special private lodging during his visits to his manor. Beside four rooms, most probably used as sleeping apartments, there was under the same roof a spacious room 54 feet by 18 feet, known as "camera major", and alluded to by William de Chambre as that in which, but two years before his death, 25 July 1404, he signed the last codicil to his will. It was in this chamber also, or in one of the apartments close by, that he drew his last breath. Jutting from the western extremity of the bishop's lodging was the beautiful porch which, with its groined ceiling, now serves the purpose of a dairy. The whole building was vaulted, and in its front were contained 9 windows of 2 lights, very likely similar to the one over the porch.'[611]

A sketch of Skirlaw's hall or palace, as it is thought to have looked in medieval times, appears in a recently published book on Howden.[612]

At the same time as Skirlaw applied for permission to establish the chantry of St. Cuthbert (see Chapter Eleven), he also applied to the king for a grant to establish a hall with chambers for the vicars of Howden Minster.[613] Permission was duly received and a bedern was built by Skirlaw to accommodate six resident vicars-choral, positions filled by local Yorkshire clerks. The six canonries and prebends were given to higher ranking ecclesiastics who were not normally resident at Howden. The house, which no longer exists, was situated in Howden between Pinfold Street and Parsons Lane, where the house called 'The Chestnuts' now stands.[614]

In his will dated 3 February 1380 Canon Henry Snaith, who was canon of Lincoln, Beverley and Howden, bequeathed the sum of £10 towards the building of a chapter house at Howden Minster. He died around 1387 and Skirlaw, who was one of his fellow canons at Beverley and also his executor, after becoming bishop of Durham, added a further amount sufficient to cover the cost of the building. The resulting structure is said to have been the last octagonal, vaulted chapter house to be built in England. It has similarities to the one at York Minster, but on a smaller scale. It has been described as follows:

'The Chapter House (now a ruin) is entered from the south aisle of the choir by a splendid arch, with canopied niches on each side ... [It] is a superb and very beautifully proportioned octagonal edifice, with buttresses at the angles; each containing two pointed arches. In each division was an elegant window of three lights, and above each window was a pedimented canopy, crocketed, and terminating in a rich finial. The finish was a pierced parapet of quatrefoils, and pinnacles at the angles. Its beautifully groined roof and octagonal spire fell in on St. Stephen's Day 1750. The diameter of the interior is only 24 feet, and it contained 30 seats, separated by clustered pillars, very small and extremely delicate, having foliated capitals of pierced work, from which rises rich tabernacle work, ornamenting pointed arches. The seats are canopied, in imitation of a groined and ribbed arch.'[615]

Hutchinson wrote:

'We may then regard A.D. 1390 as the time when the foundation stone was laid. What a day of rejoicing it must have been not only for the ecclesiastics belonging to the church, but we may well believe for the multitudes living round! With the bishop's well-known profuse liberality, no expense would be spared to render it a masterpiece in the style of architecture which then began everywhere to prevail, the early Perpendicular. You have only to take your stand within it and look around to be thoroughly convinced that he has completely succeeded.'[616]

Clarke's opinion in 1843 was:

'I speak in no exaggerated terms when I assert – indeed, I only reiterate the opinions of others – that the Chapter House, for elegance and beauty of proportion, stands without equal among the ecclesiastical structures of Great Britain. Roslyn may be more elaborate and highly finished in its detail, York may be larger, and some others may excel it in one or two particulars, but taken as a whole there is nothing equal to it, or capable of being put into competition with it. In finish and proportion it is perfect. It is universally admitted that nowhere can the architect find specimens of tracery, of mullion, of ornament, better worthy of his study, more perfect in all their parts, or more complete as a whole. It is faultless, and cannot be viewed, even by the eye of indifference, without delight . . . It is, in fine, the *chef-d'œuvre* of Bishop Skirlaw, that munificent patron of architecture . . .'[617] *(Plate 30)*

The choir end of the minster was abandoned during the seventeenth century, due to both a lack of funds and to the effects of the Civil War, and eventually the roof of the chapter house, which stands on the south of the choir, collapsed on 26 December 1750. Although now ruined, much of it still remains, and it was given a new roof in 1984 under the aegis of English Heritage, which now administers that end of the minster grounds. It is hoped that the tracery in the windows will be restored and the windows glazed.[618] Sketches of a section of the interior and of the elevation of the chapter house in their original state are included in Clarke's booklet.[619]

Plate 30. Howden Minster, chapter house.

Plate 31. Howden Minster, tower.

The east end of the ruined choir is remarkably beautiful. Two fine statues still remain, one of St. Peter, the other supporting a tabernacle, supposed to be of St. Cuthbert or Skirlaw.[620]

The tower of Howden Minster was built by Skirlaw, and work may have commenced in 1390. It seems that the tower Skirlaw funded was only the first section of the tower as it now stands – a tall and stately stage above the roofs, with great slender Perpendicular windows similar in design to those of the tower of Durham Cathedral. The hood-moulds of the windows stop on angels; each pair of angels in the middle of each side holds a shield as follows: east, Skirlaw; south, Metham; west, Langley; north, Neville.[621] Apart from those listed above in the tower there were placed shields in the corners: to the north-east, on a fess three buckles; to the south-east, three roses (probably Darcy); to the south-west, on a bend three escallops, and to the north-west, on a bend three buckles. They may have been the arms of some of those who aided Skirlaw in his work, or other benefactors or prelates.[622] The top section of the tower was added for a belfry towards the end of the fifteenth century, although it could be that Skirlaw's original bequest of £40 'towards the fabric of the bell-tower' (see Chapter Twelve) was for that purpose *(Plate 31 shows the tower and the ruined chancel in the foreground).* [623] One story suggests that Skirlaw built the tower of great height so that the inhabitants could seek refuge if the river chanced to flood. Clarke comments that is, 'doubtless the joke of some witling from a higher locality', and it can be considered unlikely, for even if the banks of the two rivers in the neighbourhood (the Ouse and Derwent) were levelled, the town of Howden could never be laid more than six or eight feet under water.[624] Skirlaw, whilst bishop of Durham, also spent large sums on repairs to the church.

Howden Grammar School was founded by Skirlaw whilst bishop of Durham, and his coat of arms was adopted by the school as its badge. His original school was built on to the minster as a low stone-vaulted room within the angle of the south porch and the west end of the south wall of the nave. In about 1500, the school was moved to a room built on top of the original school room. Skirlaw's original school is now used as a boiler-house,[625] and the later school as a Sunday school. Although it is not certain when precisely the grammar school was built, the Durham Register gives a possible clue, some schooling may have taken place in the minster before Walter's school was built but the Register for 1393 contains entries in respect of the prior of Durham as 'Ordinary of the spiritualities of St. Cuthbert in Howdenshire,' appointing masters of the song school *(scolas cantuales)* and grammar school *(scolas gramaticales)* there, 'as they have been accustomed to be conferred'. In 1394 the prior appointed masters to the combined reading and song school *(tam lectuales quam cantuales)*, and, in making a fresh appointment to the school in 1401, reserved to another person, probably the parish clerk, the right to teach eighteen boys reading. A new appointment to the grammar school in 1403 expressly directed the master to make his boys attend and sing the Lady Mass in the collegiate church 'as anciently used'.[626]

In medieval times Howden had a reputation as a centre of culture, and the school attracted boys whose education there would equip them to become clerks and administrators. In 1925 the then master, Mr. Hatt (who was also the choirmaster) died, and the pupils were transferred to Goole Grammar School. However, in 1963, when the newly created Howden County Secondary School was considering the form of its badge, it was decided to base it on that of the old Howden Grammar School. The new badge was designed by Mr. E. Stockdale and incorporated Bishop Skirlaw's coat of arms, a bishop's mitre, a market cross and a horse (representing Howden's famous horse fair).[627]

There is a saying which is still remembered by the people of Howden:

'Bishop Skirlaw was good to his people,
He built them a school house and heightened their steeple.'[628]

Hull

At an unknown date Skirlaw also established a college of prebendaries at Holy Trinity Church in the centre of the old part of the city of Kingston upon Hull. The college was dissolved at the time of the Reformation, and no traces remain.[629] A footnote to Abraham Pryme's diary suggests that the college of prebendaries was at Howden, rather than Hull, but this seems unlikely.[630]

Skirlaugh

The other building of importance created by Skirlaw was Skirlaugh Chapel. This forms the subject of Chapter Ten.

CHAPTER TEN

SKIRLAW CHAPEL

The abbot of Thornton in North Lincolnshire is known to have possessed the village of South Skirlaugh which comprised four carucates[631] in the district of Aldbrough during the reign of Henry II (1133-89), from whom he received his grant. By the time of Edward III (1312-77) it is recorded that the prioress of Swine and the abbot of Thornton held two carucates and three bovates[632] of land.[633] The priory of Swine in Holderness was founded in the twelfth century, during or before the reign of King Stephen, for fourteen or fifteen nuns of the Cistercian Order by Robert de Verle *(Plate 32 shows the remains of Swine Priory today which consist of the chancel and (rebuilt) tower of the priory church)*. The nuns built chapels of ease in the villages and hamlets in their parish. Skirlaugh then lay in the parish of Swine, and one of these chapels was built there. It would have been constructed of timber, and subject to the ravages of the elements, would have needed constant repair and renewal. There is documentary evidence of a chapel in existence in 1337[634] as well as some earlier references. The inhabitants would have maintained the chapel and hired a priest with the assistance of Swine Priory. On 10 December 1337 a dispute arose between

Plate 32. Swine Church.

the inhabitants of North and South Skirlaugh and the prioress and convent of Swine, over who should pay for the upkeep of the chapel and priest, following the withdrawal of the chantry by the prioress. Brought before the court of the archbishop of York, it was determined:

> 'Whereas a controversy arose between the inhabitants of South Skirlaugh and North Skirlaugh, Arnold and Rowton on one part, and the prioress and convent of nuns of Swine on the other, touching a certain chantry in the chapel of South Skirlaugh who submitting to the laud and arbitrament of William Archbishop of York he thus determined the same viz.
>
> That the inhabitants of [North and South Skirlaugh] should find and perpetually at their own costs maintain one fit priest every day to celebrate and serve in the chapel of South Skirlaugh, who after he has been presented by the prioress and convent of Swine, and admitted thereunto, shall without prejudice to the mother church of Swine as a stipendiary chaplain exercise cure of souls. And shall answer and satisfy the said prioress and convent out of the fruits, obventions[635] and profits belonging to the said chapel.
>
> Also the said inhabitants shall find books, chalice, vestments, lights, bread and wine and other necessaries for the said chantry, and shall repair and rebuild the said chapel, and bear all other burdens incumbent thereon.
>
> But to the sustentation of the chantry the said prioress and nuns shall pay yearly 36s 4d sterling to the stipendiary priest in the chapel for the time being. Moreover the said chaplain shall have two oxgangs of land in the territory of South Skirlaugh and the prioress and convent of Swine shall also give him one penny out of every oxgang of land which they hold in Skirlaugh and henceforth shall not require that 5s sterling which the inhabitants were wont to pay them in times past.
>
> And that the mother church of Swine might not be defrauded, he furthermore ordained, that the inhabitants of those Towns shall repair to their parish church of Swine on the feasts of Easter and Our Lady's Assumption as they were wont to do in preceding times.'[636]

Towards the end of his life, Skirlaw built (or rebuilt), the ageing chapel in the village of [South] Skirlaugh where he was born. This he dedicated to St. Augustine of Hippo. The building was Skirlaw's own design, and incorporated the latest designs in layout and Perpendicular form, quite revolutionary for a village place of worship at that time. It would be interesting to know how the villagers reacted to the new church constructed from the best materials Skirlaw could obtain.

Dodsworth, in his *Yorkshire Church Notes*, says:

> 'Remember Walter Skirlaw, borne att Skirlaw, a sivier's son, and run away from his father, being very untoward, came to the university of

[Oxford], and there was a sizer, and came to have such learning as he was made bishop of Durham, his father never knowing what was become of him, and when he came to Durham he sent his steward to inquire for his father and mother, and after notice of their being alive he sent for them, and in memory of his being borne there builded a faire chappell att Swine, where he sett his armes in every windowe, videlicet, a crosse of ther spells of a sive or riddle, in memory and acknowledgment from whence he sprunge.'[637]

For the purpose of establishing the chapel it seems that Sir Robert Hilton (lord of Swine) and John Redness quit claim to Walter Skirlaw all rights in lands and tenements in South Skirlaugh on 16 April 1401.[638] And in 1402, Walter Skirlaw was granted a licence to give to the prioress and convent of Swine a messuage (valued at 1s yearly), two tofts (each worth 4d per annum), twenty-four acres of land (each worth 3d per annum), and eleven acres of meadow (each acre valued at 5d per annum).[639] As the chapel in Skirlaugh then came under the priory of Swine, it is likely that this gift was intended for the upkeep of the chapel. The following statement from the ordinance included in Langley's register no doubt also relates to the establishment of the chapel, and is taken from the Calendar of Patent Rolls for 23 November 1402. It seems that Henry IV granted the licence to Walter, but recompensed the abbot of Thornton by granting to him some land in Lincolnshire, as follows:

'Licence for Walter, bishop of Durham, Thomas Weston, clerk, Richard Holme, clerk, and Peter de la Hay, esquire, to grant in mortmain 17 messuages, 2 tofts, 302 acres of land, 56 acres of meadow and 6s 8d rent in Barrow, Ulceby and Grimsby, of which one messuage in Grimsby is held of the king in burgage and the remainder are held of others, worth 18 marks yearly, as appears by an inquisition taken before John de la Launde, escheator in the county of Lincoln, to the abbot and convent of St. Mary, Thornton, to hold in aid of their maintenance and the support of certain charges and works of piety; in full satisfaction of a licence by letters patent dated 18 November 1 Henry IV.'[640]

Skirlaw first executed the ordinance, then procured a licence from Richard Scrope, archbishop of York, on 5 January 1403, and after obtained the consent of the chapter of York and of the prioress and convent of Swine to the establishment of the chapel and chantry. Finally, on the 2 May 1404, by his writing and under his seal, Skirlaw founded one chantry of two chaplains in the chapel of Skirlaugh, appointing two priests, Robert Brynston and William Skirlaw, as the first incumbents. At the same time he set out the regulations for the establishment and ordering of their pensions and celebrations, and of themselves, as well as for their habitation and future presentation.[641]

The register of Bishop Thomas Langley includes an ordinance of Bishop Skirlaw for the establishment of a chantry in his chapel at Skirlaugh dated 2 May 1404. The statement quotes royal and archiepiscopal licences obtained, together with confirmations given by the prioress and convent of Swine and the chapter of York.[642] Why this notice should appear here is not clear, but Storey suggests that it was probably enregistered at the instance of Richard Holme, Langley's chancellor, who was one of Skirlaw's executors.[643]

While there is no conclusive evidence as to when Skirlaw built his chapel at Skirlaugh, some writers date its completion as 1404, and the appointment of chaplains on 2 May 1404, seem to indicate that the chapel was sufficiently complete to be operating at that date. Skirlaw's will, dated 1403 (see Chapter Twelve), did include the following:

'Also I bequeath 200 marks to complete the chantry at Skirlaugh if I have not completed it before my death, and as much more as is appropriate for its completion.' [644]

The following is a translation from the Latin taken from the ordinance relating to the establishment of the chapel and chantry by Bishop Skirlaw and preserved in Bishop Langley's register:

RELIGIOUS SERVICES AT SKIRLAUGH
Appointed by
BISHOP SKIRLAW

Chapel of St. Augustine
Skirlaw Chantries
2 May 1404

Walter Skirlaw Bishop of Durham (having obtained the King's Licence dated 18 November 1402 and the Licence of Richard archbishop of York dated 5 January 1403) out of the devotion and sincere affection which he bore to the Nunnery of Swine and to the Chapelry of Skirlaugh (where he was born) and to the relief of certain poor parishioners of the said Chapel ordained created made and founded one perpetual Chantry of two Chaplains in the Chapel of Skirlaugh Instituting therein Robert Brynston and William Skirlaw Prebenders to be Chaplains thereof for term of life And willed that the said Robert and his Successors be Principals and Wardens of the said Chapel and Chantry and to have cure of all the Parishioners thereof in all things as the Stipendiary Chaplain heretofore used to have who was hired by the Prioress of Swine and these Parishioners And who shall make Oath to the said Prioress and Convent to answer them faithfully in such small Tythes Oblations and Obventions as shall be offered by the Parishioners of the said Chapel.

And in recompense for his pains the Prioress and Convent shall pay him 13s 4d instead of the 2 marks & ½ they were wont before to give to the Stipendiary Priest hereof and the residue of the said Pension being 26s 8d shall be assigned for the yearly maintenance of the Chapel in bread and candle for celebration of masses And the Chaplains shall also have 6s 8d towards the repairs of their houses and for wine in their celebrations Likewise there shall be 3s 4d given to the Vicars Priests and Clerks on the day of his Exequies and other 3s 4d and 6s 8d be distributed amongst the Nuns of the House on the day of his anniversary obit for ever to be celebrated in the Priory Church of Swine.

Furthermore ordaining that the said Chaplains shall be bound daily to say the Canonical hours and celebrate Masses according to the use of the Church of York, And that one of them do celebrate daily the Mass of the day.

And the other on every Sunday, the Mass *de Trinitate*.

And on Mondays, Wednesdays and Fridays, the Mass *de Requiem pro mortuis*.

And on Tuesdays, Thursdays and Saturdays, the Mass de *Scā Virgine*. In which (excepting on double Festivals) they shall devoutly say one Collect for the good estate of himself* while he lives, *Scil. Rege quesumus*.

And another Collect, *Scil. Deus qui Caritatis*, &c. for his* kindred friends and benefactors, then living.

And after his* decease the Collect, *Scil. Deus qui inter Apostolicos*, &c.

And the Collect, *Scil. Omnipotens Sempiterne Deus cui nunquam sine spe*, for the souls of his* Parents Kindred Friends and Benefactors.

And that every day they shall sing or say at Matins and Vespers the Canonical hours within the said Chapel.

And each of them shall say the Office of the Dead *Scil. Placebo Dirige cu commendatione aiaru*.

And that every Lord's day one of them shall celebrate in the Chapel of Skirlaugh the Great Mass with the solemn Orations thereof, and as the manner is to expound to the People touching the good Estate of himself*, and of Joan his sister while they live, and after their decease to make special mention for their Souls, &c.

Then he* granted to the said two Chaplains and their Successors that ancient habitation for the old Chaplain ordained, and one place with a Croft on the South side of the Chapel yard which were anciently assigned by the Prioress and Convent of Swine for the said old Chaplain To have and to hold the same to them and their Successors Chaplains for a mansion wherein they shall dwell eat drink and converse together.

And that each Chaplain and his Successors shall have 8 marks per annum paid out of the annual Pension of 16 marks granted to the Abbot and Convent of Thornton for that purpose.

The Principal of them who shall be called the *Warden* of the Chantry shall bear the cure of all the Parishioners of the Towns and Hamlets belonging to the Chapel as the Stipendiary Chaplain who was hired by the Prioress and Parishioners was wont to bear.

Lastly that the said Chaplains and their Successors shall be presented in all vacations by himself* during life, and after his* decease by the Prioress and Convent of Swine for the time being.

All which was confirmed by the Chapter of York 8 June 1406.[645]

(*Walter Skirlaw/Skirlaw's)

Following Skirlaw's gift of a new chapel, and the setting up of the Bishop Skirlaw Charity (as described later in the chapter), the inhabitants of Skirlaugh (and the adjacent hamlets) and the prioress of Swine would have found the financial burden of a chapel at Skirlaugh much lighter.

Walter Skirlaw's chapel, which stands in South Skirlaugh on a rise near the Lambwath Stream, was designed in Perpendicular form and built in York stone, which came from a quarry near Tadcaster. Apart from the tower, the exterior is of simple rectangular construction, with six large windows of three lights on the north and south sides of the nave, and one larger east window with five lights, each filled with tracery in the head. Between each window there is a buttress which rises above the battlements in crocketed pinnacles. Four of these windows have a shortened drop to accommodate the doors underneath them. These are a north door (in the nave), a south (or priest's) door (in the chancel), a door to a (south) embattled porch (in the nave), and a door from the chancel opening to a (north) embattled vestry (or chantry chapel) attached to the building. The tower at the west end of the building, which houses two bells, is constructed in a style similar to the rest of the building and incorporates a west window of similar dimensions and position as the large north and south windows. Above the battlemented roof line, there are the belfry windows. Apart from these, the windows and doors all have drip-tones which terminate with Skirlaw's shield, a total of thirty-four shields *(plate 33 shows the priest's door on the south side of the church)*. On the west side, between the large lower window and the belfry window, is a crocketed niche, in which it is thought a statue of St. Augustine was originally situated. A statue of the saint has recently been placed in the empty niche, and stone crosses have been added centrally above the embattled east wall and the south porch of the church where it is evident they had previously existed.[646] The parapets of the tower are elegantly carved with crocketed pinnacles in keeping with those above the nave and chancel *(Plate 34 of Skirlaw's chapel)*.

On inspection, it has been found that some stone mason's marks at Skirlaugh match those carved in the stonework of York Minster. It may be that Skirlaw employed the most skilled masons available at that time. It is also evident that the tower was built with an ashlar facing which does not

*Plate 33.
Skirlaugh
Church,
priest's door.*

*Plate 134.
Skirlaugh
Church
(exterior).*

altogether match that of the rest of the building, which otherwise appears homogeneous. The tower is usually the last part of a church to be completed, and it is noticeable also that the inside of the tower is not ashlar-faced as is the rest of the building. Moreover, the tower is a little disappointing in stature when compared with the rest of the building, and lacks Skirlaw's coat of arms on the drip-stone ends of the upper windows, as can seen on all the other windows of the chapel. It is possible that although operational from May 1404, the chapel was incomplete, and that the tower and porch were added later, possibly after Skirlaw's death in 1406.

The windows in Skirlaugh chapel are mentioned in Warburton's *Yorkshire Collections*, in the Lansdowne MSS, as having been 'all curiously painted, and set with coats of arms, but now [1656] almost all gone, and white glass in lieu thereof. Remains only Walter de Skirlaugh.' However, the manuscript later mentions that in that year the following, as well as other arms still remained in some of the windows although none of them survive today:

'A. 3 Palets crossing 3 Barrulets – frequent
A. 3 Trefoils G. in Bend between 2 Cottoises S.
A. on a Chev. sa. 3 Mullets or.
B. 3 Chevrons braced in base and a Chief or. *[Fitzhugh]*
Barry 6 or and B. *[Constable]*
A. 3 Chaplets Gu. *[Lascelles or Hilton]*
B. 5 Martlets about a Cross paty or.
England and France – quarterly.'[647]

The first shield described above must be that of Walter Skirlaw, which might have been incorporated into every window. Only a relic of the medieval glass remains. These pieces are now incorporated in the modern east window glazing of 1981, and depict what appears to be an angel, a communion cup and the letters 'W' and 'S', the initials presumably representing those of Walter Skirlaw (*Plate 35*). The other chapel windows were glazed at the same time except for one over the north door completed in 1890 as a memorial to Mary Catlin, matron of Skirlaugh workhouse.

*Plate 35.
Skirlaugh Church,
east window (detail).*

The interior of the chapel has no columns and is lofty, light and airy. The dimensions are about 80 feet from west to east (excluding the tower) and 25 feet from north to south. The only distinction between nave and chancel was the placing of a rood screen from the north to the south wall, about 25 feet in from the east end of the building, removed at some time in the past. In other respects, the interior has changed over time to suit the current customs of the church. For instance, there is now no three-tier pulpit, western gallery or boxed pews, and the old basic hand-pumped organ was replaced at the beginning of the twentieth century by a more sophisticated instrument by Forster and Andrews, which is still in use today. Evidence of the wall painting which would have been intended to illustrate aspects of the Bible's teaching to earlier worshippers still exists.

The church is sometimes referred to as the 'Prince of Holderness' with Hedon and Patrington churches been known as the 'King' and 'Queen' of Holderness respectively. Pevsner described Skirlaugh Church as 'a perfect piece of Perpendicular architecture, perfect because [it was] built not only lavishly but also quickly and entirely to one plan.' His only criticism was that the south porch sat against the building awkwardly and that the west tower was a little short for the lofty nave and chancel. He also commented that the nave and chancel were one, without structural division, which was a new Perpendicular ideal, or on the other hand it could be argued that the bishop visualised the building as a chapel, like college chapels.[648] Pugin also favourably contrasted the design of Skirlaugh Church with that of St. Pancras Chapel in London.[649]

In Scotland, in the second decade of the nineteenth century, the trend in designing church exteriors moved from medieval Gothic forms towards neo-Perpendicular lines. This fashion was directly linked to John Britton's *Architectural Antiquities,* published from 1805 onwards, which found its place in most country house libraries, and enabled clients as well as architects to be better informed. The new trend was first apparent in country churches built for discerning landed gentlemen, but soon spread to the towns. In 1813 a correct neo-Perpendicular church was built at Collace near Perth, its external form an adaptation from Britton's plate of Skirlaugh chapel. Other churches were built which followed the same design in principle, many by the same architect, J. G. Graham, although none seem to have been as correctly proportioned as the church at Collace.[650]

On 18 August 1552, a survey of church goods, plate, jewels, vestments, bells, and other ornaments of Skirlaugh chapel took place between the king's commissioners for the East Riding of Yorkshire and the people of Skirlaugh. The commissioners for the survey were Sir William Babthorpe, Sir Robert Constable, Sir Ralph Ellerker, and John Eaglesfield, and for Skirlaugh, the churchwardens of St. Augustine's – William Cole, William Maxwell, and Robert Underwodde (Underwood?) – and two villagers, James Stynte (Styche?) and Robert Chapphamsone (Clappison?). An inventory, in the form of a bill, was agreed as follows:

> 'Firstly, two bells, one hand bell.
> Also, one chrismatory, one holy water vat made of latten, one chest, one cruet.
> Also, one altar cloth, one towel.
> Also, one old surplice.'[651]

On 9 June 1415, a licence was obtained from Parliament under Henry V for Richard Holme and Peter de la Hay, executors of Skirlaw's will, to grant in mortmain three messuages, two tofts, 240 acres of land and 29 acres of meadow in South Skirlaugh and Thirkleby, not held of the king, to the prioress and convent of Swine in aid of their maintenance, and for the support of certain charges by the ordinance of Walter Skirlaw, late bishop of Durham, for which 20 marks was paid in the hanaper by the applicants.[652] This grant would have enlarged the estate of Swine Priory, but may have excluded land set aside for the establishment of the Bishop Skirlaw Charity for the maintenance of the Skirlaugh chapel.

Although there is no specific record of its foundation, Walter Skirlaw funded the Bishop Skirlaw's Charity (or Chapel Estate) comprising land in the Skirlaugh area. In the nineteenth century it comprised about eleven acres of land and five cottages. A letter from the Charity Commissioners to the trustees concerning the Chapel Estate dated 9 July 1877 states:

> 'The object of the Charity being apparently the repair and continuance of the Chapel of Skirlaugh, there would seem to be no objection in any year, where sufficient provision has been made for the repair and maintenance of the Chapel buildings and premises, to the application of such portion of the net income of the Charity as may not be required for the repair of the fabric in defraying such expenses as would have been properly chargeable to the Church Rate.'

A parcel or close of land called Chapel Carr Field, comprised nearly eight and a half acres, situated in Arnold Carr to the west of Skirlaugh, bordering Green Lane and the Benningholme and Arnold Ings Drain. It was a source of income for the church until 1943, when it was sold by the trustees and the money invested in securities. [653]

Another parcel of land of nearly two acres was situated on the north side of Vicarage Lane, Skirlaugh. The Charity received rents from the field until 1974, when it was sold as building land. It now forms a cul-de-sac called 'Little Shore' (named after the beck running along its western boundary), going northwards from Vicarage Lane and is flanked by a number of bungalows. The proceeds of the sale were used towards church restoration and the balance invested in securities.

A row of four cottages and gardens ('Vicarage Row'), on the north side of Vicarage Lane in North Skirlaugh, remains a part of the Charity from which rents continue to be received *(Plate 36)*. Another cottage belonging to the Charity, with about a third of an acre of land, is situated on the north side of Church Lane in South Skirlaugh to the south of and near St. Augustine's Church. Until recent years it was rented out but, it is now used by the church for meetings and other activities. All five cottages were built in 1862. Before then, only two cottages are listed as part of the estate.

The income from the Bishop Skirlaw Charity, whether from cottage rents or investment continues to be a valued source of funds for the repair and maintenance of the fabric of the church and its property, and contributes towards any shortfall of church income.

Skirlaugh church continues to be the centre of worship and prayer envisaged by Skirlaw, although his chantry disappeared with the Reformation. Since then, the Church of England maintained it as a chapel of ease of Swine Church until 1867, when it became a parish church in its own right with its own vicar. More recently, under the present vicar, the Reverend David W. Perry, the church has moved ecumenically with the establishment of a partnership with the Methodist Church following the closure of the village chapel in 1982.

Plate 36. Skirlaugh, Vicarage Row.

Chapter Eleven
Death of Bishop Skirlaw

Skirlaw held office as bishop of Durham until his death in the living quarters he built at Howden Manor on 24 March 1406. Skirlaw made elaborate preparations for his death by writing his will (see Chapter Twelve), and by obtaining permission for his burial in Durham Cathedral. He also set up chantries where prayers would be said in perpetuity for his soul at Durham Cathedral, York Minster, Howden Minster, Selby Abbey and Skirlaugh Chapel.

In 1398, Skirlaw began to make provision for his chantry at Durham Cathedral in the north choir aisle, where mass was to be said daily for his soul. Opposite this, he constructed a row of benches for a number of old men called bedesmen, who received a pension from him and gave him the benefit of their prayers. To fund his chantry, Skirlaw, through Peter de la Hay, of Spaldington (near Howden), transferred to the prior and convent of Durham certain lands in Wolviston once belonging to John Bishopton,[654] and other property at Auckland and Monkton.

A brief series of accounts dealing with Skirlaw's chantry from 1398 until his death records the expenditure incurred on erecting and equipping the chapel, which was completed by the autumn of 1403. The account also records income from the appropriated land and property. The expenses were partly in connection with the various properties, such as commissions to agents, but also such as items relating to the chantry itself including candlesticks. These records are now kept by the dean and chapter of Durham. A summary of the account for the year ended 1 November 1403 is given below.[655]

Account roll produced by Thomas Lyth (monk) of the Chantry of Walter Skirlaw, for the year ended the Feast of All Saints, 1 November 1403

	£ s d	£ s d
Balance: cash held by Thomas at start of year		1 10 6
Receipts:		
Rents: Wolviston: periods ending Martinmas (11 November 1402) and Pentecost (May 1403)	2 0 4	
Auckland: from Peter de la Hay	2 10 0	
Monkton: to Feast of All Saints 1403	10 0	
Total:		5 0 4
Total receipts and remittances [Lyth states it to be £6 10s 8d]		**6 10 10**

Expenses:
    Property transactions:
        Purchase of Monkton land   2 10 0
        Expenses and repairs   10 5
                                                                       3 0 5
    Chantry expenses:
        John Tudowe, stone mason   2 4
        William Pictori of Elvet, statue   3 8
        Various legal costs, compensation   8 8
        Thomas Hyndley, stone mason, for tomb   6 8
        Purchase of washing bowl of tin, for altar   2 6
        Purchase of lectern, brass candle stand and
            pair of cruets   1 3
        Purchase of 4 linen cloths and cases, to be
            used for celebrating mass   6 8
        Purchase of 4 altar napkins   1 0
        John Piercebridge for making shield of
            Bishop Skirlaw's coat of arms and other
            Ironwork, and tools used   8 6
        Purchase of 3 lead weights for making
            firm ironwork round tomb   1 6
        John Hexham for embroidery work   6
        Celebrating mass at bishop's altar for 3½
            years *(balancing figure?)*   2 2
                                                                     2 5 5
    Total expenses   5 5 10
Surplus of receipts over expenses: 1 5 0
Out of which was paid
    Amounts due on 40 acres of land and 2
        acres of meadow at Wolviston   18 0
    To Thomas South and William Homaze for
        amounts due on properties   9 8
    To Peter Dryng *(master mason in charge)*
        for an amount owing to him from the
        previous accounting period   1 0 0
Total exonerated   2 7 8
And thus the sum indebted for   (1 2 8)

Endorsement:
A summary of the altar furnishings of the bishop of Durham chantry:
    Firstly, 4 linen altar cloths with 3 frontals with fringes of silk,
    Also, 4 complete sets of priest's vestments given by the bishop, one set
       in mottled black velvet, one set of velvet robes embroidered with

gold letters, another set of gold cloth, and a green one with Cyprus gold appliqué,
Also, 1 hair cloth for the altar,
Also, 4 cloth cases with 4 linen cloths used in celebration of mass,
Also, 1 shallow washing bowl made of tin,
Also, 4 towels for the altar,
Also, 1 pair of cruets made of tin,
Also, 1 wooden lectern and 1 brass candle stand,
Also, 4 veils and curtains for Lent of dyed buckram,
Also, 1 statue of St. Blaise,
Also, 4 large pale blue curtains.

Memorandum added:
And thus the debt works out at £1 5s 4d which represents only for the labour of his property around the aforementioned incantation, during the past 6 years.[656]

Other payments recorded during the period from 1398 to March 1406 include 6s 8d to a mason and 3s 4d to William Payntour for a painted panel at the altar. In 1406 an account produced by the same monk, Thomas Lyth, records payments relating to Skirlaw's chantry made during the period 1 November 1403 to 20 March 1406, to Thomas Weston and Peter de la Hay, the bishop's executors.[657]

Skirlaw's chantry was placed in the north aisle of the choir opposite the tomb and throne of Bishop Hatfield, which still remains in the south aisle of the choir. Hatfield, who died in 1381, came from the Holderness village of that name, only a few miles from where Skirlaw was born, and no doubt the two were acquainted.

The bedesmen's stalls in the form of stone benches were constructed opposite his chantry, in the third bay below the window of the outer wall in the north choir aisle. The fronts have multifoiled circular panels containing twelve of Skirlaw's shields alternating with smaller cinquefoil-headed panels. There is a blind wall arcade of six arches supported by columns from below the window to the back of the benches (*Plate 37*). Today bedesmen still play an important role in the cathedral, although they now no longer serve Skirlaw's chantry. The men and women taking this role are appointed to help in welcoming visitors who wish to look round the cathedral or attend the many services.[658]

It was usual for the Durham bishops to be buried in the chapter house of the cathedral, but exceptionally Skirlaw applied for a licence to the prior and convent of Durham for his burial to take placed in their church. This was granted on 6 January 1404,[659] and worded as follows:

'To the most reverend Father in Christ and Lord Walter by the grace of God Bishop of Durham, his most devoted son, John the prior, and the convent of the church of Durham, obedience, reverence, and honour,

Plate 37. Durham Cathedral, bedesmen's benches.

with the most perfect mind to do his pleasure! O most reverend Father and Lord, we are bound by the institutes and precept of our order earnestly to supplicate the Lord in behalf of our benefactors, that they may receive, for the benefit which they have conferred on us upon earth, eternal rewards in heaven: and contemplating with the internal eyes of our minds, the many and great signs of your paternal affection which your most evident love towards us has displayed; in that you have often relieved our want out of the means which God has given to you; in that you have rescued our college at Oxford from decay and destruction; in that you have largely added precious vestments and ornaments to our church; and above all in that you have most liberally expended of your wealth in the construction of a dormitory, especially appropriated to our comfort, we should ourselves be obliged to remember you of all persons in our prayers.[685]

Wherefore, although all your honourable predecessors have been buried, according to ancient custom, in our chapter house (four only excepted, whose bodies are buried in the church), that ever hereafter when we shall stand to pray in the choir we may the more retentively hold the recollection of you and your benefits, we will and concede, that after you have gone to your rest, your soul being called away to the Lord, your body may be buried on the north side of our choir, in the spot which you have already chosen, in full sight of our eyes; that while we see your monument we may be incited to pray that you may receive abundantly of the favour God, saying devoutly, *'Ejus in pace cum Domino anima requiecat, qui pro nostra requie corporali divitias suas habundantes effundere consuevit.'* In witness whereof our common seal is affixed to these presents. Given in our chapter house this sixth day of January, in the year of our Lord one thousand four hundred and four.'[660]

Skirlaw died at Howden Manor on 24 March 1406. At about ten o'clock on the morning his sister Joan, who had previously been summoned to his bedside, closed his eyes. Skirlaw was already suffering from some form of paralysis in September 1402, but in March 1403 it was reported that he was 'well enough to do more than preside' at a stage in the trial of Richard Wyche (see Chapter Seven). He was specifically reported as infirm on 31 January 1406 and as ill on 15 March 1406. It seems that Howden Manor was a favourite resting place for the bishops of Durham, and some, like Skirlaw, eventually died there.

According to Hutchinson, before his bones were taken to Durham for interment, Skirlaw's entrails were removed.[661] There is said to have been a memorial stone at Howden placed (probably) on the floor near St. Cuthbert's chantry, which has since disappeared. The inscription read:

'Hic requiescunt viscera Walteri Skirlaw, quondam Dunelmsis episcopi, quæ sepeliuntur sub hoc Saxo, A.D. 1406.'[662]

Hutchinson, however, disputes considering that confusion had arisen with a previous bishop, Walter Kirkham, and relates to a broken grave slab in the cross-aisle of the church. This slab, which has now disappeared, had lettering which was partly distinguishable in that the name 'Walter' and fragments of the last letters of the surname could be seen. However, he argues that the letters interpreted as 'AW' were in fact 'AM', from a script identifiable with the period when Kirkham died (1260).[663]

In due course, Skirlaw's body was transported to its final burial place at Durham. Hutchinson recorded the customary rite for the burial of bishops as follows:

'The bishops of Durham, when they died, were brought to the abbey to be interred; and where the prior and monks met the corpse at the churchyard gates on the palace green, where they received and carried him through the church into the chapter house. Great solemnity and devotion, according to the ancient custom was used. The custom was to bury them with their alb, stole, phannel and other vestments wherein they used to say mass, a mitre on the head, and a crosier staff in his hand, and so laid in the coffin, with a little chalice of silver, other metal, or wax, placed on the breast; which wax chalice, and the knobs, and the edge of the pattern or cover, and the base were gilded. The prior and monks had the horses, chariot, and all other things that came with the deceased, due to them by ancient custom. But afterwards the bishops were buried in the church.'[664]

Skirlaw was interred in the magnificent tomb he had previously prepared in the cathedral before the altar of St. Blaise and St. John of Beverley, which afterwards was called Skirlaw's altar. Surrounded by an elaborately wrought iron lattice railing, it was covered by a beautiful marble slab carved with many images, with a brass plate in the centre portraying his own image, and on his breast was this inscription from Job Chapter 19 verses 25 and 26:

'Credo quod redemptor meus vivit, et in die novissimo de terra surrecturus sum et in carne mea videbo Deum Salvatorem meum.'

'For I know that my redeemer liveth, and that he shall stand at the latter day upon the earth: And though after my skin worms destroy my body, yet in my flesh shall I see God.'[665]

The marble slab bore the following inscription:

'Hic jacet bene memoriæ Walterus Skirlaw, primum Episcopus Coventry et Lichfield, deinde Bathon. & Wellen. & postea ad hanc sanctam sedem Dunelmens. translatus, qui obiit 24 die mensis Martii A. D. 1406. Deum pro anima ejus.'[666]

'In esteemed memory of Walter Skirlaw, firstly bishop of Coventry & Lichfield, then Bath & Wells, and later translated to the see of Durham, who died in March 1406 AD. His soul rests with God.'

A public instrument was issued concerning the hearse and horses used at the funeral of Skirlaw in 1406:[667]

'Instrument concerning the hearse and horses, with the whole of the furniture left to the sacristan of Durham, for the mortuary of Walter, Bishop of Durham.
In the name of God, Amen. Know all men by these presents, that in the year from the incarnation of our Lord, according to the reckoning of the Church of England, one thousand four hundred and six, on the seventh of May, the Reverend Masters Thomas Weston, archdeacon of Durham, Richard Holme, John Hildyard, clerks, and Peter de la Hay, executors, as was declared of the Lord Walter Skirlawe, of happy

memory, late bishop of Durham, deceased, with his late household, brought and caused to be brought the body of the said Lord Walter deceased, to the cathedral church of Durham, to be committed to Christian burial in the same, in one hearse with five great horses drawing it to the said cathedral church; and that when the body had been thus brought, and placed in the said cathedral church, in the said hearse, they took his body from the said hearse and carried and bore it into the said cathedral church. Which being done, Brother Thomas Rome, a religious, a monk, and a professed of the foresaid cathedral church, and appointed to the office of Sacristan of the said cathedral church, claimed the said hearse and the said five horses drawing it, with all the furniture to them pertaining, as of accustomed right due and belonging to the said cathedral church, and to him in the name of the same, as the mortuary of the said Lord Walter; and so took the said hearse, with the said five horses, and ordered that the said hearse should be left in the said cathedral church by his servants, and that the said five horses should be led to the Abbey of Durham: and of the said hearse and of the said five horses be ordered and disposed at his pleasure, the said executors knowing that all and singular the premises were so done by brother Thomas, and suffering it, and not gainsaying, as was at that time evidently seen of me the undersigned notary, and there were present also men of credit, Richard Ripon, and Thomas Roos, clerks of the diocese of Durham, and many others, in great numbers, who were especially called to witness of the premises, and I, Thomas Ryall, clerk of the diocese of Lincoln, etc.'[668]

The account of Brother Thomas for 1405-6 details the receipts from the disposal of assets from Skirlaw's funeral and his expenses and donations.

Summary	£	s	d
Sale of black cloth covering the hearse to Robert Lowyk	3	6	8
Exchange of 5 horses leading the hearse for 40 sheep		nil	
Sale of harness to the hearse	1	0	0
Offerings/obleys bestowed during 3 day funeral procession to the high altar	1	11	4
Sale of 8 torches (64 remain for use in the church)	2	8	6

No money was received for 716 lb wax from the funeral procession. This was used in the church.[669]

Following Skirlaw's death, a *Suffragiorum Peticio* (prayers for the souls of the departed on behalf of Walter Skirlaw) was drawn up and the names of 292 monasteries all over England appended to it. The roll measures twenty feet in length by one foot in breadth, and consists of nine membranes of parchment with the beginning of a tenth. The *Peticio* is over 600 words long and includes reference to some of Skirlaw's achievements.[670]

On the announcement of Skirlaw's death and knowing that the see of York was also vacant, the prior and chapter of Durham claimed that by common law and prescriptive right the custody of the spiritualities and jurisdiction of the city and diocese of Durham lay in their hands. On 30 March 1406 in the chapter house at Durham, John Hemingbrough (prior), Robert Ripon DD (sub-prior), John Bishopton BD, William Pocklington BD, and Thomas Rome BD, with many more monks of Durham, drew up a notarial instrument to that effect. The prior and chapter appointed Robert Ripon and John Barton (chamberlain), as keepers of the spiritualities, and Oswald (bishop of Whithorn) to act in all matters where episcopal orders were necessary. The witnesses were Thomas Ryall and John Ronchorne (clerk of the diocese of Lichfield).[671] A mandate was then drawn up, dated 5 April 1406, by Robert Ripon, to preserve the spiritualities of the see of Durham during the vacancy, and to denounce sorcerers, amongst other measures.[672]

In response, the chapter of York claimed for itself the right to the custody of the spiritualities. However, the Durham chapter succeeded in maintaining its title. The king's son, John, warden of the East March, assigned the keeping of the temporalities, gave his support to Durham against York. The register of Robert Ripon and John Barton, as keepers of the spiritualities, records their exercise of that authority throughout the vacancy, mostly in admitting clerks to benefices. The chapter had given them full jurisdictional powers, exercised in the excommunication of those persons convicted of practising witchcraft. Elsewhere a suffragan bishop was appointed, and the keepers also called a synod of the clergy of Durham.[673]

The appointment of bishops in the later Middle Ages was normally made by papal bull, but the pope's choice of English bishops was usually guided by the king. The formal election by the cathedral chapter therefore, 'was simply an act of consent to the king's choice'. The royal licence to elect a new bishop of Durham was granted on 25 April 1406, and the writ was laid before the chapter on 3 May, when it was decided to call a full meeting a fortnight later to make the election. Henry IV would have informed the two proctors (Thomas Rome and William Barry. who were sent from Durham to Westminster for this purpose on 2 April) of his wish to appoint Thomas Langley, dean of York. On 15 May 1406, a papal bull was issued appointing him bishop, and he was formally chosen on 17 May 1406.[674] There had been a second candidate for the see, Thomas Weston, archdeacon of Durham, who was Skirlaw's spiritual chancellor. Weston, however, fell in with the king's wishes, and did not oppose Langley. Langley's election by the chapter completed the canonical requirements. On 1 July, after paying £600 into the king's chamber, the temporalities of Durham were committed to his agents. In the absence of an archbishop of York, the archbishop of Canterbury consecrated the new bishop in St. Paul's Cathedral on 8 August. On the following day, the king formally released the temporalities to Thomas Langley, *vice* Walter Skirlaw deceased.[675] Langley's first commission as ordinary was to appoint the prior of Durham and Thomas Weston, as his vicars-general *in spiritualibus*.

An inquisition *ad quod damnum* was held before Percival Lindley, Bishop Langley's escheator for County Durham on Monday 16 July 1414, concerning a proposed grant in mortmain by Peter de la Hay, esquire, to the prior and chapter of Durham of lands and rents in Durham, Wolviston and Monkton, The purpose of the grant was to help the prior sustain the burdens of the altar of Bishop Skirlaw in Durham Cathedral. The inquest stated that no damage to the bishop or others would ensue by allowing Peter de la Hay to grant the land to the convent for the Bishop Skirlaw altar. The property in question included 3 messuages, 72 acres, 3 acres of meadow in Wolviston, once held by John Bishopton and held of the prior for 12s 9d a year and worth 30s a year net; 1 messuage, 56 acres, 1 acre of meadow in Monkton, once held by William Seaton and held of the prior for 2s 2d a year and worth 13s 4d a year net; 9s in rent from 1 messuage in Durham held of the bishop in burgage and paying 2d and 9d a year; leaving Peter de la Hay with holdings in Durham, Boldon, Whitburn and Whickham held of the bishop and worth £10 a year.[676] The Hostillar's Roll of 1415/16 lists a payment of 6d made for recording the ordination of Bishop Skirlaw's chantry.

The income from this property ensured that mass was celebrated daily for Skirlaw's soul until the time of the Reformation, when the practice ceased and the land was appropriated by the Crown. The rentals and other amounts received in respect of Skirlaw's chantry from land and cottages in Wolviston in 1430 are listed in the records of the prior and convent of Durham.[677] The Commoner's Inventory of 1517 and 1524 recorded the rentals received for the chantry during this period as well as a payment of £2 to the celebrant.[678]

In the railing round Skirlaw's tomb in Durham Cathedral was removed, and a stall erected in that area for women to attend divine service. Skirlaw's altar is now occupied by of the recumbent effigy of Bishop Lightfoot (d. 1891), [679] and all that now remains of his memorial is the marble stone above his tomb, without any brass ornamentation or inscription *(Plate 38)*. The bedesmen's pews, however, are still in place with Skirlaw's coat of arms beneath each one. Skirlaw's body was found in 1848, encased in a lead coffin, when his grave was removed to make way for an organ, and was placed unopened in its present position in that same year *(Plate 39)*. [680]

On the 13 June 1414, Bishop Langley ordained a chantry in honour of St. Mary and St. Cuthbert in Durham Cathedral. Langley granted permission to John Newton (clerk, rector of Houghton-le-Spring and master of Sherburn Hospital[681]) and John Thoralby (clerk, dean of Chester-le-Street[682]) to found such a chantry (at the altar of St. Mary until another altar was provided) for the souls of King Henry IV and John of Gaunt, Walter Skirlaw and Langley himself, and his parents. The chantry was to be permanent, and its two clerks

*Plate 38. Durham Cathedral,
Skirlaw's tomb.*

*Plate 39. Durham,
Skirlaw's coffin.*

were to form a corporate body capable of acquiring and holding property, and of fighting legal cases involving the chantry. The chaplains were to be paid from the rents from such property.[683]

Whilst bishop of Durham, Skirlaw founded a chantry at the altar of St. Cuthbert in York Minster with the assistance of Peter de la Hay. The altar was located in the south-east part of the south transept.[684] A certificate of chantries of 1426 states that William Garnett, the incumbent,

> 'was bound to say masses and other suffrages for the souls of the founders and all Christian souls, and to be in his habit all principal and double feasts, Sundays and nine lessons at matins, mass, evensong, and processions to help the maintenance of the service of God, and to read lessons, begin anthems and to execute at the high altar, as is appointed to him by the officers in the choir, as appeareth by foundation dated the sixteenth day of April, the year of our Lord God 1426.'

An inventory of the chantry listed:

	£	s	d
Goods, ornaments and plate	1	17	6
Plate	3	17	6

Transactions for the year were:	£	s	d
Rents received from land appropriated to the chantry	12	0	0
Less paid: King's tenth	1	4	0
Remaining	10	16	0

It was also noted that around 1548, 'there was given to the Minster by divers well disposed persons certain lands and tenements out of which there is paid yearly for obits done for the said persons . . .' And included in the list was a payment for the obit of Walter Skirlaw yearly, 26s 8d.[686]

Skirlaw also established a chantry of St. Cuthbert at Howden Minster. He wrote a letter to Roger Walden, the king's secretary, on 4 October 1394, enclosing a copy of a letter to the king, which explained that he was sending his chancellor, Thomas Weston to Rome for permission to found a chantry most probably at Howden Collegiate Church. Skirlaw asked the king for signet letters to the pope and cardinals, as he was himself out of favour with the pope for having conducted negotiations with France in 1389, 1391 and 1393. He granted a licence to found a chantry of St. Cuthbert for 10 marks paid in the hanaper on 10 February 1395.[687]

The Howden chantry was eventually established with an endowment of eight cottages in the Howden area and six marks a year from the chapter of Howden. The chantry was founded in 1404 with the appointment of Nicholas Kayser as priest.[688] On 5 February 1405, a licence was granted to

Thomas Weston (clerk) and Peter de la Hay to assign premises in Howden, Asselby, Skelton, Thorpe juxta Howden, Kilpin, Belby and Balkholme to the chapter of the collegiate church of Howden for the support of a chaplain.[689] The chantry was either situated in a small chapel in the angle between Skirlaw's chapter house (see Chapter Nine) and the south wall of the choir, or in part of the choir itself, as were many in Durham Cathedral.[690] His arms were to be seen in the parapet of the east gable and on the stop of the hood-mould on the west side of the south window of the chapel.[691] According to Clarke, Skirlaw's arms and those of others could be found over the north window;[692] they were also placed in two places over the door which leads from the chancel to the chapter house.[693]

Skirlaw founded another chantry in Selby Abbey. To this end he granted the abbey property worth ten marks per annum in 1398 to provide revenues for various purposes. Under the terms of the agreement between bishop and abbot, the monks were to appoint one priest-monk to celebrate a daily mass of St. Cuthbert in their church, and were also to celebrate a yearly obit on the anniversary of Skirlaw's death. All monks present at that obit were to share in a distribution of 50s for their efforts, whilst the priest serving at the altar of St. Cuthbert was to be paid 14s a week for celebrating the daily mass. The organisation of a regular succession of monks for the masses presumably formed part of the duties of the keeper of the chantry, for which he himself received an annual fee of 3s 4d. The Skirlaw chantry may have been administered by the almonry from its inception. In the Selby records particular monks are described simply as 'the keeper of the chantry', like Brother Robert Pygot in 1421-1422 and Brother John Ousthorp in 1423-1424, but the keepers may well also in another context have been almoners. Certainly one hundred years later, the chantry had become completely absorbed in the almoner's duties. A survey of the property of the almoner's office made in 1535 does not refer to the keeper of the chantry at all, but it does record the continuing payment of 50s as alms on the anniversary of Skirlaw's death.

The income from the property in Selby was to be used by the abbey in maintaining Skirlaw's chantry including a priest-monk The bursar of Selby Abbey, Brother Robert Selby, in his account of 1398-1399, recorded that the abbey received £4 from Richard Drax (bailiff of Selby) out of the rents from the property as part payment of £8 incurred on transferring its ownership, which had been paid by John Brun (steward of Selby and Skirlaw's agent). In 1404 it is recorded that Richard Drax received a fee from the abbey of 40s for his work. There is also a note of a payment made by the bursar to John Moslay, Skirlaw's cook, who brought news to the lord abbot about Henry, duke of Lancaster, on 2 August 1399, for which he was paid 2s. Also recorded in the bursar's account is an amount of 20d paid to a 'certain servant' of Skirlaw's by John Birne (bursar's clerk).[694]

The accounts of almoner and keeper of the Skirlaw chantry for 1434-1435 (Brother John Acastre) is given below:

	£	s	d
Receipts			
Arrears		Nil	
Rents and farms	25	5	10
Foreign receipts		16	6
Total of receipts	26	2	4
Expenditure and allowances			
Transfers of rent	3	12	8
Wages with clothing	1	11	11
Small expenses with various things		14	4½
Purchases of grains and victuals	2	16	10
Repairs of houses	5	4	3
Charitable gifts from almoner's office	2	3	4
Payments of money from the office of the chantry	5	10	8*
Allowances	2	7	0**
Total of all expenses, payments and allowances	24	1	0½
Surplus of receipts over expenditure	2	1	3½

*This figure is made up of:
    Payments made to various brethren of the convent celebrating Mass at the altar of St. Cuthbert during 52 weeks for the soul of Walter Skirlaw this year (ending St. Martin's Day, 11 November 1435) at 14d to each for every week, 60s 8d; and to the same brethren on the anniversary day of the death of Skirlaw this year 50s.

**This figure includes:
    Allowance to this accountant himself 'for his diligence in the said offices this year by courtesy', with 3s 4d for the office of keeper of the chantry, 10s.

695

CHAPTER TWELVE
SKIRLAW'S WILL

Walter Skirlaw, realising that his health was deteriorating, set about making his will (in Latin) at Auckland Castle. It was witnessed on 7 March 1404 by only two people, both incumbents of distant parishes, Thomas Wyott of Folkton in the diocese of York, and William Pisthorn who was rector of St. Andrew's parish in Eastcheap, London. The will and codicils, registered and preserved at York, have been translated as follows:

> **The will of the Reverend Father Master Walter, of blessed memory, lately Bishop of Durham**
> In the name of the Supreme and Undivided Trinity, Father, Son and Holy Spirit, and the most blessed mother of God and Virgin Mary, and also the multitude of the heavenly host. Amen.
> Thoughts of the dread of death would be rendered too bitter to a rational creature if, after the course of this journey, ever uncertain, there were no hope of a happier life in his native land. And therefore a shrewd and wise man, knowing that nothing limited by the laws of nature is more certain than death and nothing more uncertain than the time of death, was accustomed to anticipate the hour of such a dissolution not only by virtuous and meritorious works, but also by the provident stewardship of his own goods, so that this very unexpected hour, anticipated by provident arrangement, might be awaited with greater freedom from anxiety.
> Reflecting back with due consideration of my years of experience in public office, I, the miserable sinner Walter, by God's patience and mercy, servant of the holy Church of Durham, albeit useless and unworthy, being still, by the grace of God sound in mind and body, but knowing that all flesh is grass and all its glory like the flowers of the field and that, according to the saying of the wise woman,[696] we all die and are poured out like water over the earth,[697] therefore, in the one thousand four hundred and third year of the incarnation of the Lord, according to the calendar and reckoning of the English Church, in the twelfth indiction, in the fifteenth year of the pontificate of the most holy Father and Lord in Christ Boniface the Ninth, by divine providence Pope, on Friday the seventh day of the month of March, at my palace of Auckland in the Diocese of Durham, I have decided to make my will and dispose of the goods of the fortune conferred upon me by God, in the following manner.
> Accordingly, in the first place I bequeath my soul to Almighty God, my creator, and my body to be buried in the **church at Durham**, between two columns on the north side of the choir or the sanctuary of the church itself, where I have recently already arranged my

memorial. And as to how grand my funeral should be, I wish it to be carried out in accordance with the arrangements of my executors, but with less ceremony than might be possible, while observing respectability.

Also I bequeath £200 to be distributed among the **poor**, and especially **my tenants**, from the day of my death until the time when the solemn ceremonies of my burial take place, and another £200 for the hiring of priests to celebrate masses for my soul for one year immediately after my death.

Also I bequeath to the aforesaid **church at Durham** a golden chalice, as is marked in the inventory.

Also I bequeath to the same church, for the high altar, the better embroidered cloth which I have, worked on a red field with the five joys of the Blessed Virgin, of the value of 40 marks, so that the said items may remain in the same church in perpetuity for the worship and honour of God himself and St. Cuthbert.

Also I bequeath to the **same church** the gilded statue of St. Cuthbert which I have just recently had made in London.

Also I bequeath to the **prior of Durham** who presides there at the time of my death 40s, to the **sub-prior** 20s, and to **each monk of the said monastery** 13s 4d who is present at my funeral and humbly prays to God for my soul, and any who celebrates three masses for my soul.[698]

Also I bequeath to the **Durham community at Oxford,** £20, which may go some way towards improving the building or repairing their chapel there, so that in their masses and devotions, they themselves may pray to God for my soul.

Also I bequeath to my **sister Joan**[699] £40 and a lidded cup of gilded silver, from the better ones.

Also I bequeath to **Ellen,**[700] **the widow of my brother,** a silver cup and 10 marks, and a suit of clothes, as in the inventory.

Also I bequeath to **every house or monastic community of mendicant monks within the Diocese of Durham** 40s, amongst which I wish to be included priories dependent on the church at Durham. That thus each priest living in the said places may celebrate 30 masses for my soul within a year of the time of my death.

Also I bequeath to **each house of an order of mendicants within the same Diocese** 40s, amongst whom I wish to be included those from **Alverton,**[701] so that they may themselves all pray for my soul and that every priest living in the said places may celebrate thirty masses for my soul within a year of the time of my death.

Also I bequeath to **every house of an order of mendicants and nuns within the Diocese of York** 40s. Also every priest living in the said places may celebrate thirty masses for my soul within a year of the time of my death will receive ... (bequest missing).

Also I bequeath for the fabric of the **church at York** 100 marks.

Also I bequeath to the **same church** my whole set of vestments embroidered with crowns and stars, namely five copes, a chasuble and four tunicles or dalmatics, a frontal and underfrontal with hangings, a cloth for the lectern, albs, amices, stoles and the maniples to go with them, bought in London for 120 marks; as long as the canons in residence there are friendly and well disposed to the executors in the execution of my will.[702]

Also I bequeath for the fabric of the **church at Beverley** £40.

Also I bequeath for the frontal of the high altar in the **same place** my cloth embroidered with the apostles and tabernacles on a red ground, of the value of £20.

Also I bequeath to the **monastery of community of nuns at Swine** £100, so that they may commemorate my death there in perpetuity, and on the day of my death pay 4d to each nun and sister living there; and double to the Prioress and 6s 8d to the chaplains and clerks of the parish church in Swine for likewise commemorating my death there, and I wish the same to be guaranteed to them by the bond of their own seal.

Also I bequeath 200 marks to complete the **chantry at Skirlaugh** if I have not completed it before my death, and as much more as is appropriate for its completion.

Also I bequeath to **each squire of my household** who remains with me in my household at the time of my death 100s, to **each valet** 50s, to **each servant with the position of groom** 33s 4d, and to **each junior page** 20s. Also I wish £20 to be distributed amongst the **poorer members of my household** whatever their position, according to the discretion of my executors.

Also I bequeath to **Thomas Fishburn**[703] 20 marks.

Also I wish and instruct that 100 marks be distributed amongst the **poorer members of my family** of the fourth degree and below, according to the discretion of my executors.

Also I bequeath to **each of my executors** who is willing to assume and complete the administration of my will a gilded silver cup and 20 marks.

Also I bequeath £100 to **Peter de la Hay**,[704] for his good and loyal service devoted to me, to give some improvement in his condition and for the labours and expenses which he has borne and will bear in my service.

Also I bequeath £10 to **Hugo the barber**, as some recompense for his service.

Also I bequeath 10 marks to **John my chamberlain**, in addition to the allotment left to him among the other servants.

Also I wish a disposition of my ecclesiastical vestments to be made **in accordance with the list of the same which will be found in my inventory**, and I wish the same to be done with my clothes and other chattels.

Also, with respect to paying dilapidations to **my successor**, whom may God cause to prosper, in the interests of preserving the rights of the church I wish my executors, having regard to what I received from my predecessor and the expenses which I have incurred in my own time in restorations and new buildings, to come to some sort of reasonable agreement with the said successor, if possible. But if he is unapproachable I wish my executors themselves to defend themselves against him as far as they can legally do so for as long as my fortune lasts, always preserving the instructions and ordinances above and below, which I do not wish to be prejudiced in any way at all. In order to observe this clause as closely as possible I do not wish my aforementioned executors to be prevented by the bond of their oath from considering this wish of mine and freely exercising their judgement to make a better and more sensible disposition if they can.

Also I bequeath 100 marks for the fabric of the **Priory at Durham**, if the work is not completed before my death.

Also I bequeath £40 for the fabric of the bell-tower of the **church at Howden**.

Also I bequeath to the Most Reverend Father Master **Thomas Archbishop of Canterbury**[705] my best garment of arras fabric; to the Most Reverend Father Master **Richard Archbishop of York**[706] my second best piece of arras, and to the Reverend Father Master **Robert Braybrooke, Bishop of London**[707] my third best item of arras fabric.

Also I bequeath to Master **Ralph Eure**[708] knight, Masters **John Newton**[709] Treasurer of York, **William Waltham**[710] Canon of York and **John Conyers**,[711] and to **Elizabeth de la Hay**,[712] to each of these a silver ewer and basin, according to the discretion of my executors.

Also I bequeath to Master **Robert Conyers**[713] knight, Master **Walter Cook**,[714] **Simon Gaunstead**[715] and **Robert Malton**,[716] to each of them a silver flagon, according to the discretion of my executors.

Also I bequeath to Master **Oswald Bishop of Whithorn**[717] a mitre, of the lighter sort, and a pontifical, according to the discretion of my executors.

Also I bequeath to Master **William Yarum**,[718] Rector of Boldon, Brother **Robert Selby**[719] of the Carmelite order, **Robert Gare** of York, **Alice his wife**[720] and **John Strech**,[721] to each of these a silver flagon, or a silver cup, of the value of 5 marks or less, according to the discretion of my executors.

Also I bequeath to **John Mawson**[722] of Kilpin 40s.

Also I bequeath to **each priest of my household chapel** at the time of my death one of my suits of clothes, according to the inventory.

Also, if I have unduly injured anyone or anyone's goods have been unjustly received by me or my agents, I wish my executors, having God before their eyes, to give due satisfaction to anyone making a complaint in this respect and to settle my debts in full, as is just and fair, having first received a true examination.

Also I wish and instruct that the books, vestments, suits of clothes, cups and other objects, precious and useful, described in the inventory accompanying this my sealed will, be given and distributed to the **persons and places and for the purposes to which and for which they are assigned in the said inventory.**

Also I wish my **household, with the members of my staff** who wish to remain, to be kept intact from the time of my death for one full month after the solemn ceremonies of my funeral; so that in the meantime they may look for new patrons and masters for themselves, if they are not self-supporting.

Also I bequeath to the **College of the Great Hall of the University of Oxford**[723] my books listed in the same inventory.

Also I bequeath to **each priest who is a fellow of the same** 40s; so that he may celebrate masses and pray for my soul during the year immediately following my death.

Also I bequeath to **Robert Blundell**[724] my chaplain my small portable missal and the small breviary over which I have been accustomed to say private morning and evening prayers.

Also I bequeath to **Alan Kirkton**,[725] **John Kirkeby**,[726] **William Lincoln**[727] and **John Selby**,[728] my clerks, to each of them 50s.

Also I bequeath to **William Lincoln**, the clerk of my hospice, for the next seven years after my death, 60s per annum, to help him in his studies. Provided that, for the duration of the said seven year period, he persists continuously with his studies of literature at Oxford or Cambridge and does not in the meantime succeed in receiving preferment to an ecclesiastical benefice of the value of more than 100s per year.

Also I wish and instruct that the administration of this my will be carried out as quickly as possible. Indeed concerning the residue of my estate I wish my executors to dispose and act in accordance with the instructions in any codicil or document to be made by me in the future.

Also I wish, with respect to whatever is **owed to me by my tenants** in bondage, wherever they are, that my executors may have the power of remitting to them a part or the whole of the aforesaid debt, taking consideration of their poverty and in accordance with what they believe will be more pleasing to God and more expedient for the salvation of my soul.

Also I wish **my executors** to have the authority freely and legally to make purchases from my goods for their own use, as they are valued by intelligent and trustworthy men, and that my goods be not handed over to any purchaser to be sold, or to another on his behalf, until full satisfaction has in fact been given to my executors for the price owed for them.

Furthermore I appoint the undermentioned **executors** of this my will, jointly and severally, namely the Reverend Father in Christ and Master **Robert Braybrooke**, by the grace of God **Bishop of London**, Masters **Thomas Weston**,[729] Archdeacon of Durham, **Richard Holme**,[730] rector of the parish church of Wearmouth in the diocese of Durham and **Robert Wycliffe**,[731] rector of the parish church of Rudby in the diocese of York, Master **Alan Newark**,[732] canon of the collegiate church of Lanchester in the said diocese of Durham, **Peter de la Hay** personal attendant, **John Hildyard**[733] and **John Burgh**,[734] canons of the collegiate churches of Auckland and Chester-le-Street, jointly and separately in the dioceses of York and Durham.

Upon all my executors I particularly enjoin that, with God's blessing and mine, they continually foster and keep harmony amongst themselves, and remain unanimous in all their counsels and acts concerning the present will. For just such a charge is St. Cuthbert, my blessed patron, known to have enjoined upon his brothers in his last farewell and testament. And for this reason I wish and instruct that, if some discord or difference of opinion arises amongst the aforesaid executors about the administration of this my will, which I pray it may not, the opinion of the majority of the executors will always prevail and keep that validity which has been prescribed by a majority of the same. And I wish those who refuse to accept the administration of the present will to be supervisors of those who do, to see that these my final wishes are duly fulfilled according to God.

In testimony and proof of all this my seal is attached to the present will together with the signature of **Robert Blundell**, notary public, named below.

Given in the year of the Lord, the indiction, the pontificate and the place aforesaid, on the aforesaid Friday the seventh day of March, in the presence of the distinguished gentlemen Master **William Pisthorn**,[735] rector of the parish church of St. Andrew in Eastcheap, London, and **Thomas Wyott**,[736] perpetual vicar of the parish church of Folkton in the Diocese of York, specially summoned and invited as witnesses to what is set out above.

(*Notarial act of Robert Blundell of Chichester, chaplain and Notary Public*)

The first codicil then follows on 25 July 1404 when Skirlaw was resident in Howden Manor.

In the name of God, Amen.

I, Walter, by the grace of God Bishop of Durham, albeit unworthy, wishing to make a fuller disposition and disposal of goods bestowed upon me, add and append this my present codicil or last wishes to the will made and sealed by me on another occasion, wishing both to be firmly observed insofar as individual items are contained in them.

First I give and bequeath for pious purposes, according to the disposition of my **executors**, £1,000, without prejudice to other dispositions and bequests in my will and this codicil.

Also I wish my executors to distribute 1,000 marks amongst a **thousand poor people** for beds and other necessaries, according to their discretion.[737]

Also I bequeath £20 to Brother **Stephen Patrington**,[738] of the order of Carmelites, Master of Theology.

Also I bequeath to Brother **Robert Selby**, of the order of Carmelites, £40 to celebrate masses for my soul for a period of three years.

Also I bequeath to **Alan of Kirkton** £4 per annum for seven years.

Also to **Elizabeth de la Hay** a silver pot and a gilded cup.

Also to **John, Thomas** and **Peter**, sons of Peter **de la Hay**, and to **William Bowes**,[739] to each of them a silver cup, of the value of 40s.

Also I make bequests to each member of **my household**, namely to **each attendant** 100s, to **each valet** 50s, to **each groom** 33s 4d and to **each page** 20s. And to each of **my clerks** who is not a priest such a sum as I bequeathed him in my will.

Also to **John my chamberlain** and **John Biry**,[740] 10 marks to each, and to **William the cellarer** and **Robert the butler**, 100s to each, beyond the bequests made to them in my will.

Also I bequeath to **Thomas Fishburn** as much as I bequeathed him in my will.

Also I bequeath £40 for the fabric of the **church of the Carmelite brothers at York**, if it is not completed before my death.[741]

In testimony of which I have had this present codicil signed and published by Master **Robert Blundell**, by apostolic authority notary public and my secretary, and confirmed by the addition of my seal.

Given in the greater chamber in my palace at Howden, on the 25th day of the month of July, in the year of our Lord 1404, in the twelfth indiction, in the fifteenth year of the pontificate of the most holy father in Christ and Master, by divine providence Pope, Boniface IX, in the presence to the honourable gentlemen **Thomas Weston**, archdeacon of Durham and **Richard Holme**, canon of York and **Peter de la Hay**, personal assistant, of the diocese of York, as witnesses to the above specially summoned and invited.

(Notarial act)

The next codicil Skirlaw made was witnessed on the 30 July 1404, again at Howden Manor.

In the name of God. Amen

In the year 1404 from the incarnation of the same, in the twelfth indiction, in the fifteenth year of the pontificate of our most holy master in Christ Master Boniface, by divine providence ninth Pope of that name, on the penultimate day of the month of July.

Being personally drawn up in the presence of his notary public and the undersigned witnesses, the Reverend Father in Christ Master Walter Bishop of Durham, in the larger chamber situated in his palace of Howden in the Diocese of Durham, sound in memory and fit in mind, has bequeathed to **Thomas, the son of Peter de la Hay**, a breviary, and to Master **William Pisthorn** a set of decretals, as they are listed in the inventory.

And he has bequeathed to **Ada Tirwhit**,[742] his housekeeper, such a sum as he has set out in his inventory to discharge completely expenses incurred in managing his manor-house at Nesbit,[743] unless given to her at other times by her master, provided that it not exceed 40 marks. That in the meantime she may serve her said master the bishop faithfully and well.

In the presence of Masters **Stephen Patrington**, provincial of the Carmelites, **Thomas Weston**, **Richard Holme**, Canon of York and Master **William Cross**,[744] rector of the parish church of Stanhope in the diocese of Durham.

The next codicil was dated 1 August 1404, this time in the presence of Skirlaw's sister, Joan, and other honourable gentlemen, and signed in the great hall of Howden Manor.

And subsequently, on the first day of August, in the same year of our Lord, indiction, pontificate and place as before, the aforementioned Lord Bishop bequeathed 100s to Mistress **Catherine Punde**,[745] nun of the Priory of Swine, in the said diocese of York. And to his attendant **John Roos**[746] as much as he bequeathed to the other squires of his household in his will and codicils, and to **Robert Bolton**[747] as much as to the other yeomen.

In the presence of the Religious woman Mistress **Joan, Prioress of Swine**, the sister of the said Lord Bishop, and the above-mentioned honourable gentlemen Masters **Stephen Patrington**, **Thomas Weston** and **Richard Holme**.

On the 18 September 1404, Skirlaw produced another codicil, this time at Wheel Hall.

And then, on the eighteenth day of September, in the aforementioned year of our Lord, indiction and pontificate, the said Lord Bishop, in an inner room in his palace at Wheel Hall, situated in the said diocese of York, named and appointed as his executor Master **Thomas Langley**, Dean of York,[748] and bequeathed to the said Thomas the golden cup with a lid, and piece of arras cloth from which he had bequeathed to Master Robert Braybrooke, the late Bishop of London.

In the presence of the aforementioned Masters **Thomas Weston** and **Richard Holme**, and Masters **William Pisthorn** and **Thomas**

Wyott rectors of the parish churches of St. Andrew in Eastcheap, London, and Birkby in the diocese of York.

And afterwards in the year of our Lord 1404, in the thirteenth indiction, in the first year of the pontificate of the most holy Father in Christ and our lord, Master Innocent, by divine providence seventh Pope of that name, on Monday the eighth day of the month of December, the aforesaid Lord Bishop, in the larger room situated in his aforesaid palace at Wheel Hall, considering the labours of the aforesaid Masters **Thomas, Richard** and **Peter**, which they would be likely to have in administering his estate, as much during his life as after his death and in the execution of his will, bequeathed £100 to each of them, after a calculation of everything which he had previously bequeathed to them in his will and codicils for their labours in the execution of his will. And furthermore he wished and enjoined upon the same men that they should respect and remunerate the labours of all his other executors who worked effectively for the administration of his will according to the extent of their work involved. Except that remuneration of this sort should not exceed the sum of 50 marks, after calculation of everything left to the same men in his will and codicils.

In the presence of the aforesaid Masters **Stephen Patrington, Thomas Weston, Richard Holme** and **Peter de la Hay** and Masters **William Pisthorn** and **Thomas Wyott**.

Another codicil was witnessed on 2 March 1405, again at Wheel Hall.

Subsequently indeed, on the second day of March, in the aforesaid year of our Lord, pontificate and indiction, the aforesaid Lord Bishop in his oratory in the said palace at Wheel Hall, bequeathed to his kinsman **Robert Custeby**[749] 100s per annum for a period of three years for his studies in grammar. And if he succeeded in grammar and had an aptitude for other subjects according to the supervision of Master Richard Holme, present there at the time, who promised to be a guardian of the said Robert, then the same Lord Bishop wished the same Robert to study in some subject discipline for a period of ten years. And he bequeathed to the said Robert for his support for the duration of the said period of ten years 10 marks per annum, according to the supervision and discretion of the said Master Richard and his own executors. And the same Lord Bishop bequeathed to **Ellen Sheffield**[750] £20 on her marriage, and to the **daughter of Edmund Metham**[751] £10 on her marriage.

In the presence of the said Master **Richard Holme**, Master **Alan Newark** and **Peter de la Hay**.

On 26 March 1405 a further codicil was witnessed at Wheel Hall

And then on Thursday 26th March in the year of our Lord 1405, in the indiction and pontificate recently aforesaid, being present in the inner room situated in his aforesaid palace at Wheel Hall, the same Lord Bishop added and gave as a supplement to the bequest of 60s per annum for seven years, which had been left by him to **William Lincoln**, 20s for the same time. So that thus, while his general studies continue, he may have 6 marks per annum in all; and he wished and decreed that the above-mentioned legacies should be paid to the aforementioned William on condition that, and for as long as, he lived chastely and honourably in the standing and demeanour of a clergyman, not entering a religious order. And if he did not fulfil the conditions or did the opposite, from then the aforesaid annual bequests should not be paid to him further, but should be completely and entirely denied him. Furthermore the same Lord Bishop wished and instructed that the obligation undertaken by Master Richard Holme to pay to the aforesaid William 40s per annum for the aforesaid time on the aforesaid conditions, thus coming into being, and that the said William be unaware of the aforesaid obligation, depending on his observing the aforesaid conditions. Furthermore the aforesaid Lord Bishop wished and instructed that the annual bequest which he himself left to his kinsman **Robert Custeby** to maintain himself in his studies should be owed and paid to him only provided that he observed in his own character the aforesaid conditions, and that otherwise he should be completely and wholly deprived of it. And the aforesaid Lord Bishop wished that the aforesaid William and Robert should remain under the control and guidance of the aforesaid Richard Holme during the aforesaid time.

In the presence of the aforesaid Masters **Richard Holme, William Cross** and **William Pisthorn**.

Skirlaw then added another codicil on 14 April 1405.

And on Tuesday 14th April, in the year of our Lord, indiction, pontificate and place recently aforesaid, the same Lord Bishop wished and decreed that the aforesaid Master **Thomas Weston** should be preferred to all others, if he could pay the money promptly, in the purchase of two beds covered with arras fabric, one white and one green, and of two pieces of arras cloth from that not bequeathed to be chosen by himself, and a certain painted picture of the Blessed Virgin of Italian workmanship.

In the presence of the aforesaid Master **Richard Holme, Hugo the barber** and **Robert the butler**.

Skirlaw's final codicil was added to his will on 23 April 1405, again at Wheel Hall.

And next, on the 23rd day of April, in the year, indiction, pontificate and place already given, the aforesaid Lord Bishop wished and arranged and added to the will and codicils made by him at other times and supplemented them with the following article and terms, namely that none of his executors who might be his debtor in any sums of money or in any other way whatever, or who might be obliged to render an account concerning any receipt or administration, should be admitted to the administration and execution of his will and his estate unless he should first in fact pay to the executors appointed by him the money and suchlike things, and render an account of his receipts and administration, within a time to be set by the testator, and that otherwise he should be totally excluded from such administration and execution and from any legacy left by the testator to him, and they may choose a willing deputy for such person. And the same said Lord Bishop willed that his wishes be observed by all in testamentary instructions whereby he had bequeathed anything in the aforesaid will and codicils.

Also finally he wished and instructed that all his officers, members of his household, servants and ministers, inside and outside his household, remain with him and in his service, as they were accustomed, until the day on which the solemn funeral obsequies were due to take place and be celebrated for him. And if any of them should withdraw from his office, household, service and ministry before the day of his funeral obsequies without the permission of the Lord Bishop himself or his executors, thereafter no legacy whatsoever left to him in the aforesaid will or codicils should be paid to him at all, but he should be completely and wholly deprived of it.

In the presence of the discreet gentlemen Masters **William Ryall**,[752] **Henry Beswick**[753] and **William Pisthorn**, priests of the dioceses of York, Durham and Lincoln, specially summoned and invoked as witnesses.

In addition to which, as a whole and in detail, the aforesaid Lord Bishop charged me, the undersigned notary public, his registrar and secretary, to compose one or more public instruments. These documents have been enacted, as a whole and in detail, as is written and recounted above, in the years of our Lord, the indiction, the pontificate, the months, the days and the places recorded above in the individual acts. In the presence also of the witnesses described in the individual acts.

(Notarial act.)

(Probate in the presence of the Spiritual Guardian of the Archbishopric of York, the Seat being vacant, on the 21st April 1406. Administration is granted to **Thomas Weston**, Archdeacon of Durham, **Richard Holme, Alan Newark, Peter de la Hay** and **John Hildyard**.)

Here follows a detailed summary of all Skirlaw's possessions which were bequeathed on his death to those persons written in his will and codicils.

Inventory of all the possessions of the said Reverend Father bequeathed to diverse persons in his will and codicils.

First of all one golden lidded cup fashioned in the shape of a bell, engraved overall with vine branches and leaves inside and out, with one small pearl on the knob. *To be given to **Robert Bishop of London.***

Also one large gilded lidded cup, with a circular foot, fashioned with a chaplet of white, cream and red roses on the bottom and a hind on the middle, and over the whole of the outer area with eagles, lions, crowns and other grotesque figures, and on the knob a nest and three men taking young birds, from the nest, 18 marks in weight. *To be given to my sister.*[754]

Also another lidded gilded cup, in the form of a chalice, having a circular foot standing on three angels, fashioned on the outside with figures, flower, leaves and letters, having on the knob a gilded eagle, 12 marks in weight.

Also another lidded gilded cup, fashioned in the shape of a bell, having a foot in the shape of a rose, engraved on the outside with lilies and with a plain, circular knob, (?) in weight.

Also another gilded lidded cup, fashioned in the shape of a bell, having a foot in the form of a rose, engraved inside and out, having a border and a knob on the lid in the form of a crown, and in the middle of the lid white flowers on a green ground, 10 marks in weight.

Also another lidded gilded cup, fashioned in the shape of a flower, with a circular foot, having arms on the knob circumscribed with '**Alby ese**', 9 marks 4 ounces in weight.

Also another lidded gilded cup, broad, inscribed on the side and the lid with the words '*utinam*' and the arms of the Bishop above on the knob, 8 marks 4 ounces in weight.

Also another lidded gilded cup, of Parisian workmanship, having a circular foot, engraved on the outside with an ornament, engraved with diverse flowers, 11 marks 7 ounces in weight.

Also one gilded cup, standing on a large foot in the shape of a castle, with a gilded silver lid, having on the knob a white silver angel, 11 marks in weight.

These seven cups to be given to my **seven executors**, one to each, according to their choice. And the choice to be given to them successively according to the order in which they are written in my will, beginning from the first after the Lord Bishop of London and so descending to the last executor.

Also a gilded boat of silver, with a turreted lid, standing on three lions, 2 marks 1 ounce in weight. *To be given to Master **W. Hull.***[755]

Also three cups shaped like coconuts, of which the largest has a lid and a foot of gilded silver, the other two lids and white silver feet, 6 marks 1 ounce in weight. *The best to be given to **John Tuddoe**,[756] the second to **Nicholas Cayser**[757] and the third to **T. Athereston**.[758]*

Also one silver cup with a lid, standing on three golden lions, and on the knob the arms formerly of the Bishop of Lincoln, 4 marks 5 ounces in weight. *To be given to **Ellen**, the widow of **William**,. the Bishop's brother.* Also two basins of gilded silver and a cover for one, having on the bottom the arms of the Prince of Wales, 14 marks 5 ounces in weight. *To be given to **Robert Bishop of London**.*

Also a mazer cup, standing on a foot of gilded silver, movable, carried on three lions, with a silver gilded border and a likeness of St. John Baptist on the bottom, a lid bordered with gilded silver eagles and a blue enamelled knob with a green garland and four white roses. In weight (?). *To be given to **Stephen Patrington**.*

Also a belt of gilded silver on rich webbing, 1 mark 7 ounces in weight. *To be given to **Thomas Burgh**,[759] priest, of London.*

Chapel books.

Also one inscribed missal, painted vermilion with gold overlay, which was once the property of John de Grandissono, having in each month of the calendar appropriately drawn figures, and the first column of the second page begins 'primis mandantem' and the first column of the last page ends in red 'postea revertentes clerici de tumulo dicant'. *To be given to **Robert, Bishop of London**.*

Also another small missal for an oratory, covered with silk material lined with leather, painted vermilion interspersed with blue, having the sequences of the year together at the end of the book, and the third page in the calendar begins 'tercius occidit' and the first column of the last page begins 'in missis cotidianum'. *To be given to **Robert Blundell**.*

Also one ancient breviary with a full lectionary, with music, coloured vermilion overall with tooled design of old royal fern, with a cover of white leather, and the first column of the first page begins 'Te Deum laudamus', with the music, and the third column of the last page 'xl[ta] annis proximis fui'. *To be given to **W.Pisthorn**.*

Also a small portable breviary, in which the Bishop says his daily office, coloured with blue, and with letters of gold for the principal festivals, covered with red velvet embroidered on the upper part with chains and roses and with silver clasps, of which the last column of the first page begins 'per totum annum' in red letters, and the last page written in cursive script, with 'expediar ergo' in the first column. *To be given to **R. Blundell**.*

Also one annotated antiphonar, coloured overall in blue, except the psalter, which is coloured with scarlet intermixed, covered in white leather, and the second column of the first page begins 'Clerico autem incipiatur'; the third column of the penultimate page begins 'mater illa concepit'. *To be given to **William Ryall**.*

Also one antiphonary with musical notation, coloured overall in blue, except the psalter, which is coloured with scarlet intermixed, having at the end of the book the Office of the Blessed Virgin, and the second column of the first page begins 'benedictus Dominus Deus', annotated; the third column of the last page begins 'stirps Jesse clara diluit'. *To be given to* **Henry Beswick**.

Also another gradual with musical notation, coloured in blue, covered with white leather, of which the second column of the first page begins 'Salve mater salvatoris' and the last page 'Agnus Dei'. *To be given to* **John Biry**.

Also another gradual with musical notation, coloured in blue, covered with white leather, having golden letters in the principal festivals and Sundays. On the second page it begins in the text 'Exorcizo te, creatura salis', and ends in the first column of the penultimate page with 'si quis cordis et oculi non senti'. *To be given to* **T. Wyott**.

Also one large new gradual, covered in red parchment, and it begins in the second column of the first page 'per totum annum' in red, and ends on the last page 'percipientes domin'. *To be given to* **William Marnhull**.[760]

Also another large gradual with music, covered in white parchment, and it begins in the second column of the first page 'dominator Dominus' and ends in the first column of the penultimate page 'in Dei presencia'. *To be given to* **W. Graundesden**.[761]

Also another, small gradual, covered in white parchment, and it begins in the first column of the second page 'ra nos requiem eternam' and ends in the first column of the last page 'vere filius Dei erat iste'. *It is to be handed over to the* **chapel at Skirlaugh** *by the order of the Bishop.*

Also a large breviary with music, covered in white parchment, and the first column of the first page begins 'sacerdos in eternum' and it ends in the fourth column of the last page 'gloriae magnificat', and afterwards follows the responses and antiphons missing above. *To be given to* **Robert More**,[762] *clerk.*

Also a small breviary with music, covered in white parchment, and the second column of the first page begins 'ecce dies veniunt', and the first column of the last page ends 'gloria nominis Dei'. *To be given to* **John Gille**.[763]

Chapel vestments

First a set of vestments of red velvet, embroidered in gold with crowns and stars, consisting of one chasuble and four tunics, together with six stoles, three maniples, three amices with apparels and three girdles to go with them, and with a frontal and subfrontal bearing the likeness of the crucifix, the Blessed Virgin and St. John, and a cloth for the lectern, with five copes having golden orphreys with figures standing on tabernacles, all of the same set. Also a case for a corporal, worked with the salutation of the Virgin Mary on one side and the coronation of the same on the other. Also two hangings of red tartarin, with golden crowns and stars on top, and one altar cloth with a close fitting frontal of the same workmanship. *To be given to the* **church at York**.[764]

Also a set of vestments of white brocade, embroidered with white stars, having a chasuble, two tunics and six hoods with green orphreys worked with golden tabernacles and figures, and seven copes with orphreys worked in gold with tabernacles and figures in silk, with the arms of the Bishop on the lower part, together with four albs and four amices and their apparels, two stoles and three maniples, together with a frontal, an underfrontal, a close fitting frontal, a cloth for the lectern and a cushion for the altar, of the same material and two hangings of white tartarin, worked with golden stars. *To be given to the* **church at Beverley**.

Also a set of vestments of red velvet, embroidered with gold trefoils, orphreys of silk with adornments of gold, a chasuble, two tunics, three albs, three amices with apparels, two stoles, three maniples, four copes, a frontal, a subfrontal, a closely fitted frontal, a covering for the lectern of red sarsenet, embroidered with gold trefoils, together with two hangings of red silk rayed with gold. *To be given to the* **church at Howden**.

Also another set of vestments of velvet, striped with white and green, with golden rays, consisting of one chasuble, two tunics, three albs, three amices with apparels, two stoles, three maniples, one principal cope, with golden orphreys and worked with figures in silk, and four other copes with orphreys of red velvet embroidered with flowers, together with a frontal, underfrontal and closely fitted frontal, a cloth for the lectern of the same material and two hangings of silk material striped with red and white, rayed with gold. *To be given to the* **church at Wells**.

Also another set of vestments of white silk material, worked with vine branches and leaves and clusters of grapes and small dragons, all in white, consisting of one chasuble, three copes with golden orphreys, having figures of the Saints in tabernacles, and twp other copes having orphreys of gold and ultramarine material, and two tunics edged with orphreys, together with three albs, two amices, two stoles and three maniples, and with a frontal having the salutation of the Blessed Virgin, a plain underfrontal and a cushion of the same material. Also two hangings of white and cream tartarin, tastefully striped, with gold between the lines. *To be given to the* **church at Darlington**.

Also a set of vestments of white and gold material, worked in white silk with vines and golden flying creatures, of which the chasuble and three tunics have orphreys worked with figures of the Saints and tabernacles and two tunics with flowing orphreys, together with three albs, three amices, two stoles and three maniples, and also a large frontal having a representation of the Crucifix, the Blessed Mary and St. John, a plain subfrontal of the same material and two long striped hangings. *To be given to the* **church at Chester-le-Street**.

Also one set of vestments of red and gold material, of which the chasuble and three copes have orphreys of Mauritian gold, two tunics having flowing orphreys, together with a frontal having a representation of the Crucifix, St. Mary and St. Joseph, a plain subfrontal of the same material, together with four albs, four amices, two stoles, four maniples and an altar cloth, and also a close fitting frontal and two hangings of red tartarin. *To be given to the* **church at Auckland**.

Also another set of vestments of white satin, embroidered with small golden leopards, lined with green muslin, consisting of a chasuble with narrow gold orphreys, two tunics, a cope with orphreys of red velvet embroidered with rectangular patterned garters, three albs, three amices, two stoles and three maniples. *To be given to the* **church at Norton**.

Also two thuribles of gilded silver, of the same shape, with silver chains. 13 marks 2 ounces in weight. *To be given to the* **Archbishop of York**.

Clothing and materials in the wardrobe.
First a suit of clothes of Oxford mixed silken cloth, consisting of a cloak and hood lined and trimmed with fur, another hood lined with ermine, a chimere lined with a mixture of cloths and a cloak lined with various materials. *To be given to* **Oswald, Bishop of Whithorn**.

Also another suit of murrey, consisting of a cape and hood, lined and trimmed with fur, another hood lined with ermine, a chimere lined in the middle with fur and a cloak lined with fur. *To be given to the* **Prioress of Swine**.

Also a suit of blood-red cloth from London, consisting of a cape, a chimere and two hoods, lined and trimmed with fur and a cloak of poplin. *To be given to* **Ellen, my brother's widow**.

Also one surcoat of mixed white Oxford, lined with fur, and a hood lined and trimmed with fur. *To be given to* **William Marnhull**.

Also a white mantle lined in monastic grey, elsewhere with grey. *To be given to* **William Ryall**.

Also one overdress of grey, called monstrevillers, with a hood lined with grey, and another similar hood from the same material. *To be given to* **Henry Beswick**.

Also one chimere of violet for riding, lined with fur, another chimere of the same material lined with poplin and a hood lined and trimmed with fur. *To be given to* **R. Blundell**.

Also one chimere of murrey for riding, lined and trimmed with fur, with an overdress lined with poplin and a hood lined with the same fur trim as the garment. *To be given to **W. Pisthorn**.*

Also one chimere and cloak with two hoods of green Monstrevillers cloth, all lined with tartarin and plunket. *To be given to M. **John Dalton**[765] Offic.*

Also one chimere and cape with two hoods of rich fabric in violet (and) black, all lined with red tartarin. *To be given to **John Cohen**.*[766]

Also one mantle with a chimere without a cape with two hoods of mixed London murrey, lined with tartarin and plunket. *To be given to **Thomas Hexham**.*[767]

Also one cloak with a hood lined with green material, similar to the livery of 1402. *To be given to **W. Graundesden**.*

Also one surcoat of London Monstrevillers, plain, with dark lining, with a hood lined with grey. *To be given to **William Cross**.*

Also one cloak of mixed variegated cloth from the winter livery with a hood lined with fur, and another similar hood from the year 1403. *To be given to **John Gille**.*

Also one cloak of motley, from the livery, lined with fur, with a lined hood. *To be given to **T. Wyott**.*

Also one cloak with a green hood, from the livery, lined with tartarin and plunket. *To be given to **John Biry**.*

Also one cloak with a hood of white, from the livery, lined with tartarin and plunket. *To be given to **John Catton**.*[768]

Also one cloak with a hood of white mixed York, from the livery, lined with green tartarin. *To be given to **John Tuddoe**.*

Also one cloak with a hood of plunket, from the livery, lined with white tartarin and a similar hood in the same material. *To be given to **W. Husthwaite**.*[769]

Also one cloak with a hood of russet, from the livery, lined with green tartarin and a similar hood in the same material. *To be given to **Amandus**.*[770]

Also one cloak with a white hood, from the summer livery of the year 1403, lined with tartarin (and) plunket, and a similar hood of the same material. *To be given to **Nicholas Cayser**.*

Also one cloak of red mixed cloth, from the livery, with coloured lining, with a hood lined and trimmed with fur and a similar hood. *To be given to **Robert More, clerk**.*

Also one red bedcover, woven, worked with the inscription IHS and MAR in cream letters, together with a tester. *To be given to **W. Husthwaite**.*

Also one bedcover with a woven tester with a white ground bordered with red, worked with a green tree and cream and red birds standing on it. *To be given to **Amandus**.*

Books
First, a dictionary in three volumes, of which the first volume begins on the second page, 'apposita aur' and ends on the penultimate page with 'dolorosum'. Also the second volume begins on the second page, 'firmamentum' and ends on the penultimate page with 'Nativitas b.' Also the third volume begins on the second page with 'egipti' and ends on the penultimate page with 'super quo non moneatur'. *To be given to the College of the Great Hall of the University of Oxford.*

Also Lira[771] in three volumes, of which the first volume begins on the second page, 'qui sine fine', and ends on the penultimate page 'pe^{mo} incipientibus'. Also the second volume begins on the second page, 'Judex vel Doctor', and ends on the penultimate page 'ante faciem'. Also the third volume begins on the second page, 'habeatis in nimine ejus', and ends on the penultimate page, 'equalis meriti'. *To be given to the College of the Great Hall of the University of Oxford.*

One set of decretals which begins on the second page in the text 'q' privileg', and ends on the penultimate page in the text 'patrem'. *To be given to Master W. Hull.*

Also another set of decretals begins on the second page in the text 'legem tulerunt', and ends on the penultimate page 'exheredata'. *To be given to William Cross.*

Also a psalter with glossary which begins on the second page 'quid igitur' and ends on the penultimate page 'H.I.' Likewise *The Pupil of the Eye*[772] which begins on the second page 'recipiunt gratiam' and ends on the penultimate 'mortali'. *To be given to Thomas Hexham, Dean of Chester.*

Also a lecture of Jo. de Ligno on Clement. Also a Minorica of Bartholi and a commentary by W. de Landino on some Extravagances;[773] in one volume. It begins on the second page 'set totum'. *To be given to John Dalton.*

Also 'Jo. An. In No^{la} super Decr^{bus} et sexto', in three volumes, of which the first begins on the second page 'aliquibus utilibus', the second begins on the second page 'nil exigat', the third begins on the second page 'et determinacionem'. Also six books with three commentaries. A book which begins on the second page in the text 'vitae cancellarium'. Also Nottingham on the Gospel, which begins on the second page 'fr. iiij ebdomadae predictae'. Also a Catholicon; it begins on the second page 'adde notand'. *To be sold to M. Richard Holme as they are valued among my other goods.*

Beds, etc.
First one bed of arras tapestry work, worked with green trees and grey clouds on a white ground; having a cover, a tester and a complete canopy in each corner, and in the middle two figures of a man and a woman, with six pillows of the same workmanship and three complete

hangings of white serge. *To be given to* **Ralph Eure,**[774] *knight.*

Also one bed of tapestry work with a stag standing under a large tree on a white ground, and on each side lilies and a red border, with a complete canopy and three hangings of white bolting-cloth. *To be given to my* **sister** *the Prioress of Swine.*

Also one bed with a plain red arras tapestry with a cover, a tester and a central canopy, worked with branches of white roses and floral design, with cream flowers, with tester and canopy lined with Westuala, and in the middle of each piece is a parrot in a cage, hanging in a tree, with six pillows, one bench cover of the same workmanship, and three curtains of red serge with ties. *To be given to* **Catherine de la Hay.**[775]

Also four dozen new dishes, marked with a small shield with the arms of the Bishop, made recently in London. *Twelve of these to be given to each of* **Thomas Weston, Richard Holme** *&* **Peter de la Hay.**

Also one bed of red silk worked in cream, with a complete canopy in hangings of red tartarin, once the property of Robert Archbishop of York, with eight pillows and one long pillow in the same set, with three whole pieces and two half pieces of side curtains of red serge. *To be given to* **Thomas Langley,** *Dean of York.*

THE END

At some time before his death, Skirlaw gave to the prior and chapter of Durham 'the opportunity of choosing the best set of vestments which he had. In order to make this choice the monk Thomas Lyth was sent to the palace at Auckland. He chose a set of cloth of gold with precious orphreys. In this set were one chasuble, two tunics, three albs and five copes.' Skirlaw also gave them a chalice of gold, and a statue of St. Cuthbert of gilded silver, on the foot of which was his coat of arms.[776]

In administrating Skirlaw's estate, his executors made certain distributions which were not specified in the will or codicils. These included 100s to the prior, 40s to the sub-prior and 20s to individual monks of Durham who took part in Skirlaw's funeral. The executors, with the co-operation of the prior and chapter, also provided the church with a hearse and horses to carry the body of Skirlaw from the palace at Howden to Durham, together with a cloth of gold from which was made a cope, and a sumptuously embroidered cloth for the high altar. The prior himself and the chapter undertook to provide in perpetuity a monk to celebrate mass at Skirlaw's altar dedicated in honour of St. Blaise and St. John of Beverley, in return for which the executors assigned to the prior and chapter a consideration of 50s. The executors gave £400 towards the completion of the cloister which had begun before Skirlaw's death. They later agreed with the prior and chapter to fund any further costs involved in completing the cloister. The executors paid 8 marks for the glazing of a window above the altar of St. Cuthbert near the Nine Altars in Durham Cathedral. They also gave to the community of monks in [Durham College] Oxford solemn vestments of cloth of gold, consisting of one chasuble, two tunics, three albs and two copes in one set, together with stoles and maniples to go with them.[777] Further amounts paid by the executors, not specified in Skirlaw's wil,l included £150 to the church of Wells.[778] The executors also appear to have granted Swine Priory lands in South Skirlaugh in or soon after 1415 which increased the priory's holdings in the village.[779]

CHAPTER THIRTEEN
SKIRLAW REMEMBERED

From the many sources available it has been possible to gain some insight into the life of Walter Skirlaw. Some official documents, which are still available, relate to his presence on official diplomatic missions abroad. Other records cover his term as Prince Bishop of Durham, although his register has disappeared and with it the records of his various official activities. His registrar would have copied into it reports and letters received and correspondence sent by the bishop, and in particular his official acts, letters and commissions of appointment, wills and ordination lists. Other records of a non-diocesan nature may also have been included. The content of registers varied in detail from one bishop to another so comparison with other sees is of little help here, although it is probable that correspondence concerning both the spiritual proceedings and the temporal government of the diocese would have been included.[780]

Skirlaw became a very rich man, and as bishop could afford to fund many building projects out of his vast income. He has been described as an architect and builder, and without doubt he designed some remarkable edifices. He was obviously very proud of these, and wished the world to know of his creations and generosity by placing his coat of arms on them at strategic points for all to see. Skirlaw's will and inventory provide a glimpse of the money he had accumulated over the years, not already devoted towards his various building projects. In his will he bequeathed over £4,000 to various people and to a number of causes, which today would add up to the considerable figure of over £1.5 million. In addition, he gave away a substantial amount of silverware, many sets of vestments, best quality suits of clothing and bedding, and also valuable chapel and other books which were still rare at the times. By today's standards he would have been classed as a millionaire.

In the late 14th century York was a comparatively large city with a population which came close to that of London. On 18 May 1396 a new charter of privileges was granted to York which gave full internal self-government and elevated it to county status. It had been known that Richard II had plans for York to become the capital city to replace London.[781] On the feast of Corpus Christi (1 June 1396) Richard II attended a civic reception in the chapter house of the minster. An extensive scheme of redecoration had taken place about this time, in particular round the area of the chapter house where Richard was to visit. Much of the painting applied to the walls consisted of heraldry relating to the history of the minster and its benefactors. Around the time of Richard II's planned visit to York for the purpose of establishing the city as the prospective new capital of England an arrangement of shields and inscriptions was painted on the blank window above the entrance on the south end wall of the first arm of the vestibule of the chapter house leading out of the north transept. These comprised twenty-four shields with the owners' names on flowing ribbons above them, including the arms of the united houses of York and Lancaster, Roos, England, Old Percy and France. Although these paintings are only just discernible now, those on the bottom row, representing Skirlaw, St. William, St. Edward the Confessor and Archbishop Scrope can be more clearly identified.[782] According to Norton, the vestibule shields cannot be dated precisely, the first use of the Scrope shield next to that of Skirlaw's suggests a date of at least 1398.[783] The arms of Skirlaw are described as 'eight osier twigs interlaced in cross' with the inscription 'Walterus Skyrla(w)'. Skirlaw was throughout his career a friend of York Minster and no doubt as was considered worthy of recognition both as a benefactor and a high ranking bishop in the province.[784]

York Minster houses a number of memorials to Skirlaw, placed there since his death. His shield appears in the third window from the west on the south side of the choir clerestory, together with the shields of Thomas Portington (Minster treasurer 1477-1485), Thomas Langley (bishop of Durham), Harrington and Courtney, and John Nottingham

Plate 40. *York Minster, statue to Skirlaw.*

(York Minster treasurer 1415-1418).[785] His shield was also placed in the new library at the Minster.[786] Skirlaw's coat of arms is again depicted in the spandrels of the arches of the main arcade on the south side of the choir together with those of Archbishop Richard Scrope, Scrope of Masham, Percy and Lucy, Mowbray(?), Ulf, Mortimer, St. Edmund, St. Edward the

Confessor, and St. George.[787] The north aisle of the choir includes Skirlaw's arms among many others,[788] and Skirlaw's shield can also be seen near the top of the west side of the arched entrance to the south choir transept, with that of Archbishop Scrope on the east side.[789]

In the early 1900s George Frederick Bodley, the Hull-born architect, well respected for his designs of many well-known churches, houses and other buildings including some at Oxford and Cambridge universities, was specially commissioned to design monumental sculptures of persons with connections with York Minster. These were to be attached to the four inner or interior columns of the Lady Chapel between the screen behind the high altar and the east wall of the church. Those commemorated were William Wykeham (1324-1404, a canon of York from 1362 among other preferments), John Thoresby (archbishop of York 1352-1373 and benefactor of the minster), Henry Lord Percy of Alnwick (1322-1368, also a benefactor of York), and Walter Skirlaw, well-connected with York and responsible for substantial amounts of building work *(Plate 40)*. At eye-level, below each sculpture there is a brass tablet.[790] The inscription on Skirlaw's tablet reads:

"HANC EFFIGIEM IN PIAM MEMORIAM GUALTERI DE SKIRLAW CANONICI + HUJUS ECCLESIÆ CATHEDRAL IS MCCLXX USQUE AD ANNUM MCCCLXXXVIII DEINDE EPISCOP ~ DUNELM + QUI HUIC SACRARIO SUMMAM DILIGENTIAM PERI IAMQUE IMPENDEBAT P.C. FRANCISCUS DARWIN ARMIGER EBORIENSIS MCMIII."

Translated from the Latin the tablet states "This statue was donated by Frederick Darwin of York, esquire, in 1903, in pious memory of Walter de Skirlaw, canon of this cathedral church from 1370 until 1388 and afterwards Bishop of Durham, who devoted the greatest diligence and skill to the construction of this chapel."[791]

Again, Skirlaw has been remembered in recent years in the great window above the choir vestry in the north transept of Howden Minster, which was glazed in 1953. In the topmost panel a dove symbolises the Holy Spirit, and below, a number of glass panels depicting various notables associated with Howden's past. The left-hand panel shows Skirlaw holding his tower *(Plate 41)*.[792]

Skirlaw's relationship with the University of Oxford has been commemorated in a number of ways. Although it is impossible to prove that Skirlaw studied here, as records date only from the 1380s, it is more than likely that he did.[793] He may have attended Balliol College, where he is commemorated in the medieval stained glass of the upper library *(Plate 42)*.[794] To be remembered thus Skirlaw must have been a past scholar of great distinction, and one who also made some contribution to the college by way of books for the library or funds for building.

Plate 41. Howden Minster, window to Skirlaw.

Plate 42. Oxford, Balliol College library window, Skirlaw's shield.

At some time before his death, Skirlaw also presented a book by Thomas Aquinas, *Prima Pars Summe* to the library of New College, Oxford.[795] Skirlaw's relationship with William Wykeham, the founder of the college in 1379, has been described earlier in this text. Hutchinson states that a manuscript apparently written by Skirlaw on the Aristotelian treatise, *De Generatione et Corruptione*, one of the books prescribed for the Arts course at Oxford, was in the Bodleian Library.[796]

Wood argues that Skirlaw might have studied for his doctorate at University College, citing Skirlaw's gift to the Masters and Fellows in 1403 of Marks Hall manor, in Margaret Roding, a village on the east side of the Vale of Roding, eight miles from Chelmsford in Essex, for the purpose of funding three fellows at the College, who were to be in priest's orders, with preference for natives of the dioceses of York and Durham. They were not required to be Masters of Arts when elected (unlike the founder's fellows) and were to receive 6s 8d on the anniversary of the founder's death and on St. Cuthbert's Day. The bursar's roll for 1406-1407 shows that the three priests received 30s for one term (Easter to St. John Baptist), and each of the six fellows received 13s 4d *de ordinacione domini episcopi Dunelmensis*. The profit from Marks Hall was hardly adequate during the year, due to heavy expenses in restocking and building repairs.[797] At University College, a library was incorporated in the first floor of the chapel range, probably as a result of Skirlaw's gift of books in his will, although some money had also been spent on books in 1401/2.[798] By the time Skirlaw would have begun his studies at University College, investment had already been made in land and buildings in High Street, where the college still stands. Prior to 1343, the college properties were scattered about Oxford, but a substantial gift from Robert Riplingham MA DTh, an Oxford graduate who came from the now deserted village of Riplingham some seven miles south-west of Beverley in the East Riding of Yorkshire, made it possible to purchase the High Street property.[799] The present buildings date only from 1634.

Skirlaw's shield, among others, can be seen below the first floor windows of the University College buildings facing High Street *(Plate 43)*, and is also incorporated in the fan vaulting of the street entrance lobby to the front quadrangle. The chapel and hall are on the opposite side of the front quadrangle. Skirlaw is commemorated in the painted glass of the chapel. His coat of arms is in the top panel of a window on the south side of the chapel below which there is a painting of Abraham offering Isaac as a sacrifice (Genesis 22).

On the Commemoration Days of University College, namely the Festivals of St. Cuthbert (20 March) and St. Simon and St. Jude (28 October), on the first and last Sundays of each term in the academic year, at the service held at the College Gaudy, and at the Annual Meetings of Old Members of the College, the prayer for the Founder and Benefactors of the College is said. This starts:

Plate 43. Oxford, University College, High Street, Skirlaw's shield.

'O Merciful God and most loving Father, we praise thy Holy Name for the memory of King Alfred and for his advancement of learning in the land; we give thanks for the blessings bestowed upon us of this House by the bounty of William of Durham; King Henry IV; Walter Skirlaw, Bishop of Durham; Henry Percy, Earl of Northumberland; Robert Dudley, Earl of Leicester...'

Playing the part of the Chancellor of the University of Oxford in a recent episode of Inspector Morse, Sir John Gielgud remarked to a potential benefactor of a new college:

'If you want your name to go down to posterity you have to get it in the bidding prayer, something we say at the beginning of each academic year naming our benefactors and thanking God for them. Your name does get recited and the wardens and fellows have to listen.'

A more recent reminder of Skirlaw's benevolence comes in the name *'Skirlaw Building'* given to one of a number of halls of residence built in the 1960s for students of University College in Stavertonia in North Oxford.

Bishop Skirlaw has also been remembered in the names of a number of roads in Yorkshire and Durham; they include:

Skirlaw Close, Chilton, Ferryhill
Skirlaw Close, Howden *(Plate 44)*
Skirlaw Road, Newton Aycliffe
Skirlaw Close, Washington
Skirlaw Road, Yarm.

Plate 44. Howden, Skirlaw Close.

The Durham Cathedral Chorister School is divided into houses named after past bishops, including Skirlaw House. Some well-known old boys of the school include Rowan Atkinson (Langley House), Tony Blair (Pudsey House) and Peter Vardy (Skirlaw House).[800]

Skirlaw's coat of arms is incorporated in the badge of Howden County Secondary School established in 1963 (see Chapter Nine). Various organisations and clubs in the village of Skirlaugh itself have also adopted Skirlaw's coat of arms including the Church of England Primary School. Approaching Skirlaugh along the A165, the village name sign incorporates his coat of arms, a reminder to those entering the village of its famous son and benefactor.

Hence, Skirlaw is commemorated in different ways in various parts of the country which came under his influence during his lifetime six hundred years ago. However, an attempt to assess his character is more difficult, and must rely on clues and assumptions from literature, and research into the role of churchmen in medieval times in England. Our knowledge of Bishop Skirlaw and his character is less complete than several of his near contemporary bishops because of the disappearance of his register as bishop of Durham.

Skirlaw was obviously a person of high intelligence and ambition who made the most of the opportunities open to him to better himself. The traditional view that he came from a lowly background has been called into question, with some commentators contending that no-one could have undertaken the necessary education to launch a career in Church and state unless he came from a family of some standing in the community. Although little is known about his early years, he came under the influence of John Thoresby, the archbishop of York, who was scouting for promising recruits to fill the vacancies in the Church caused by the devastating effects of the Black Death. A number of East Riding and Lincolnshire clergymen obtained high office around this time; possibly the archbishop liked to surround himself with men whom he could trust, and whose backgrounds he knew well, many of whom were his relatives. The huge reduction in the number of clergy no doubt worked to Skirlaw's advantage. Government departments were short-staffed for the same reason. By pursuing an appropriate university degree course, Skirlaw was able to follow a career similar to that of Thoresby. However, he just failed to gain his ultimate goal, the archbishopric of York, despite his investment in the fabric of York Minster and the vote of the York chapter in his favour, probably because the opportunity only arose when Skirlaw was considered by the Crown too old for the job, or perhaps it was felt his character did not fit. It may be that Richard II was exerting his own authority, and vetoed Skirlaw's appointment to the job because he favoured Scrope.

In the world of government, there is no doubt that Skirlaw was a shrewd operator and a remarkable survivor for over twenty-five years in those perilous times. He showed himself to be skilled in administration, law and diplomacy. His skill in negotiating treaties and trade agreements was acknowledged by the Crown (in particular by Richard II, with Skirlaw even finding a bride for him), and he was from time to time a member of the king's council under both Richard and Henry. Because of his well-recognised capabilities, he continued to make an important contribution to his country's government throughout his life, despite the changes in regime. It might be suggested that to save his own skin he changed his allegiances when events were threatening. He became one of Richard II's close advisers when the king was young, but when the Lords Appellant ousted the king's council, Skirlaw soon found himself on the committee of the ruling magnates. Despite his association with Michael de la Pole, he managed to avoid the disgrace of the latter, and quickly gained favour with the new regime. Later, when Henry Bolingbroke claimed the throne from Richard, Skirlaw voted for the new king and became a member of his council, leaving Richard to die in Pontefract Castle.

With his background and experience in diplomatic service, Skirlaw's approach to his position as Prince Bishop was less confrontational than that of some of his predecessors. His treatment of Richard Wyche, the heretic, for example, could have been much more draconian than his use of patient persuasion to try and change Wyche's beliefs. For some, Skirlaw was not a strong ruler of the palatinate, allowing the king to appropriate lands of renegade barons which should, by tradition, have been transferred to him. His leadership in war was not tested in battle as was that of Fordham and other earlier bishops. Some indications of Skirlaw's personality found their way into the occasional document. A member of his household once described him as 'headstrong and impatient'.[801] He was also known to be 'a bit testy',[802] and on one occasion a negotiator approaching him on a sensitive issue was urged to take 'a gentle approach'.[803] Yet he was described by another in more complimentary terms as an 'eloquent and discrete doctor'.[804] Like many clerics of this period, Skirlaw for a great number of years focused more on his political and diplomatic duties, in the course of which he amassed a large fortune, lived the life of a prince, and became one of the most powerful territorial magnates in England. As a consequence it may be said that he neglected his ecclesiastical role, delegating his pastoral duty to deputies, and spending long periods out of his diocese.

The opening paragraphs of his will leave no doubt that Skirlaw had a deep religious faith and he wrote of himself in humble terms as 'a miserable sinner'. A feature of medieval Catholic doctrine was the belief in purgatory, ie. the state in which souls are purified after death to make them fit for Heaven. Masses or prayers for the dead were believed to shorten a soul's purgatorial suffering. Thus a substantial allocation of Skirlaw's money went towards provision for his afterlife through the creation of chantries and in the legacies to various religious groups including bedesmen to pray for his soul, which he believed would shorten his life in purgatory. The terms in which he referred to himself in his will would also help in this respect.

Surtees describes Walter Skirlaw as 'a pious and humble prelate, whose name is transmitted to posterity only by his works of charity and munificence'.[805] In fact Skirlaw can be remembered in many ways, although they remain centred on the fact that he was the Prince Bishop of Durham, who gave generously towards creating many beautiful buildings in Durham and Yorkshire, and contributed to education at both Howden and Oxford. Perhaps this book will also draw attention to Walter Skirlaw the statesman, with the talents of a highly skilled negotiator and administrator, who advised his king and his government on matters affecting the nation, and so in some ways helped to shape its destiny.

Appendix A
John Danby (Kinsman of Walter Skirlaw)

1363: 21 May, was vicar of Burneston (near Bedale) of the abbey and convent of St. Mary's, York, in the archdeaconry of Richmond, exchanged with the vicar of Kirkby Stephen, on the resignation of Peter de Morland *[Thompson (YAJ) p. 170].*

1368: 15 June, was chaplain and cantor, church of St. Radegund, Scruton (near Northallerton) in the archdeaconry of Richmond, at the altar of St. Mary, on falling vacant *[Thompson.(YAJ) p 173].*

1378: 12 July, noted as prebendary of Crophill (Cropwell Bishop) Nottinghamshire, Southwell (diocese of York) *[CPR 1377-1381 p. 299].*

1379: 8 March, nominated canon of Bosham in the diocese of Chichester, the first *[CPR 1377-1381 p. 330].*

1380: Canon and prebendary of Lichfield until 1386, presumably of Stotfold *[Surtees (139) p 34; CPR 1385-1389 pp. 229, 230].*

1382: Clerk (personal assistant) to Walter Skirlaw, keeper of the privy seal *[Tout vol.5 p. 78].*

1383: Noted as chaplain of convent of St. Mary's, York *[CPR 1381-1385 p. 332]* (may not be the same person).

1386: Canon and prebendary of Fauconers, Good Easter in Essex (St. Martin-le-Grand) *[CPR 1385-1389 pp. 229, 230],* (but not known when acquired).

1386: 29 October, exchanged prebend of Stotfold in Bedfordshire (Lichfield) for the prebendary of Bole in Nottinghamshire (diocese of York) from Thomas Brandon *[CPR 1385-1389 pp. 229, 230; Le Neve vol. 6 p. 35].*

1388: 26 May, ratification of the estate of John Danby as prebendary of Bole (Bolom) in York *[CPR 1385-1389 p. 445].*

1388: 3 June, ratification as above *[CPR 1385-1389 p. 453].*

1392: Prebendary of Oxton (Southwell), held in 1396 and resigned in 1397 (as John de Dandeby) *[Le Neve Vol. 3 p. 450].*

1397: Rector of Wearmouth *[Surtees (139) p.34];* was also recorded as rector of Wearmouth and canon of Durham on 27 March 1400 *[Surtees (9) p. clxxxiii].*

1399: 11 July, Laurence Middleton became vicar of Burneston and John Danby moved to Faceby as rector in the archdeaconry of Cleveland. It may be that the move took place in 1380 as in that year Thomas Reynard was inserted as vicar of Burneston according to *Richmondshire Churches 13* although A Hamilton Thompson disputes this. *[Thompson (YAJ) p. 198]*

1400: 2/13 May, died. *[Le Neve vol. 6 p. 35]*

APPENDIX B
John Skirlaw (Kinsman of Walter Skirlaw)

1379: 8 March, nominated canon in collegiate chapel of St. Mary and Holy Angels (within the cathedral church of York), the first *[CPR 1377-1381 p. 329]*.
1379: noted as prebendary of Fauconers (Good Easter), St. Martin-le-Grand for poll tax 1379 *[McHardy p. 4]*.
1382: prebendary of Ampleforth (York) *[Le Neve vol. 6 p 28]* Collated 11 Sept. *[Le Neve vol. 3 p 169)]*.
1383: resigned before 23 March *[Le Neve vol. 6 p 28]*.

BIBLIOGRAPHY

Sources and key to short titles used in the notes

Primary Sources

British Library. MS Ch 982Skirlaw accounts and expenses ADD-24511
Durham Archives. Use has been made of the University of Durham Library Archives and Special Collections using summary translations of records as accessed on the internet (dur.ac.uk/library/asc/) Archiepiscopalia Cartulary Financial Material Locelli Miscellaneous Charters Papalia Pontificalia
ERYC. East Riding of Yorkshire Council, Archives and Records Service, *Register of Deeds*

Printed Primary Sources

Amb Ang. Les Ambasades Anglais Pendant la Guerre de Cent Ans, 1327-1450 (ed.) L Mirot & E Déprez (Ecole des Chartes)
Cal Let. Calendar of Letter-books Preserved Among the Archives of the Corporation of the City of London at the Guildhall, A-L (ed.) R R Sharpe (London: John Edward Francis 1899-1912)
Cal Pap. Calendar of the Entries in the Papal Registers Relating to Great Britain and Ireland (ed.) W H Bliss (& J A Twemlow) (London: HMSO)
CCR. Calendar of the Close Rolls: Edward III, Richard II, Henry IV Public Records Office (London: HMSO)
CFR. Calendar of the Fine Rolls Public Records Office (London: HMSO)
CPR. Calendar of the Patent Rolls: Edward III vols. 10-16; Richard II vols. 1-6; Henry IV vols. 1-3, Public Records Office (London: HMSO)
Col Wills. A Collection of All the Wills, Now Known to be Extant, of the Kings and Queens of England (ed.) J Nichols (London: Society of Antiquaries 1780)
Dip Cor. The Diplomatic Correspondence of Richard II E Perroy (ed.) Camden 3rd series vol. 48 (Royal Historical Society1933)
Eccl Cause. Ecclesiastical Cause Papers at York: the Court of York, 1301-1399 (ed.) D M Smith (York: University of York 1988)
Mon & Soc. Monastery and Society in the Late Middle Ages (ed.) J H Tillotson (Woodbridge: The Boydell Press 1988)
Not Signs. Notarial Signs from the York Archiepiscopal Records (ed.) J S Purvis (London: St. Anthony's Press 1957)
Reg Court. Register of William Courtenay (Canterbury)
Reg Nev. Register of Alexander Neville (York)
Reg Scrope. Register of Richard Scrope (York)
Reg Thoresby. Register of John Thoresby (York)
Rolls Parl. Rolls of Parliament: Reigns of Richard II and Henry IV Vol. 3 (London)
Rotuli Scotiæ. Rotuli Scotiæ in Turri Londinensi et in Domo Capitulari Westmonasteriensi Asservati vol. 2 (London: 1819)
Rymer. Rymer's Foedera (trans.) Sir T D Hardy (London: Longman 1873)
Surtees (2). Wills and Inventories Illustrative of the History, Manners, Language, Statistics, &c. of the Northern Counties of England from the Eleventh Century Downwards, Part 1 (Surtees Society 2, 1835)
Surtees (4). Testamenta Eboracensia: Wills Registered at York, Part I (Surtees Society 4, 1836)
Surtees (6). The Charters of Endowment, Inventories, and Account Rolls of the Priory of Finchale in the County of Durham (Surtees Society 6, 1837)
Surtees (9). Historiæ Dunelmsis Scriptores Tres: Gaufridus de Coldingham, Robertus de Graystanes, et Willielmus de Chambre J Raine (ed.) (Surtees Society 9, 1839)
Surtees (21). Depositions and Other Ecclesiastical Proceedings from the Courts of Durham, 1311 to Elizabeth I (Surtees Society 21, 1847)
Surtees (31). The Obituary Roll of William Ebchester and John Burnby, Priors of Durham J Raine (ed.) (Surtees Society 31, 1856)

Surtees (35). *The Fabric and Rolls of York Minster* (Surtees Society 35, 1858)
Surtees (54). *The Diary of Abraham de la Pryme, the Yorkshire Antiquary* A de la Pryme (Surtees Society 54, 1870)
Surtees (58). *Feodarium Prioratus Dunelmensis* (Surtees Society 58, 1872)
Surtees (69). *Cartularium Abbathiae de Whiteby* (Surtees Society 69, 1881)
Surtees (91). *The Certificates of the Commissioners Appointed to Survey the Chantries, Guilds, Hospitals, etc., in the County of York*, Part I (Surtees Society 91, 1894)
Surtees (92). *The Certificates of the Commissioners Appointed to Survey the Chantries, Guilds, Hospitals, etc., in the County of York*, Part II (Surtees Society 92, 1895)
Surtees (95). *Memorials of St. Giles, Durham* (Surtees Society 95, 1896)
Surtees (97). *The Inventories of Church Goods for the Counties of York, Durham, and Northumberland* (Surtees Society 97, 1897)
Surtees (98). *Memorials of Beverley Minster: the Chapter Act Book*, vol. 1 (Surtees Society 98, 1898)
Surtees (100). *Extracts from the Account Rolls of the Abbey of Durham*, vol. 2 (Surtees Society 100, 1899)
Surtees (103). *Extracts from the Account Rolls of the Abbey of Durham*, vol. 3 (Surtees Society 103, 1901)
Surtees (107). *Ancient Monuments, Rites and Customs of the Monastic Church of Durham* (Surtees Society 107, 1903)
Surtees (108). *Memorials of Beverley Minster: the Chapter Act Book*, Vol. 2 (Surtees Society 108, 1903)
Surtees (113). *The Records of the Northern Convocation* (Surtees Society 113, 1907)
Surtees (127). *Miscellanea* Vol. 2 (Surtees Society 127, 1916)
Surtees (139). *Fasti Dunelmenses* (Surtees Society 139, 1926)
Surtees (164). *The Register of Thomas Langley Bishop of Durham, 1406-1437*, Vol. 1 (ed.) R L Storey (Surtees Society 164, 1956)
Surtees (192). *York City Chamberlains' Account Rolls, 1396-1500* (ed.) R B Dobson, (Surtees Society 192, 1980)
Surtees (194). *Northern Petitions Illustrative of Life in Berwick, Cumbria and Durham in the Fourteenth Century* (ed.) C M Fraser (Surtees Society 194, 1981)
Surtees (198). *Durham Cathedral Priory Rentals*, Vol. 1 *Bursars' Rentals* (ed.) R A Lomas & A J Piper (Surtees Society 198, 1989)
West Chron. The Westminster Chronicles, 1381-1394 (ed.) L C Hector & B F Harvey (Oxford: Clarendon Press 1982)

Unpublished work and theses

Calkin. S W Calkin, *'Alexander Neville, Archbishop of York (1373-1388): a study of his career with Emphasis on the Crisis at Beverley in 1381'*, D.Phil. dissertation (University of Nebraska, 1971)
Carr. D R Carr, *'The Role of the Episcopy in English Municipal Politics During the Middle Ages: the Example of Four Bishoprics'*, dissertation (University of Nebraska, 1971)
Snape *(Notes)*. M G Snape, *Notes on Walter Skirlaw* (unpublished 1999)

Secondary sources

AA (3rd). *Archaeologia Aeliana, Third Series* (Society of Antiquaries of Newcastle upon Tyne)
AA (4th). *Archaeologia Aeliana, Fourth Series* (Society of Antiquaries of Newcastle upon Tyne)
Adams. M Adams: *Feudal terms* (internet [22.02.01]: geocities.com/abrigon/terms)
Armitage-Smith. S Armitage-Smith, *John of Gaunt* (London: Constable 1904/64)
Aston & Faith. T H Aston & R Faith, 'University and College endowments', *The History of the University of Oxford*, vol. 1, (ed.) J I Catto, (Oxford: Clarendon Press 1984)
Aylmer. G E Aylmer, 'Funeral Monuments and other Post-Medieval Sculpture', *A History of York Minster* (ed.) G E Aylmer & R Cant (Oxford: Clarendon Press 1977)
BAA *Conf* 1977. The British Archaeological Association Conference Transactions 1977, *III Medieval Art and Architecture at Durham Cathedral (1980)*
BAA *Conf* 1983. The British Archaeological Association Conference Transactions 1983,

Medieval Art and Architecture in the East Riding of Yorkshire
Baines *(York)*. E Baines, *History, Directory and Gazetteer of the County of York* Vol. 2 *(East and North Ridings)* (Leeds: Baines 1823)
Baldwin. J F Baldwin, *The King's Council in England During the Middle Ages* (Oxford: Clarendon Press 1913)
Balfour-Melville. E W M Balfour-Melville, *Edward III and David II* (London: The Historical Association 1954)
Barrell. A D M Barrell, *The Papacy, Scotland and Northern England, 1342-1378* (Cambridge: Cambridge University Press 1995)
Beckett & Hornak. L Beckett & A Hornak, *York Minster* (London: Scala Books 1981)
Bell *(London)*. W G Bell, *The Great Fire of London in 1666* (London: Bodley Head 1920)
Bell *(York)*. G Bell, *The Cathedral Church of York* (London: George Bell & Sons 1909)
Bennett. M Bennett, 'Edward III's Entail and the Succession to the Crown, 1376-1471', *EHR* vol. 113, (1998)
Benson. G Benson, *Later Medieval York* (York: Coultas & Vollans 1919)
BIHR. Bulletin of the Institute of Historical Research, Vol. 44 (London: University of London)
Bilson *(YAJ)*. J Bilson, *'Howden Church, Some Notes on its Architectural History'*, *YAJ* Vol. 22 (1913)
Bird. R Bird, *The Turbulent London of Richard II* (London: Longmans 1949)
Blashill. T Blashill, *Sutton–in–Holderness* (London: Elliot Stock 1900)
Boyle. L E Boyle, 'Canon Law before 1380', *The History of the University of Oxford*, vol. 2, (ed.) J I Catto & R Evans, (Oxford: Clarendon Press 1984)
Brown. S Brown, *The Medieval Courts of the York Minster Peculiar* (York: University of York 1984)
Browne. J Browne, *A Description of the Representations and Arms on the Glass in the Windows of York Minster, also the Arms on Stone* (Leeds: Richard Jackson 1859)
Bulmer *(EY.)* Bulmer, *History and Directory of East Yorkshire* (Preston: 1892)
Butler & Powls. S Butler & K Powls, *Howden, an East Riding Market Town* (Howden: Gilberdyke Local History Group 1994)
Bygate. J E Bygate. *The Cathedral Church of Durham* (London: George Bell & Sons 1900)
Bythell. D Bythell (& M Leyland), *Durham Castle, University College, Durham, an Illustrated Guide Book* (Norwich: Jarrold 1992)
Camden. W Camden, *Remains Concerning Britain* (London: John Russell Smith, 1870)
Carr. D R Carr, dissertation: *The Role of the Episcopacy in English Municipal Politics During the Middle Ages: the Example of Four Bishoprics* (Lincoln: University of Nebraska 1971)
Cassan. S H Cassan, *Lives of the Bishops of Bath and Wells from the Earliest to the Present Period* (London: Rivington 1829)
Cath Encyc. *Catholic Encyclopedia*: (internet [various dates]: newadvent.org/cathen/)
Chorister School. The Chorister School Durham Alumni (internet [22.02.01]: Choristers.durham.sch.uk/Alumni)
Chaplais. P Chaplais, 'English Diplomatic Documents, 1377-99', *The Reign of Richard II: Essays in Honour of May McKisack*, (ed.) F R H du Boulay & C M Barron (London: University of London 1971)
Chute. M G Chute, *Geoffrey Chaucer of England* (New York: Dutton 1946)
Clarke. T Clarke, *History of the Church, Parish, and Manor of Howden* (Howden: W F Pratt 1850)
Clay. J W Clay, *The Extinct and Dormant Peerages of the Northern Counties of England* (London: James Nisbet 1913)
Cobban. A B Cobban, *The Medieval Universities: Their Development and Organization* (London: Methuen 1975)
Col Encyc. Colombia Encyclopedia 6th ed. (2001), (internet [26.07.02]: bartleby.com/65/jo/Joanna1.html
Copsey *(Northallerton)*. R Copsey, *The Medieval Carmelite Priory at Northallerton, a Chronology* (internet [22.02.01]: carmelite.org/chronology/northallerton)
Copsey *(York)*. R Copsey, *The Medieval Carmelite Priory at York, a Chronology* (internet [22.02.01]: carmelite.org/chronology/york)

Page 193

Cross. C Cross, *The End of Medieval Monasticism in the East Riding of Yorkshire* (Beverley: East Yorkshire Local History Society 1993)
Cullum. P H Cullum, *Cremetts and Corrodies: Care of the Poor and Sick at St. Leonard's Hospital, York, in the Middle Ages* (York: University of York 1991)
Darwall-Smith. R Darwall-Smith, *The Great Mastership Dispute* (internet [22.02.01]: univ.ox.ac.uk/News/Record99)
Davies *(Spec)*. R G Davies, *The Episcopate and the Political Crisis in England of 1386-1388* (Reprint from *Speculum – a Journal of Medieval Studies* LI, no. 4)
DCC. Durham County Council, Visitor Information 1997: *The Prince Bishops County Durham* (Durham: DCC 1997)
Denton. J H Denton, *English Royal Free Chapels, 1100-1300* (Manchester: Manchester University Press 1970)
Dickens. A G Dickens, *The English Reformation* 2nd edition (London: Batsford 1964)
Dickinson. J C Dickinson, *The Origins of the Austin Canons and Their Introduction into England* (London: SPCK 1950)
DNB. *Dictionary of National Biography* (Oxford: Oxford University Press 1885-1900)
Dobson *(Beverley)*. R B Dobson, 'Beverley in Conflict: Archbishop Alexander Neville and the Minster Clergy, 1381-1388', *BAA Conf* 1983
Dobson *(Durham)*. R B Dobson, *Durham Priory 1400-1450* (Cambridge: Cambridge University Press 1971)
Dodds. M H Dodds, 'The Bishops' Boroughs', *AA* 3rd vol. 12 (1915)
Dodsworth *(YAS)*. R Dodsworth, 'Yorkshire Church Notes 1619-1631', (ed.) J W Clay, *YAS* Record Series vol. 34 (1904)
Durham Network. *Durham Network – Cathedral Bedesmen Retire* (internet [22.02.01]: durham.anglican.org/refrence/network/network99-3/articles/07_cathedral_bedesmen_retire)
Durham Archives. University of Durham Archives
Edwards. G F Edwards, *Auckland Castle Co. Durham, a Guide and History of the Castle and Chapel* (Crawley: undated)
EHR. *The English Historical Review* (London: Longman)
Emden. A B Emden, *A Biographical Register of the University of Oxford to AD 1500*, vols. 1-3 (Oxford: Clarendon Press 1957)
Emsley *(YAJ)*. K Emsley, 'The Yorkshire Enclaves of the Bishops of Durham', *YAJ* Vol. 47 (1975)
Evans. T A R Evans, 'The Number, Origins and Careers of Scholars', *The History of the University of Oxford*, vol. 2, (ed.) J I Catto & R Evans, (Oxford: Clarendon Press 1984)
Foss .E Foss, *Foss's Judges of England 1377-1485* vol. 4 (London: Murray 1974)
Fowler *(YATJ)*. J T Fowler, 'On a window Representing the life and Miracles of St. William of York', *YATJ* vol. 3 (1875)
Gagnière. S Gagnière et al, *The Pope's Palace Avignon* (Pusignan: FOT 1998)
Gee. E A Gee (introduction for RCHM), *York Minster, Sculpture in the Central Tower* (London: HMSO 1981)
Goodman *(JofG)*. A Goodman, *John of Gaunt* (London: Longman 1992)
Goodman *(Loyal Con)*. A Goodman, *The Loyal Conspiracy* (London: Routledge & Kegan Paul 1971
Grassi. J L Grassi, 'Royal Clerks from the Archdiocese of York in the Fourteenth Century', *North Hist* vol. 5 1970
Green. V H H Green, *A History of Oxford University* (London: Batsford 1974)
Greenwell. W Greenwell, *Durham Cathedral* 7th edition (Durham: Andrews & Co 1913)
Greenwell & Blair. W Greenwell & C H H Blair, *Catalogue of the Seals in the Treasury of the Dean and Chapter of Durham* (Newcastle upon Tyne: Antiquaries Society 1917, internet: dur.ac.uk/library/asc)
Hamilton. R Hamilton, *Walking the History of Durham's Prince Bishops* (Darlington: D E Hamilton 1988)
Harvey J. J Harvey, *English Medieval Architects* (Worcester: Alan Sutton 1984)
Harvey J H. J H Harvey, 'Richard II and York', *The Reign of Richard II: Essays in Honour of May*

McKisack (ed.) F R H du Boulay & C M Barron (London: University of London 1971)
Haselock. J Haselock and D E O'Connor, 'The Medieval Stained Glass of Durham Cathedral', *Architectural History of Some English Cathedrals, 1842-1863* (ed.) R Willis (Chicheley: Minet 1972-73)
Hilton. O N Hilton *History of Colorado* (internet [22.10.99]: ftp.rootweb.com/pub/usgenweb/co/denver/bios/hiltonon.txt)
HIT.C Hurworth IT Consultants, *Along the River Bank* (internet [22.02.01]: hitc.co.uk/tees/croft1)
Holmes. G Holmes, *The Good Parliament* (Oxford: Clarendon Press 1975)
Hovannisian. R Hovannisian (edited and translated), *The Armenian People from Ancient to Modern Times* (Basingstoke: Macmillan Press 1997)
HQEYP. The Hull Quarterly and East Yorkshire Portfolio (Hull: A Brown & Sons)
Hughes. J Hughes, *Pastors and Visionaries: Religion and Secular Life in Late Medieval Yorkshire* (Woodbridge: The Boydell Press 1988)
Hutchinson *(Durham)*. W Hutchinson, *The History and Antiquities of the County Palatine of Durham* Vols. 1-3 Durham: G Walker 1823)
Hutchinson *(Howden)*. W Hutchinson, *A Guide-book to St. Peter's Church, Howden* (Hull: William Andrews & Co 1892)
Hutchinson *(YATJ)*. W Hutchinson, 'The Ancient Manor-House of the Bishops of Durham at Howden, Yorkshire', *YATJ* vol. 9 (1886)
Jones M W. M W Jones, *Walk Around the Snickelways of York* (York: M & A Jones 1993)
Judd. A F Judd, *The Life of Thomas Bekynton, Secretary to King Henry VI and Bishop of Bath and Wells, 1443-1465* (Chichester: Moore & Tillyer 1961)
Keeton. B Keeton, *A Guide book to Howden Minster 3rd ed.* (Howden Minster 2000)
Kirby. J L Kirby, *Henry IV of England* (London: Constable 1970)
Knowles. J A Knowles, *The York School of Glass-Painting* (London: SPCK 1936)
Lapsey. G T Lapsey, *The County Palatine of Durham* (New York: Harvard 1899)
Laurie. B Laurie, *The Listed Bridges of Bishop Auckland* (Durham City: Durham County Council (undated))
Le Neve *(London)*. J le Neve (various compilers), *Fasti Ecclesiae Anglicanae 1300-1541* vols. 1-12 (London: Athlone Press 1963)
Le Neve *(Oxford)*. J le Neve (with T D Hardy), *Fasti Ecclesiae Anglicanae* vols. 1-3 (Oxford: Oxford University Press 1954)
Leach. A F Leach, *The Schools of Medieval England* 2nd edition (London: Methuen 1915)
Leach *(YAS)*. A F Leach, 'Early Yorkshire Schools', vol. 2 *YAS* Record Series vol.33 (1903)
Lee J E. J E Lee, *St. Romald's Church, Romaldkirk in Teesdale* (St. Romald's Church 1999)
Legge. M D Legge, *Anglo-Norman Letters and Petitions* (Oxford: Basil Blackwell 1941)
Leland. J Leland, *The Itinerary of John Leland In or About the Years 1535-1543* London: Centaur Press 1964)
Lomas .R Lomas, *North-East England in the Middle Ages* (Edinburgh: John Donald 1992)
Lumley. *Lumley Castle, County Durham* (internet [22.02.01]: Members.nbci.com/AndrewMuller/lumley)
Lynch. T D Lynch, *The History of Income Tax* (Edinburgh: The Accountants' Publishing Co Ltd 1964)
Martin. G H Martin (edited and translated), *Knighton's Chronicle, 1337-1396* (Oxford: Clarendon Press 1995)
McCall. J P McCall, *Chaucer and John of Legnano* (*Speculum* vol. 40 issue 3 1965)
McDermid *(YAS)*. R T W McDermid, 'Beverley Minster Fasti' *YAS* Record Series vol. 149 (1990)
McFarlane. K B McFarlane, *Lancastrian Kings and Lollard Knights* (Oxford: Clarendon Press 1972)
McHardy. A K McHardy, *The Church in London, 1375-1392* (London: London Record Society 1977)
McKinnell. J S McKinnell, *The Sequence of the Sacrament at Durham* (internet [22.02.01]: sdu.dk/hum/midlab/theatre/papers/mckinnell)

McKisack. M McKisack, *The Fourteenth Century, 1307-1399* (Oxford: Clarendon Press 1959)
Myers. B A Myers, *The Rectors of the Ancient Parish Church of Bishopwearmouth* (internet [23.01.02]: citysun.ac.uk/minster/rectors1.htm)
Neave *(Howden)*. D Neave, *Howden Explored* (Howden: Mr. Pye (Books) 1991)
Nicholson. R Nicholson, *Scotland, The Later Middle Ages* (Edinburgh: Oliver & Boyd 1974)
Nordberg. M Nordberg, *Les Ducs et la Royauté* (Stockholm: Scandinavian University Books 1964)
North Hist. Northern History: A Review of the History of Northern England vols. from 1966 (Leeds: University of Leeds)
Norton. C Norton, 'Richard II and York Minster', *The Government of Medieval York*, (ed.) S R Jones (York: University of York 1997)
Nott Med. Studies Nottingham Mediaeval Studies Journal (Nottingham: University of Nottingham)
O'Connor. D E O'Connor & J Haselock, 'The Stained And Painted Glass', *A History of York Minster* (ed.) J E Aylmer & R Cant (Oxford: Clarendon Press 1977)
OED. Oxford English Dictionary (Oxford: Oxford University Press)
Palmer *(BIHR)*. J J N Palmer, 'The background to Richard II's Marriage to Isabel of France (1396)', *Bulletin of the Institute of Historical Research* (University of London)
Palmer *(TRHS)*. J J N Palmer, 'The Anglo-French Peace Negotiations,1390-1396', *(TRHS)* 5th series vol. 16 1966
Parkes. M B Parkes ','The Provision of Books', *The History of the University of Oxford* vol. 3 (ed.) J McConica (Oxford: Clarendon Press 1986)
Pattison & Murray. I R Pattison & H Murray, *Monuments of York Minster* (York: The Friends of York Minster 2001)
Pevsner *(City)*. N Pevsner (revised S Bradley), *The Buildings of England: London 1, the City of London* (London: Penguin 1997)
Pevsner *(London)*. N Pevsner (revised B Cherry), *The Buildings of England: London I, the Cities of London and Westminster* (London: Penguin 1973)
Pevsner & Neave. N Pevsner (revised D Neave), *The Buildings of England: Yorkshire, York and the East Riding* (London: Penguin 1995)
Pevsner *(North Riding)*. N Pevsner, *The Buildings of England: Yorkshire, the North Riding* (London: Penguin 1966)
Piper. A J Piper, *The Diocese of Durham and its Organisation: Historical Sketch* (internet [23.07.01]: durham.anglican.org/reference/diocesanhistory/)
Poole. G A Poole, *Chapel of St. Augustine Skirlaugh* (Hull: Malet Lambert Local History Reprints (1981): Extra Volume no.10, originally 1855)
Poulson. G Poulson, *The History and Antiquities of the Seigniory of Holderness in the East Riding of the County of York*, vols. 1 and 2 (Hull: Thomas Topping 1841)
Proud. K Proud, *The History of the George Hotel at Chollerford* (internet)[22.02.01]: georgehotel-chollerford.com/history)
Pugin. A W N Pugin, *Contrasts* (Leicester: Leicester University Press 1969)
Purvis *(Tudor)*. J S Purvis, *Tudor Parish Documents of the Diocese of York* (Cambridge: Cambridge University Press 1948)
Raine. A Raine, *Mediæval York* (London: John Murray 1955)
Reaney. P H Reaney, *The Origins of English Surnames* (London: Routledge & Kegan Paul 1967)
Rich III Found. The Richard III Foundation, Inc., *Richard III — a Man and his Time* (internet [2003]: richard111.com/richardiii.htm.)
Robertson. D W Robertson Jr., *Chaucer's London* (New York: Wiley 1968)
Rogers. A Rogers, 'Hoton Versus Shakell: a Ransom case in the Court of Chivalry, 1390-5', *Nott Med Studies* vol. 6 1962
Rothery. G C Rothery, *Concise Encyclopedia of Heraldry* (London: Senate 1994)
Ruding. R Ruding, *Annals of the Coinage of Great Britain and its Dependencies* vol. 2, 3rd edition (London: John Hearn 1840)
Saul. N Saul, *Richard II* (Yale University Press 1997)
Saul *(York)*. N Saul, 'Richard II and the City of York', *The Government of Medieval York* (ed.) S R

Jones (York: University of York 1997)

Sheahan *(HQEYP)*. J J Sheahan, 'The Monastic Institutions of Hull and its Vicinity', *HQEYP* (ed. W G B Page vol. 1 1884)

Sheahan & Whellan. J J Sheahan & J Whellan, *History and Topography of the City of York, the Ainsty Wapentake and the East Riding of Yorkshire* (Beverley: J Green 1855)

Simpson. D A Simpson, *North East England History Pages, Elvet (Durham City)* (internet [16.04.03]: thenortheast.fsnet.co.uk)

Snape *(Buildings)*. M G Snape, *'Documentary Evidence for the Building of Durham Cathedral and its Monastic buildings'*, BAA Conf 1977

Snape *(Lollard)*. M G Snape, 'Some Evidence of Lollard Activity in the Diocese of Durham in the Early Fifteenth Century', *AA* (4th) vol. 39 (1961)

Snape *(Maps)*. M G Snape, 'Durham, circa 1440x1445', *Local Maps and Plans from Medieval England*, (ed.) R A Skelton & P D A Harvey (London: Clarendon Press 1986)

Solloway. J Solloway, *The Alien Benedictines of York* (Leeds: Richard Jackson 1910)

Steel. A Steel, *Richard II* (Cambridge: Cambridge University Press 1941)

Storey. R L Storey, *Thomas Langley and the Bishopric of Durham, 1406-1437* (London: SPCK 1961)

Stow. J Stow, *A Survey of London, Reprinted from the Text of 1603*, vols. 1-2 (Oxford: Clarendon Press 1908)

Stranks. C J Stranks, *This Sumptuous Church: the Story of Durham Cathedral* (London: SPCK 1993)

Thompson *(Clergy)*. A H Thompson, *The English Clergy and Their Organisation in the Later Middle Ages* (Oxford: Clarendon Press 1947)

Thompson *(Swine)*. T Thompson, *A History of the Church and Priory of Swine in Holderness* (Hull: Thomas Topping 1824)

Thompson *(YAJ)*. A H Thompson, 'The Registers of the Archdeaconry of Richmond, 1361-1442', *YAJ* Vol.25 (1920)

Tout T F Tout, *Chapters in the Administrative History of Mediaeval England*, Vols. 1-6 (Manchester: University Press 1920-1933)

Toy. J Toy, *A Guide and Index to the Windows of York Minster* (York: Dean and Chapter of York 1985)

TRHS. *Transactions of the Royal Historical Society* (London: Royal Historical Society)

Tuck. A Tuck, *Richard II and the English Nobility* (London: Edward Arnold 1973)

VCH *(Buckingham)*. *The Victoria History of the Counties of England: Buckinghamshire* Vols. 1-4 (London: Constable etc. 1900-1927)

VCH *(Durham)*. *The Victoria History of the County of Durham* Vols. 1-3 (London: Constable 1900)

VCH *(East Yorkshire)*. *The Victoria History of the County of York East Riding* Vols. 1-7 (London: Oxford University Press 1969-2002)

VCH *(London) The Victoria History of the Counties of England: London* Vol. 1 (Folkstone: Dawson 1974)

VCH *(Oxford)*. *The Victoria History of the County of Oxford* Vol. 3 (London: Oxford University Press 1954)

VCH *(York)*. *The Victoria History of the Counties of England: Yorkshire* Vols. I-3 (London: Constable 1907-2002)

Walker. D M Walker, *Govan Old: its Place in Nineteenth and Early Twentieth Century Church Design* (internet [22.02.01]: govanold.org.uk/reports/1993_church_design)

Wardell. J W Wardell, *A History of Yarm, an Ancient North Riding Town* (Sunderland: Thomas Reed & Co. Ltd. and J W Wardell 1957)

Wathey. A Wathey, 'John of Gaunt, John Pycard and the Amiens Negotiations of 1392', *England and the Low Countries in the Late Middle Ages*, (ed.) C Barron & N Saul, (Stroud: Alan Sutton Publishing 1995)

Waugh. S L Waugh, *England in the Reign of Edward III* (Cambridge: Cambridge University Press 1991)

Weir. Y E Weir, *A Guide to the Heraldry in York Minster* (York: Dean and Chapter of York 1986)

Welldon & Wall. J E C Welldon & J Wall, *The Story of Durham Cathedral* (London: Raphael Tuck 1900)
Wells Palace. Bishop of Bath & Wells, *The Bishop's Palace, Wells* (The Bishop's Palace, Wells and Jarrold 1991)
Whellan *(Durham)*. *Whellan's History, Topography and Directory of Durham (and Newcastle)* (London: Whittaker 1856)
White W White, *History, Gazetteer and Directory of the County of Essex* (1848) (internet [22.02.01]: dunmow.co.uk/margaret-roothing)
Wilkinson. B Wilkinson, *The Chancery under Edward III* (Manchester: Manchester University Press 1929)
Williams. G A Williams, *Medieval London from Commune to Capital* (London: Athlone 1963
Willis. R Willis, 'The Architectural History of York Cathedral', *Architectural history of some English Cathedrals, 1842-63* (ed.) R Willis (Chicheley: Minet 1972-73}
Wylie. J H Wylie, *History of England under Henry IV*, vols. 1-4 (London: Longmans 1884)
YAJ. Yorkshire Archæological Journal (Yorkshire Archæological Society)
Yarm history. Yarm & Eaglescliffe History (internet [22.02.01]: thenortheast.fsnet.co.uk/Yarm)
YAS Record. Record Series (Yorkshire Archaeological Society)
YATA Record. Record Series (The Yorkshire Archaeological & Topographical Association)
YATA (Wills). Index of Wills at the York Registry, 1389-1514, YATA Record Series vol. 6 (1889)
YATJ. The Yorkshire Archæological & Topographical Journal (Yorkshire Archæological & Topographical Association)
York Minster. *History of York Minster, Eastern Arm* (internet [22.02.01]: yorkminster.org/chron6)

NOTES

1. *CPR* Richard II (1377-81) p.364
2. *VCH (East Yorkshire)* vol.7 p.156
3. Thompson *(Swine)* pp.186, 188
4. Poulson vol.2 p.261
5. Bulmer p.504
6. Reaney p.32
7. Emden vol.3 p.1709
8. Wylie vol.2 p.481
9. *VCH (EY)* vol.7 pp.159, 163: Swine Priory possessed windmills at South Skirlaugh (rebuilt 1560s) and Rowton (1241), and there was a water mill at North Skirlaugh (1536).
10. Leland vol.8 p.9
11. *VCH (York)* vol.3 p.476 (Sellers)
12. Blashill p.83
13. Clay pp.68-71
14. *CPR* Richard II (1385-89) p.88
15. *Surtees* (4) p.309
16. *Surtees* (4) p.311
17. Thompson *(Swine)* pp.54, 55
18. *VCH (York)* vol.3 p.182 (Fallow)
19. *Surtees* (4) p.308
20. Thompson *(Swine)* p.197
21. British Library MS Ch. 482
22. Camden p.153
23. Or Skyrbau, Skyrlaw, Skyrlawe, Skyrlo, Skyrlowe. Emden gives further alternatives: Schirlawe, Shirlagh, Skarlawe, Skirlagh, Skirlawe, Skirlowe.
24. *YATA* (Wills) pp.150-52 records the surnames 'Shirlagh' and Skyrlawe 'at Long Riston, 'Skirlay' and 'Skyrlay' at Hornsea, and 'Skyrlagh' at Beverley.
25. Reaney p.32
26. Bulmer p.506
27. Leach p.183
28. Robertson pp.111-12
29. Cross p.14
30. Pattison & Murray p.17
31. *OED*: 'very untoward' = arch. perverse.
32. Dodsworth, (YAS) p.156
33. Green p.25
34. Originally the Lincoln University Campus of the University of Lincolnshire and Humberside (now renamed University of Lincoln}.
35. Cobban p.98
36. *VCH (Oxford)* vol.3 p.2 (Gibson)
37. *VCH (Oxford)* vol.3 p.3 (Gibson)
38. Green pp.12, 13
39. Green p.28
40. Dodsworth (YAS) p.15
41. *OED*: 'sizar' = an undergraduate receiving an allowance from college to enable him to study and to perform certain menial duties.
42. Aston & Faith p.286
43. 1 mark = 13s 4d (67p)
44. *VCH (Oxford)* vol.3 p.12 (Gibson)
45. Green p.20
46. Green pp.22, 23
47. Emden vol.3 p.1708
48. *VCH (Oxford)* vol.3 p.82 (Hunt)

49 *VCH (Oxford)* vol.3 p.104 (Garrod)
50 Aston & Faith map 4
51 *VCH (Oxford)* vol.3 p 93 (Davis)
52 *Not Signs* plate 21; Reg Thoresby f100v
53 *Not Signs* p.vi.
54 Durham Archives: Archiepiscopalia Box 2, 4.2.Archiep.2a
55 Hughes p.166
56 *DNB* : Skirlaw (Tait)
57 *DNB* : Skirlaw (Tait)
58 Dickinson p.286
59 Green p.8
60 *VCH (Oxford)* vol.3 p 61 (Oswald)
61 Aston & Faith p.291
62 Green p.8
63 Aston & Faith p.290
64 *DNB*: Pagula (Fotheringham)
65 Aston & Faith p.290
66 Information supplied by Dr R Darwall-Smith (Oxfordshire Archives) 17 February 1998
67 *VCH (Oxford)* vol.3 p.63 (Oswald)
68 *VCH (Oxford)* vol.3 p.71 (Oswald)
69 Boyle p.540
70 Emden vol.3 p.1708
71 *OED*: letters dimissory = bishop's authorisation of a candidate's ordination outside his own see.
72 Emden vol.3 p.1708
73 Green p.15
74 Boyle pp.528-30
75 Boyle p.526
76 *VCH (Buckingham)* vol.4 p.219 (Jenkinson)
77 *VCH (Buckingham)* vol.4 p.215 (Jenkinson)
78 *VCH (Buckingham)* vol.4 p.218 (Jenkinson)
79 *VCH (Buckingham)* vol.4 p.220 (Jenkinson)
80 *VCH (Buckingham)* vol.4 p.215 (Jenkinson)
81 Thompson (*Clergy*) p.103
82 Waugh p.142
83 *Snape (Notes)*
84 *CPR* Edward III (1370-74) p.25
85 le Neve (*London*) vol 6 p.22
86 Snape (*Notes*)
87 *OED*: prebend = part of the revenue of a cathedral or collegiate church granted to a canon or member of chapter as a stipend; portion of land or tithe from which this stipend is drawn.
88 Thompson (*Clergy*) p.106
89 British Library: Skirlaw accounts and expenses ADD-24511
90 *OED*: common-weal = general well-being or common good.
91 Robertson p.11
92 *OED*: assoiling = releasing from excommunication.
93 Robertson pp.113, 114.
94 *OED:* Significavit = a form of writ used by a bishop granting or supporting the arrest of an excommunicated person.
95 Waugh p.141
96 Thompson (*Clergy*) pp.61, 62
97 *OED*: procuration = provision of necessary entertainment on visiting a parish, or payment of money in lieu.
98 Thompson (*Clergy*) p.61

99 Reg Nev I f86
100 Reg Nev I f87
101 Reg Nev I f74
102 Reg Nev I f3
103 *Eccl Cause* p.52
104 Reg Nev I f47
105 Lawton p.388
106 *OED*: official (official principal) = the presiding officer (or judge) of the archbishop's court.
107 *Rolls Parl* p.363
108 Thompson (*Clergy*) p.60
109 Poulson vol.1 p.360
110 le Neve (*London*) vol.6 p.22
111 Snape (*Notes*)
112 Gagnière p.30
113 *Rymer* p.468
114 Reg Nev I f15
115 Rymer p.484; *Cal Pap* Papal letters vol.4 (Greg XI) p.132
116 *OED*: pallium = transfer of the office or dignity of an archbishop.
117 Reg Nev I f16
118 *CPR* Edward III 1374-77 pp.226, 227
119 Hughes p.170
120 *OED*: eloigned = removed property (out of legal jurisdiction).
121 *OED*: corrody = provision for maintenance, especially as given regularly by a religious house.
122 *CPR* Edward III 1374-77 pp.226, 227
123 Cullum p.5: Petercorn = thraves from the York diocese (Peter = St. Peter, York Minster?)
124 Cullum pp.8-9: cremett = a word used in the 1399 Visitation documents of St. Leonards and York wills around that time to denote the weak or infirm poor people of the hospital of St. Leonards, also referred to as the 'cremethouse' of St. Leonards. The cremetts were the main constituents of the hospital's care and protection.
125 Cullum pp.5, 8-11, 20-30.
126 *CPR* Edward III 1364-77 pp.239, 240, 348
127 McDermid (YAS) p.xxiii
128 Barrell pp.110, 245
129 *CPR* Edward III 1374-77 pp.473; CPR Richard II 1377-81 p 32
130 *Surtees* (108) p.lxviii
131 Reg Nev ff8/9
132 *CPR* Richard II 1377-81 p.553
133 Calkin p.171
134 *OED*: one thrave = two stooks of corn, each containing twelve sheaves, used as a measure of straw, fodder, etc.
135 McDermid (*YAS*) p.xxvii: *Berefellarii* = minor canons peculiar to Beverley who were later known as the parsons or rectors of the choir.
136 Hughes p.162
137 Dobson (*Beverley*) p.163
138 Hughes p.162
139 McDermid (*YAS*) p.10
140 *OED*: contumacious = wilfully disobedient to the summons or order of the court.
141 *Surtees* (108) pp.216-65
142 *Surtees* (108) p.lxxxi
143 *OED*: Cave of Adullam = derived from 1 Samuel, 22:1,2 where David hid from Saul; hence, 'Adullamite', a member of any dissident political group.
144 Thompson (YAJ) p.252
145 McDermid (YAS) p.135

146 *OED*: possessioner = endowed ecclesiastic.
147 Dobson (*Beverley*) p.163
148 Reg Court ff. 198/9
149 *Surtees* (108) p.lxxx
150 *CPR* Richard II 1377-81 p.623
151 le Neve (*Oxford*) vol.2 p.89
152 le Neve (*Oxford*) vol.2 p.89
153 Cassan p.179
154 *CPR* Richard II 1377-81 p.623
155 Reg Court ff. 217/8; Hughes p.167
156 Hughes p.184; le Neve (*London*) vol.6 p.22
157 *CPR* Edward III 1374-77 p.398
158 Grassi, p.14
159 *VCH (London)* vol.1 p.555
160 Denton p.35
161 Denton p.39
162 Chute p.34
163 Denton p.40
164 *Cal Let* H p.56
165 *Cal Let* H p.56
166 Bell (*London*) p.110
167 Pevsner (*City*) p.48
168 Williams pp.172, 177
169 Dickens p.239
170 Stow vol.1 p.309
171 Bell (*London*) p.110
172 Pevsner (*City*) pp.296, 591
173 *VCH (London)* vol.1 pp.559, 560 (Reddan)
174 *CPR* Edward III 1374-77 p.487
175 Tout vol.5 pp.70-73
176 *CPR* Richard II 1381-85 p.285
177 *Col Wills* p.64; Bennett p.583
178 Sir Robert Ashton became admiral of the Narrow Seas, 1369; King's chamberlain, 1373; constable of Dover and warden of Cinque Ports, 1380 (*DNB*); also captain of Guines, 1380 (Rymer p.491)
179 *CPR* Edward III 1374-77 pp.353-354
180 Holmes p.159
181 Bennett pp.580-90
182 *CPR* Richard II 1377-81 p.339
183 *CPR* Edward III 1374-77 p.410
184 *CPR* Edward III 1374-77 pp.487, 488
185 *CPR* Edward III 1374-77 pp.494, 495
186 Wilkinson p.178; *CPR* Edward III 1374-77 p.438
187 Wilkinson p.71
188 Wilkinson pp.178-80
189 Wilkinson pp.72, 73
190 *VCH* (London) vol.1 p.560 (Reddan)
191 *OED*: mendicant = designated or belonging to any of the religious orders whose members (known as friars) lived solely on alms.
192 McHardy p.x
193 McHardy p.4
194 McHardy p.xi
195 *CPR* Richard II 1377-81 p.619
196 *CPR* Richard II 1381-85 p.375
197 Robertson p.147

198 *OED*: questmonger = one who made a business of conducting inquests.
199 Saul pp.64, 65
200 Bird p.53
201 *VCH (London)* vol.1 p.561 (Reddan); Lynch p.3
202 Rich III *Found Richard III — a Man and his Time*
203 *VCH (London)* vol.1 p.561 (Reddan)
204 Tout vol.5 p.78n
205 *CPR* Richard II 1377-81 p.330
206 *Dip Cor* pp.xi – xvii
207 Tout vol.5 pp.50-54, 205-11; Storey pp.11, 12
208 Tout vol.5 ch. 16
209 Tout vol.5 p.60
210 Tout vol.5 plate III
211 Storey pp.11, 12
212 Tout vol.6 .p 16
213 *CPR* Richard II 1381-85 pp.197, 261
214 *OED*: wool-fell = hide of sheep etc. with fleece attached.
215 *CPR* Richard II 1381-85 p.212
216 *Surtees* (69) pp.537, 538
217 *CPR* Richard II 1381-85 p.285
218 *CPR* Richard II 1381-85 p.322
219 *CPR* Richard II 1381-85 p.495
220 Stow vol.2, p 400; Pevsner (*London*) vol.1 p.324
221 Pevsner (*London*) vol.1 p.38
222 *CCR* Richard II 1381-85 pp.292, 293
223 Le Neve (*Oxford*) vol.2 p.89
224 *CPR* Richard II 1381-85 p.281
225 Tout vol.5, p.215
226 *Surtees* (103): proventus = profit.
227 *CCR* Richard II 1381-85 p.267
228 *CPR* Richard II 1381-85 pp.291, 335
229 *Cal Let* H p.219
230 *Cal Let* H p.267; *CPR* Richard II 1385-89 p.5
231 Chaplais p.35
232 Tout vol.3 p.446; Richard II 1377-81 p.168
233 *CPR* Richard II 1381-85 pp.509, 584, 587-88
234 *CPR* Richard II 1381-85 pp.556-57
235 Saul p 116; Goodman (*JofG*) pp.104, 105
236 Saul p 182; Goodman (*JofG*) p.42
237 Davies (*Spec*) pp.659-60
238 Davies (*Spec*) pp.660-64
239 Tout vol.5 p.50
240 Davies (*Spec*) pp.665-67
241 Steel pp.122, 123
242 Davies (*Spec*) p.667
243 *Rolls Parl* p.210
244 Davies (*Spec*) pp.668-69
245 Steel p.140
246 Davies (*Spec*) pp.669-70
247 Davies (*Spec*) pp.673-74, 681
248 Snape (*Notes*)
249 Saul pp.15, 28-34, 40; Holmes p.163
250 Saul p.84; McCall p.488
251 *Rymer* p.484
252 Saul pp.39-41

253 *Rymer* p.485
254 Saul p.99
255 *Amb Ang* p.198
256 McCall p.488
257 Saul pp.42, 43
258 *Rymer* p.491
259 Saul p.15
260 *Amb Ang* p.204
261 Saul p.44
262 *Amb Ang* p.204
263 *Rymer* p.491
264 *Rymer* p.492
265 *Rotuli Scotiæ* vol 2 p.28
266 Armitage-Smith pp.244, 245; Nicholson p.195; Goodman (*JofG*) p.77
267 *Amb Ang* p.202
268 Saul pp.85-87
269 *Amb Ang* p.202
270 *Amb Ang* pp.201-3; Dip Cor p.191
271 Saul pp.87, 88
272 *Rymer* p.497
273 *Rymer* p.497
274 *Rymer* p.497
275 *Dip Cor* p.191
276 Saul pp.85-87
277 *Dip Cor* p.191
278 Saul pp.88-90
279 Saul p.92
280 *Rymer* p.504
281 *Rymer* p.501
282 *Col Encyc*
283 *Amb Ang* p.206
284 *West Chron* pp.522-25; Goodman (*JofG*) p.98
285 Tout vol.5, p.48
286 *Amb Ang* p.206; Tout vol.5 p.48
287 *West Chron* p.88, 89
288 *West Chron* pp.88, 89
289 Saul p.137; Goodman (*JofG*) p.101
290 *Rymer* p.508; Tout vol.5 p.48; Saul p.124
291 Tout vol.5 p.48; Saul p.145; Nicholson pp.196, 197; Armitage-Smith pp.295, 296
292 *Rymer* p.51
293 *Amb Ang* pp.207, 208
294 *West Chron* pp.160, 161
295 *West Chron* pp.160, 161
296 Saul pp.148-58; Armitage-Smith pp.92, 93
297 McKisack pp.462, 463
298 *Dip Cor* pp.211, 212
299 Goodman (*Loyal Con*) pp.49, 50; *West Chron* pp.374, 375
300 *Dip Cor* p.214
301 *West Chron* pp.406, 407; *Rymer* p.518
302 *Rymer* p.519
303 *West Chron* pp.436, 437
304 Martin pp.542-45
305 Goodman (*JofG*) pp.150, 151; Wathey pp.30-34
306 *West Chron* pp.486, 487
307 *Dip Cor* p.216

308 *Rymer* p.523
309 *Rymer* p.524
310 Martin pp.548, 549
311 *AmbAng* p.214
312 Palmer (*TRHS*) pp.81-84
313 *Dip Cor* pp.147, 161, 246, 247, 251
314 *Rymer* p.527; Saul p.225
315 *Rymer* p.527
316 Palmer (BIHR) pp 1, 2
317 Saul pp.225, 457
318 Wylie vol.1 p.20
319 Snape (Notes)
320 Wylie vol.1 p.86
321 Kirby p.80
322 Kirby pp.82-84
323 Wylie vol.1, pp.354, 355
324 *Rymer* p.536, Thompson (Swine) p.202
325 *Rymer* p.537
326 *Rymer* p.538
327 *Rymer* p.537
328 *Rymer* p.538
329 Wylie vol.1 p.154; vol.4 pp.259, 260
330 *Rymer* p.541
331 *Rymer* p.541
332 Kirby p.121
333 Kirby pp.120, 121
334 Wylie vol.1 pp.206-209
335 *Rymer* p.542, Nordberg p.114
336 Jacob p.67
337 Jacob pp.67, 68
338 *Rymer* p.542
339 Rogers pp.74-81
340 Legge pp.466, 467
341 Le Neve vol.1 pp.550, 551
342 Reg Court Fo. 320; *West Chron* pp.118, 119
343 *Cath Encyc*: Chester, Lichfield (Burton)
344 *CPR* Richard II 1385-89 p.23
345 *CPR* Richard II 1385-89 p.37
346 *CPR* Richard II 1385-89 p.96; *Rymer* p.510
347 Le Neve vol.1 p.551
348 *West Chron* p.157
349 Hovannisian vol.1 p.287
350 Storey p.10
351 *CPR* Richard II 1385-89 pp.145, 146
352 *OED*: enfeoff = convey freehold property by putting a person in possession of property, rents, etc.
353 *OED*: tail = the limitation of succession of property so that it cannot be disposed of but must pass to the holder's descendants or reverts back to the donor's heirs.
354 *OED*: remainder = an interest in an estate that becomes effective in possession only on the ending of a prior interest.
355 *CPR* Richard II 1385-89 p.162
356 *CPR* Richard II 1385-89 p.216
357 *CPR* Richard II 1385-89 pp.226, 227
358 Le Neve vol.1 p.551
359 *Rymer* p.512

360 *Dip Cor* p.219
361 *Cath Encyc*: Bath and Wells (Burton)
362 *Wells Palace*
363 *Rymer* p.513
364 *CFR* Richard II 1383-91 p.165
365 *CFR* Richard II 1383-91 pp.223, 224
366 Solloway pp.227-43, 324; Pevsner & Neave p.162
367 Davies (*Spec*) pp.675-76
368 Steel p.164
369 Hutchinson (*Durham*) vol.1 pp.390, 391
370 Steel p.117
371 Tuck pp.69-70
372 Tuck p.70
373 Davies (*Spec*) pp.660-87
374 Davies (*Spec*) pp.686-87
375 *CPR* Richard II 1385-89 p .483
376 *Rymer* p.514
377 Durham Archives: Papalia, 1.2.Pap.21
378 *Rymer* p.516
379 Durham Archives: Cartulary I, f. 118r
380 Poole p.38
381 Lomas p.76
382 Lomas p.21
383 Rothery p.125
384 Cassan p.191
385 Carr p.235
386 *Surtees* (139) p.63; *Surtees* (164) pp.xiv, xv, xxxxvi
387 Storey pp.169, 170
388 *Surtees* (139) p.15; *Surtees* (4) p.319; *Surtees* (164) p.xviii; Myers
389 Piper p.5; Storey pp.169, 170
390 Judd p.116
391 *OED*: dignities = persons holding official positions.
392 Durham Archives: Pontificalia, 1.3.Pont. 10
393 *Surtees* (9) pp.clix, clx
394 Storey pp.175, 176
395 *Surtees* (4) p.310; Storey p.175
396 Piper pp.5-7
397 Le Neve vol.6, p.113
398 Greenwell & Blair: seal 3260
399 Greenwell & Blair: seal 2611
400 Durham Archives: Pontificalia, 1.6.Pont. 7
401 *Surtees* (164) pp.xii, 45
402 Le Neve vol.6, p.114
403 Storey pp.172, 173, 174
404 Storey pp.92-104
405 Storey pp.52-6
406 Hutchinson (*Durham*) vol 1, p.396
407 Bythell pp.1, 2
408 Emsley (*YAJ*) p.108
409 Bulmer (*EY*)
410 Storey p.94
411 Adams
412 Hutchinson (*YATJ*) pp.388, 389
413 Greenwell & Blair: seal 2716
414 Lee p.10

415 Durham Archives: Indentures, I/A5/1/18
416 *OED*: keel = flat-bottomed boat used on the Rivers Tyne and Wear to transport coal and loading colliers.
417 Durham Archives: Indentures, I/A5/1/17
418 Durham Archives: Indentures, I/A5/1/19
419 *Surtees* (9) p.clxxxiii
420 Durham Archives: Indentures, I/A5/1.24
421 Durham Archives: Indentures, (various)
422 Durham Archives: Indentures, I/A5/1/36
423 Durham Archives: Indentures, I/A5/1/27
424 Durham Archives: Indentures, I/A5/1/7
425 Durham Archives: Indentures, I/A5/1/22
426 Durham Archives: Indentures, I/A5/1/26
427 Durham Archives: Indentures, I/A5/1/10
428 *OED*. amercement (imposition of) discretionary penalty or fine.
429 Durham Archives: Indentures, I/A5/1/34
430 Durham Archives: Indentures, I/A5/1/66
431 Harvey J pp.88-9
432 *OED* novel desseisin = recent wrongful appropriation of land of another.
433 Durham Archives: Miscellaneous Charters, Misc.Ch. 6461
434 Hutchinson (*Durham*) vol.2 p.550
435 Hutchinson (*Durham*) vol.2 p.651
436 Hutchinson (*Durham*) vol.1 p.395
437 Storey pp.206, 207
438 Storey p.209
439 Piper p.4
440 Piper p 4
441 *Surtees* (113) pp xxxi, 118, 119, 344, 345, 361
442 Lomas p.99
443 Dobson (*Durham*) pp.218, 219
444 York Minster
445 Baldwin pp.134-37, 490-515
446 Kirby p.82
447 *Rymer* p.521
448 Balfour-Melville pp.13-22
449 Saul pp.277, 279
450 Legge p.60, 209-11
451 Goodman (JofG) p.15
452 Tuck pp.195, 196; Saul p.408
453 *Rolls Parl* pp.426, 427
454 Kirby p.84
455 Kirby pp.92-98
456 Kirby p.174
457 Wylie vol.1, p.476
458 Wylie vol.1, pp.354, 355
459 Wylie vol.2 pp.116, 117
460 *Surtees* (9) pp.clx – clxii; Storey pp.144-46
461 Durham Archives: Miscellaneous Charters, Misc.Ch. 972
462 *Dip Cor* p.249
463 Whellan (*Durham*) pp.497-99
464 Wylie vol.3 p.466
465 Snape (*Lollard*) AA (4th) vol.39 p.361
466 *DNB*, John (d. 1379), called Of Bridlington; *Cath Encyc*, St. John Twenge
467 Storey pp.176, 177; Lomas pp.108, 109; Piper pp.6-8
468 Storey pp.179, 190, 181

469 Storey p.185-187, 196; Hutchinson (*Durham*) vol.2 p.754
470 Piper pp.9-10
471 *Surtees* (194) pp.201, 202
472 *Surtees* (194) pp.202, 203, 204
473 *Surtees* (194) pp.204, 205
474 *Eccl Cause* pp.74, 78
475 Stranks p.16
476 Storey pp.192, 193
477 Storey pp.194-201
478 *Surtees* (103) pp.i-vii
479 Dobson (*Durham*) p.231, 232, 254, 255
480 Durham Archives: Pontificalia, 1.4.Pont. 4
481 Durham Archives: Pontificalia, 2.5.Pont. 7
482 Durham Archives: Pontificalia, 4.6.Pont. 10
483 Durham Archives: Pontificalia, 3.6.Pont. 15.I
484 Durham Archives: Pontificalia, 3.6.Pont. 15.III
485 Durham Archives: Pontificalia, 3.2.Pont. 11
486 *Surtees* (95) pp.xxxii, 238, 239, 257
487 Hutchinson (*Durham*) vol.2 pp.402, 403
488 Durham Archives: Pontificalia, 4.6.Pont. 6
489 Durham Archives: Cartulary I, f. 157r-v
490 Durham Archives: Pontificalia, 2.4.Pont. 6
491 Durham Archives: Pontificalia, 2.4.Pont. 5(c); 1.5.Pont. 3
492 Durham Archives: Pontificalia, 2.7.Pont. 2(d)
493 Durham Archives: Pontificalia, 12.8.Pont. 2
494 Durham Archives: Miscellaneous Charters, Misc.Ch. 7217
495 *Surtees* (9) pp clxiii, clxiv; Durham Archives: Locelli, Loc XIII.8
496 Durham Archives: Pontificalia, 2.6.Pont. 4
497 Durham Archives: Pontificalia, 1.6.Pont. 7
498 *Surtees* (9) pp.clxiii-clxviii
499 *OED*: procuration = the provision of necessary entertainment for a bishop or other visitor by a parish or religious house visited; a payment of money in lieu.
500 Durham Archives: Pontificalia, 2.8.Pont. 3
501 Durham Archives: Pontificalia, 1.8.Pont. 18
502 *Laetare Jerusalem* = fourth or middle Sunday in Lent.
503 Durham Archives: Pontificalia, 2.7.Pont. 2(c)
504 Durham Archives: Cartulary I, f. 21r
505 Durham Archives: Pontificalia, 2.8.Pont. 15
506 Durham Archives: Cartulary I, f. 98r; f. 98r – v
507 Durham Archives: Cartulary I, f. 21v – 22r; Pontificalia, 2.9.Pont. 1
508 *OED*: mortmain = the condition of lands or tenements held inalienably by an ecclesiastical or other corporation; land or tenements so held.
509 Durham Archives: Pontificalia, 3.9.Pont. 22a
510 Durham Archives: Pontificalia, 3.9.Pont. 21(a); 1.10.Pont. 5
511 Durham Archives: Miscellaneous Charters, Misc.Ch. 6637; *Surtees* (9) p.clxxv
512 *Surtees* (9) p.cxcii
513 Durham Archives: Miscellaneous Charters, Misc.Ch. 7307/1/2
514 Dobson (*Durham*) pp.348, 349
515 Dobson (*Durham*) p.347
516 Dobson (*Durham*) pp.69-71
517 *OED*: intablying = entering or inscribing in a table or list.
518 Dobson (*Durham*) p.72
519 *Surtees* (2) pp.43, 44
520 McKinnell
521 *OED*: burgage tenure = a tenure by which lands, tenements, etc., in towns or cities were

held from the lord for an annual rent or service.
522 Dodds *AA* 3rd vol.12 pp.81, 120-37
523 Lomas p.79
524 Hutchinson (*Durham*) vol.1 pp.391, 392
525 Storey pp.57-64
526 Hutchinson (*Durham*) vol.1 p.397
527 *Surtees* (164) pp.xii, 12
528 *Rolls Parl* p.578
529 Piper p.4; Greenwell & Blair: seals 3144, 3145, 3146
530 Greenwell & Blair: (royal seals)
531 Greenwell & Blair: seal 3147
532 Hutchinson (*Durham*) vol.1 p.397
533 Ruding pp 164, 165; Dodds pp.100, 101
534 Fordyce p.45
535 Ruding p.100
536 Lomas p.79
537 Lapsley p.278
538 Storey pp.68-91
539 Storey pp.104-14
540 Storey p.147
541 Storey pp.135, 136
542 Hilton
543 Lumley
544 Hutchinson (*Durham*) vol.2 p.506
545 Storey pp.136-41
546 *West Chron* pp.346-51
547 Durham Archives: Locellus XIX, 131
548 *Surtees* (107) p.110; Hutchinson (*Durham*) vol.2 p.294n
549 Haselock pp.110-13
550 Haselock p.116
551 Welldon & Wall p.53
552 *Surtees* (4) p.306
553 Snape (*Buildings*) pp.29, 30
554 Harvey J p.194
555 Harvey J p.156
556 Harvey J pp.245, 311
557 Hutchinson (*Durham*) vol.2 p.339; Dobson (*Durham*) p.296
558 Knowles pp.10, 11
559 Hutchinson (*Durham*) vol.2, p.341
560 *VCH* (*Durham*) pp.124, 125; Knowles p.10
561 *Surtees* (4) p.306
562 Hutchinson (*Durham*) vol.1 p.394
563 Bygate pp.32, 33
564 Hutchinson (*Durham*) vol, 2, pp.335, 336
565 *Surtees* (9) pp.clxxx-clxxxii
566 *Surtees* (9) pp.clxxxvii – cxc
567 Welldon & Wall pp.52, 53; Harvey J pp.84, 87, 88, 204
568 Snape (*Buildings*) pp.28, 29
569 Hutchinson (*Durham*) vol.2, p 342
570 *Surtees* (21) p.141
571 *VCH* (*Durham*) vol.3, p.23
572 *VCH* (*Durham*) vol.3 pp.2, 23; Simpson
573 *Surtees* (21) p.141
574 *VCH* (*Durham*) vol.3, p.64
575 Leland parts IX-XI pp.128, 129

576 *VCH (Durham)* vol.3 pp.148, 154
577 Hutchinson *(Durham)* vol.1 p.393
578 Hutchinson *(Durham)* vol.2 p.413
579 Snape *(Maps)* p.207
580 Hamilton pp.31, 32
581 Leland parts I-III p.70
582 Edwards p.14
583 Laurie pp.2, 10
584 Hamilton pp.13, 14; HITC
585 Proud
586 Hutchinson *(Durham)* vol.1 p.393
587 *Yarm History*
588 Wardell pp.118-22
589 Baines *(York)* p.36
590 Sheehan & Whellan vol.1 p.411
591 Beckett & Hornak pp.66, 67
592 *Surtees* (35) p.32; Gee p1
593 Weir pp.22-24
594 Sheehan & Whellan vol.1 p.430
595 O'Connor pp.364, 365
596 Knowles p.40
597 Bell *(York)* pp.136, 137
598 Toy p.7
599 Beckett & Hornak pp.59, 60
600 Browne p.184
601 Knowles pp.219, 220
602 Knowles pp.212-21
603 Sheehan & Whellan *(York)* vol.1 p.442
604 Reg Nev ff. 8/9
605 *CPR* Richard II 1377-81 p.553
606 £13 8s 10d *less* £3 equals £10 6s 10d, *not* £10 8s 9d as stated.
607 *Surtees* (91) p.531
608 Neave pp.6, 7
609 Bilson *(YAJ)* pp.256-69
610 Hutchinson *(YATJ)* pp.389, 390
611 Hutchinson *(YATJ)* pp.389, 390
612 Butler & Powls p.20
613 Durham Archives: Archiepiscopalia Box 1, 3.1.Archiep.2a & 2b
614 Dobson *(Durham)* pp.152-55
615 Sheehan & Whellan vol.2 pp.601, 602
616 Hutchinson *(Howden)* pp.22, 23
617 Clarke pp.41, 42
618 Keeton p.4; Bilson *(YAJ)* pp.163, 164
619 Clarke pp.40, 41
620 Hutchinson *(Durham)* vol.3 p.568
621 Bilson *(YAJ)* p.163, 164
622 Clarke pp.30-35
623 Keeton p.4
624 Sheehan & Whellan *(York)* vol.2 p.600
625 Keeton p.5
626 Leach p.166; Leach (YAS) pp.84-88
627 Butler & Powls pp.56-59
628 Bulmer *(EY)* p.651; Clarke p.46
629 Sheehan *(HQEYP)* p.122
630 *Surtees* (54) p.253

631 *OED*: carucate = a measure of land equivalent to the area that could be ploughed in a year by one plough and eight oxen. Adams: carucate = (theoretically) 8 x 15 acres = 120 acres.
632 *OED*: bovate = an oxgang of land. Adams: bovate = a unit of measurement for assessment of tax, theoretically fifteen acres. It is the share of each ox in a team of eight, ie. one eighth of a carucate.
633 Poole pp.33, 34
634 Thompson (*Swine*) pp.191, 192
635 *OED*: obvention = an incoming fee or revenue, especially one of an occasional or incidental character.
636 Thompson (*Swine*) pp.191, 192
637 Dodsworth (*YAS*) p.156
638 Poulson vol.2 p.261
639 Poulson vol.2 p.204
640 *CPR* 1401-5 pp.177, 178
641 Poulson vol.2 pp.262, 263
642 *Surtees* (166) pp.81-90
643 *Surtees* (164) p.xxxvi
644 Poole p.47
645 Thompson (Swine) pp.193-96
646 Edward Brown (1924-2003), a retired parishioner who acquired skills in stone carving, was responsible for these additions, together with the cleaning and renewal of the external stonework, as well as certain improvements within the church. The time he spent on this work which covered normal working hours over the period 1981 to 1991, was given free to the church. These operations uncovered a stone with a carving of a bishop, which may predate Skirlaw's building, in a wall of the vestry.
647 Thompson (*Swine*) p.198
648 Pevsner & Neave (*East Riding*) p.689
649 Pugin, plate of contrasted chapels
650 Walker
651 Surtees (97) p.35
652 *CPR* Henry V 1413-16 p.327; VCH (*East Yorkshire*) vol.7 p.162 (Kent); OED: hanaper = the department of the Chancery into which fees were paid for the sealing and enrolment of charters, etc.
653 ERYC: register of deeds vol.668 no. 210
654 Durham Archives: Miscellaneous Charters, Misc.Ch. 6541
655 *Surtees* (103) pp.lix-lxi; Harvey J pp.87-88; Lomas & Piper vol.1 p.202
656 *Surtees* (103) pp.lix-lxi
657 Durham Archives: Miscellaneous Charters, Misc.Ch. 7169
658 Durham Network
659 *Surtees* (9) p.cxciii
660 Poole pp.42-45; *Surtees* (9) p.cxciii
661 Hutchinson (*Howden*) p.52
662 Hutchinson (*Howden*) p.29; Cassan pp.181, 182
663 Hutchinson (*Howden*) pp.568, 569
664 Hutchinson (*Durham*) vol.2 p.340
665 Thompson (*Swine*) p.201
666 Thompson (*Swine*) p.202
667 *Surtees*(9) pp.cxcvi, cxcvii
668 Poole pp.45, 46; *Surtees* (9) p.cxcvi
669 *Surtees* (100) pp.400, 401
670 *Surtees* (31) pp.56-63
671 Durham Archives: Pontificalia, 1.12.Pont. 6
672 *Surtees* (9) pp.cxciv-cxcvi
673 Storey pp.164, 165
674 *Surtees* (9) pp.cxcvii, cxcviii; Wylie vol.2 .p 483

675 *Rymer* p.556; Durham Archives: Regalia, 1.5.REG. 3
676 Durham Archives: Pontificalia, 1.11.Pont.10
677 *Surtees* (58) pp.29, 86, 316
678 *Surtees* (103) pp.lix, lxi
679 *VCH (Durham)* p.107
680 *Surtees* (31) pp.xxii, xxiii
681 *Surtees* (139) p.94
682 *Surtees* (139) p.128
683 Durham Archives: Pontificalia, 3.3.Pont. 7
684 Willis p.46
685 *Surtees* (91) p.13
686 *Surtees* (91) p.449
687 Legge pp.56-58
688 Durham Archives: Archiepiscopalia Box 1, 3.1.Archiep.2a
689 *Surtees* (92) p.559
690 Keeton p.4
691 Bilson (*YAJ*) pp.163, 164
692 Clarke p.44
693 *Surtees* (54) p194
694 *Mon & Soc* pp.44, 45, 51, 63, 64
695 *Mon & Soc* pp.236-49
696 That is, of Tekoah. 2 Samuel 14:14
697 Those of sensitive piety, who were readers of the contemplative literature of the north, prefixed their wills with lamentations on the different aspects of death. Other examples were Thomas Dalby, John Newton and Henry Lord Scrope [Hughes p.268].
698 Skirlaw's executors gave 100s to the prior, 40s to the sub-prior and 20s to individual monks who took part in the funeral [*Surtees* (2) pp.23, 44].
699 Joan: (Johanna) sister of WS may have used the surname Skirlaw, prioress of Swine [*Surtees* (4) p.317].
700 Ellen: or Elena, see footnote [750] below.
701 Alverton = Northallerton. There were over twenty friaries in Yorkshire alone.
702 These bequests were made despite his failure to achieve his ultimate ambition of becoming archbishop of York. Skirlaw bequeathed all his rich vestments to York Minster. Although he was a Yorkshireman, and was archdeacon of the East Riding and prebendary of York, his vestments had not been acquired from embroiderers in York [Knowles p.40].
703 Thomas Fishburn: a native of the district round York, who had been a squire in his earlier days, possibly taking part in the rising of 1405 and who helped to make the Royal Brigittine foundation of Syon a centre for the study of Rolle's writings. He had been made the General Confessor at the Brigittine convent and was a cousin of Bishop Clifford of London. [Hughes p.92; Wylie vol.2 pp.360-381].
704 Peter de la Hay: was WS's domicellum (asquire or personal attendant), of Spaldington, guardian of the heirs of Thomas Claxton, steward of the bishop's manor of Howden; became knight with property at Laytham near Selby, in East Yorkshire [*Surtees* (127) pp.122-24] His seal was an octagonal signet, a scallop shell, 1398-1403 [Greenwell & Blair: seal (1221)].
705 Thomas Arundel: formerly archbishop of York [*Surtees* (4) p.310].
706 Richard Scrope: beheaded 8 June 1405 [*Surtees* (4) p.310].
707 Robert Braybrooke: died before the testator 27 August 1404 [*Surtees* (4) p.310].
708 Sir Ralph Eure: of Witton Castle, bishop's seneschal, a near neighbour of the bishop at Auckland [*Surtees* (4) p.310].
709 John Newton: treasurer of York, canon and prebendary, York 1384 [*Surtees* (139) pp.93, 94].
710 William Waltham: rector of Wearmouth 1387 [*Surtees* (139) p.135].
711 John and Robert Conyers: both of the Conyers family of Sockburne. Robert was high sheriff of the Palatinate [*Surtees* (4) p.310].

712 Elizabeth de la Hay: probably the wife of Peter de la Hay, one of the bishop's executors [Surtees (4) p.310]. See footnote [704] above.
713 See footnote [711] above.
714 Walter Cook: no information.
715 Simon Gaunstead: no information.
716 Robert Malton: no information.
717 Oswald: suffragan to the testator [Surtees (4) p.310]. He continued as suffragan to Bishop Langley as bishop of Galloway [Storey p.175].
718 William Yarum: rector of Boldon 1392, rector of St. Nicholas, Durham, 1405; resigned 1406 [Surtees (139) p.146].
719 Robert Selby: connected with Michael de la Pole in establishing the Hull Charterhouse and Hospital under the Carthusian monks together with Richard Scrope, Walter Fauconberg and Richard Ferriby [Hughes p.72], bursar of Selby Abbey [*Mon & Soc* p.44].
720 Robert and Alice Gare: no further information.
721 John Strech: appears as executor in the will of Thomas Weston, archdeacon of Durham, dated 1407 [Surtees (4) p.310].
722 John Mawson: from Kilpin near Howden.
723 In 1280 University College, as it is now named, received its first statutes, first as a Hall of the University and later, many years after moving to its present site, as *Collegium Magnae Aulae Universitatis* (The College of the Great Hall of the University).
724 Robert Blundell: may be Robert Blondell sometime rector of Wearmouth [Surtees (139) p.15]. The domestic chaplain, notary and scribe seemingly at his elbow of WS for two or more years before his death [Surtees (4) p.319]. He is described as registrar to WS and was a notary of the diocese of Chichester [Surtees (164) p.xviii]. Was rector of Farnborough, exchanged for Wearmouth, exchanged for Bishopbourn, exchanged for Monks' Risborough (no dates), resigned 1409 [Surtees (139) p.15].
725 Alan Kirkton: clerk to WS, no information (Kirkton near Hawick?).
726 John Kirkeby: clerk to WS, no information.
727 William Lincoln: clerk to hospice of WS, no other information.
728 John Selby: clerk to WS, no information.
729 Thomas Weston: spiritual chancellor to WS, master of Gretham Hospital, provided to Sedgefield 1393, canon and prebendary of Southwell and York 1397-1408 and Howden 1404-1408, [Surtees (139) p.139]. Thomas Langley, in his will, bequeathed to Weston a silver gilded communion cup with white interior which once belonged to WS [Surtees (164) p.98]. Private seal (2611): round, armorial, a saltire formed of six interlacing bastons, the shield hangs from the branches of a tree, dated 1405 [Greenwell & Blair].
730 Richard Holme: rector of Wearmouth 1401, commissary to WS [Surtees (139) p.63]. He was a Yorkshireman, a scholar of King's Hall, Cambridge, and a bachelor in both laws; he had been an abbreviator of letters at the Roman Curia, chancellor to John Waltham (bishop of Salisbury) and a royal clerk and diplomat. He received a canonry of York in 1391, and was a prebendary of York, a position he held until his death. He was spiritual chancellor to WS, and continued in that office under Bishop Langley until 1422. The ordinance for the chantry of WS at Swine was probably enregistered at the instance of Holme [Surtees (164) pp.xiv, xv, xxxvi].
731 Robert Wycliffe: rector of Hutton Rudby, Kirby Ravensworth and Romaldkirk (in North Yorkshire/Durham), appointed temporal chancellor to WS, constable of the Castle and receiver general 1390, master of Kepier 1405, [Surtees (139) p.144, Lee p.10]. Wycliffe also held high offices under the bishop [Surtees (9) pp.311, 312], as constable of Durham [Surtees (9) p.clxxxiii.] Private seal: round, armorial a chevron between three crosses crosslet, dated 1415 [Greenwell & Blair: seal 2716].
732 Alan Newark: obtained a grant of £40 p.a. to stay with the king 1390, advocate at court of York 1397, canon and at Lanchester 1399, vicar of Norton 1401, master of Sherburn Hospital 1403-1409 [Surtees (4) pp.311, 312; Surtees (139) p.92].
733 John Hildyard: canon and prebendary of Auckland, Darlington and London 1403, master of St. James's Hospital Northallerton and of St. Giles by Richmond [Surtees (139) p.62].

734 John Burgh: from Lincoln diocese, was a proctor of Cambridge in 1370, a doctor of divinity in 1384, and later a member of the collegiate church of Auckland after obtaining preferment to the York diocese, probably under the influence of Arundel, rector of Ryton (near Newcastle) 1402-1407, canon and prebendary of Chester-le-Street 1404 [*Surtees* (139) p.21]. He was also appointed as an executor of Skirlaw's will. He adapted Pagula's *Oculus Sacerdotis* to meet the special requirements of an elite group of Cambridge graduates, benefice holders and northern clergy, providing information on such technicalities of priestly life as the correct office to follow in cases where a priest holds several benefices, and adding civil law citations useful for consistory court officials, such as an extra chapter on the conduct of matrimonial cases and cases of consanguinity, and information on tithes, vows, mortuaries and funerals. The book was distributed widely in Cambridge and York. He also wrote *The Pupil of the Eye* [Hughes pp.193, 194].

735 William Pisthorn: rector of St. Andrews, East Chepe (Cheap) London, who witnessed Skirlaw's will [*Surtees* (4) p.313].

736 Thomas Wyott: rector of Folkton, Yorkshire (near Hunmanby) [*Surtees* (139) p.144] and later of Birkby (North Yorkshire) 1404 [*Surtees* (127) p.302].

737 This amounts to 13s 4d per pauper [*Surtees* (4) p.313]. See Fowler comments, 'This splendid but indiscriminate charity increased, as we know, the number of beggars and vagabonds enormously, until they swarmed in England, as they do now in some continental cities. That they were not, as a class, regarded with disfavour, is, I think, shown by the fact that by far the great majority of the subjects of miracles in this remarkable window (that of St. William of York in the Minster) evidently belonged to that class of society.' [Fowler (YATJ) p.260.

738 Stephen Patrington: became bishop of Winchester and was a student of contemplative literature in the north east of England [Hughes p.360].

739 William Bowes: probably Sir WB [Storey pp.61, 155].He may be the WB who was mayor of York 1417 [Surtees (192) p.209].

740 John Biry: may be the John Brun or Birne of Selby Abbey (see Chapter Eleven).

741 The priory had originally been situated in Bootham near the Horsefair, but in 1295 it moved to a new site with boundaries of Stonebow Lane to the north, the river Foss with its quay on the south, Mersk (Marsck?) Lane (no longer existing) on the west and Fossgate on the east. The church was to be located in the northern part of the grounds of the friary which was within St. Saviour's parish, and building appears to have commenced in 1392. It is not clear whether the church was completed before Skirlaw's death, but his generosity was acknowledged and commemorated in the wall of the priory gatehouse entrance in Fossgate (near its junction with Pavement and within the parish of St. Crux), where his coat of arms and others including that of Archbishop Neville were displayed. Little now remains of the priory apart from a stretch of stone wall (surmounted by Victorian brick) along Black Horse Passage off Stonebow Lane. This wall later provided cover for Victorian clients on their way to and from the red light district of Hungate. [*VCH (York)* vol.3 p.293 (Little); Benson p.59; Jones M W pp.52, 53; Raine p.64; Copsey (*York*)].

742 Ada Tirwhit: no further information.

743 Nesbit (Nebbet) manor: no information, possibly in the parish of either Hart (Hartlepool) or Haughton le Skerne [Surtees (4) p.314].

744 William Cross: also canon and prebendary of Auckland 1403 [*Surtees* (139) p.32].

745 Catherine Punde: (Katerina) no further information.

746 John Roos: no further information.

747 Robert Bolton: no further information.

748 Thomas Langley: was Skirlaw's successor to the see of Durham [*Surtees* (4) p.314].

749 Robert Custeby: cousin of WS [*Surtees* (4) p.308n].

750 Ellen Sheffield: could she be an in-law of WS?

751 Daughter of Edmund Metham: The Methams were a family of great antiquity and rank in the East Riding of Yorkshire [*Surtees* (4) p.315], many are buried in Howden Minster.

752 William Ryall: (Ryell) clerk of the diocese of Lincoln and notary, portioner of Norton

parish church [*Surtees* (194) pp.202-204].
753 Henry Beswick: Skirlaw's vicar-general in 1381 when canon of Beverley Minster.
754 Sister: Joan, see footnote [699] above.
755 William Hull: rector of Wearmouth 1390, prebendary of Darlington 1400 and rector of Stanhope [*Surtees* (139) p.65].
756 John Tuddoe: vicar of Hartburn near Morpeth [*Surtees* (139) p.131].
757 Nicholas Cayser: no information.
758 T. Athereston: no information.
759 Thomas Burgh: no further information.
760 William Marnhull: vicar of Hesilden and rector of Meldon [Surtees (4) p.320], probably *Marunhull* or *Marimhill*, rector of Whitburn 1402 [*Surtees* (139) p.85].
761 W Graundesden: probably *Grandisden*, canon of Auckland and portioner of Norton 1403 [*Surtees* (139) p.52].
762 Robert More: may have become rector of Ryton 1407 [*Surtees* (139) p.89].
763 John Gille: rector of Elwiek 1400 [*Surtees* (139) p.50].
764 The advent of this precious bequest is duly recorded on the contemporary roll of the chamberlain [*Surtees* (35) p.213].
765 John Dalton: one of Rolle's disciples? [Hughes p.333], Archdeacon of Northumberland 1400-1405 [le Neve vol.6 p.115]; canon and prebendary of Darlington 1405 [*Surtees* (139) p.33]; official [*Surtees* (9) p.clxxxiii].
766 John Cohen: no information.
767 Thomas Hexham: chaplain to Henry IV, vicar of Haltwhistle 1391, bishop's receiver in Norham and Island shires [*Surtees* (139) pp.61, 62], dean of Chester(-le-Street).
768 John Catton: vicar of Heighington (Durham) 1401-19 [*Surtees* (139) p.24].
769 W Husthwaite: no information.
770 Amandus: no information
771 Probably the Postils of Nicholas de Lyra on the Books of Holy Scripture [*Surtees* (103) p.933].
772 *The Pupil of the Eye*: the author was John Burgh (see note [734] above).
773 *constitutio extravagans* - a papal constitution not embodied in the decretals.
774 Ralph Eure: owner of extensive lands in Durham and held posts under WS [Storey p.71].
775 Catherine de la Hay: (Katerina) no doubt a member of Peter de la Hay's family, see note [704] above.
776 *Surtees* (2) pp.43, 44
777 *Surtees* (2) pp.43, 44
778 Hutchinson (*Durham*) vol.1 p.394
779 *VCH (East Yorkshire)* vol.7 p.162 (Kent)
780 Storey p.170
781 Saul (*York*) p.1
782 Browne p.31
783 Norton pp.57, 71, 72
784 Harvey J H pp.212, 213
785 Browne p.245; Toy p.37
786 Norton p.63
787 Norton p.79 pl 8 ; Browne p.250
788 Browne p.250
789 Weir p.24
790 Aylmer p.481
791 Pattison & Murray p.20
792 Keeton p.6
793 Information supplied by Dr R Darwall-Smith (Oxfordshire Archives) 17 February 1998
794 *VCH (Oxford)* vol.3 p.93 (Davis)
795 Emden (*Oxford*) p.1710
796 Hutchinson (*Durham*) vol.1 p.396; Wylie vol.2 p.482
797 *VCH (Oxford)* vol.3 p.63 (Oswald); White

798 Parkes p.461
799 Catto p.291
800 Chorister School
801 Snape (*Notes*)
802 Wylie vol.2 p.482
803 Durham Archives: Pontificalia, 2.8.Pont. 15
804 Durham Archives: Pontificalia, 2.6.Pont. 15; Wylie vol.2 p.482
805 Foss p.96

INDEX

A
Abberbury, 36, 44, 46
Allerton, 76
Allertonshire, 73, 78, 89
Alnwick Abbey 84, 87
Alnwick, Henry, Lord Percy of, 181
Amiens, 51
Ampleforth, 32, 190
Angle, Guichard d', 42-3
Anne, queen of Richard II, 41, 46-47, 52, 58
Ardres, 52
Arnold, 1, 136, 144
Arundel, Richard Fitzalan, 4th Earl of, 35, 37, 39, 40
Arundel, Bishop Thomas, 39-40, 53, 56, 62, 64, 78-81
Ashton, Sir Robert, 29, 30, 35, 42, 44
Atkinson, Rowan, 186
Auckland (also see Bishop Auckland)
Auckland Castle, 73-7, 82-3, 114, 115, 159, 177
Auckland Collegiate Church, 84-85, 164, 174,
Auckland, Skirlaw's Bridge, 115
Avignon, 14, 18-19, 82

B
Babthorpe, Sir William, 143
Bacon, John, 32, 34, 36
Balliol College, 7-8, 181, 182
Balliol, John de, 98
Bamburgh Castle, 45
Barnard Castle, 98
Barrow, 137
Bath, 59, 61-3
Bath and Wells, Bishop of, 29, 35, 37, 40, 59, 61-64, 77, 151
Beauchamp, Sir Roger, 29
Beauchamp, Sir William, 48-51
Berry, duke of, 48, 52, 54
Berwick, 45, 51, 79, 82, 104, 116
Beswick, Henry, 22, 24, 169, 172, 174
Beverley, 1, 4, 10, 14-15, 21-22, 45, 127, 183
Beverley, John, 29
Beverley Minster, 9, 20-25, 127, 130, 161, 173
Beverley, Richard, 20
Beverley, Robert, 20
Beverley, St. John of, 24, 151, 177
Beverley, Thomas, 19, 21
Bishop Auckland, 74, 76, 98, 114-16
Bishop Skirlaw Charity, 144-45
Black Death, 2, 5, 19, 28, 31-32, 186

Black Prince, 29, 42, 44, 46, 56
Blair, Tony, 186
Blanche, daughter of Henry IV, 56
Blanchland, 84, 87
Blundell, Robert, 69, 163-65, 171, 174
Bodley George Frederick, 181
Bohemia, 46-47, 83
Bolingbroke, Henry, (also see Henry IV) 38-40, 47, 53, 77, 80, 157, 187
Boniface VIII, 87
Boniface IX, 64, 82, 93, 159, 165
Bosham, 3, 33, 189
Bouland, John, 30
Boulogne, 48
Bowes, Sir William, 100, 165
Boynton, Sir Thomas, 100
Brabant, 46
Brantingham, Bishop Thomas, 39, 82
Braybrooke, Robert, 35, 40, 46, 64, 70, 80, 162, 164, 166
Brest, 43-44
Bridlington, 1, 84
Bridlington, St. John of, 84
Briggs, Charles, 128
Brinkburn Priory, 84, 87, 90
Brinton, Thomas, Bishop of Rochester, 44
Brittany, 41, 44, 53
Brittany, John IV, duke of, 43, 47
Bruges, 18-19, 42-43, 46, 48
Brynston, Robert, 137-138
Burgeys, John, 85
Burgh, John, 77, 122, 164
Burgh, Thomas, 17
Burgundy, Philip, Duke of, 48, 50-52
Burley, Sir John, 29
Burley, Sir Simon, 36, 37, 39, 45-47, 49
Burstall, William, 22, 28

C
Cade, Jack, 33
Calveley, Sir Hugh, 35, 44
Cambridge
  Edmund, Earl of, 37
  Parliament, 40,
  University, 5, 37, 69, 163, 181
Canterbury, 54, 87
Canterbury, archbishop of, 18, 21, 29, 32, 35-36, 39, 53, 56-58, 61, 72, 78-81, 153, 162
Canterbury, Court of, 33
Canterbury, St Thomas of, 106
Canterbury Tales, 26
Carlisle, 51, 117
Carlisle, bishop of, 16-17, 51, 84

Page 217

Castile, 38, 44, 49-50
Catlin, Mary, 142
Catton, John, 175
Cawood, 74
Cawood Castle, 16, 20, 74
Chambre, William de, 128, 130
Chapphamsone, Robert, 143
Charles III, King of Naples, 47
Charles IV, Holy Roman Emperor, 41, 45
Charles V, King of France, 41-42, 44
Charles VI, King of France, 47-48, 50-52, 54, 81, 105
Charles the Bad, King of Navarre ,43
Charter House, 16-17
Chartres, John, Bishop of, 55
Chaucer, Geoffrey, 15, 26, 42
Cherbourg, 43
Chester, 34, 57
Chester-le-Street, 64, 66, 73, 83-84, 86, 104, 154, 164, 174, 176
Chesterfield, Richard, 20, 22-25
Chichester, bishop and diocese of, 3, 33, 36, 40, 62-63, 69, 164, 189
Chilton, 99, 184
Chilton, Hugh, 94
Chollerford, 117
Clanvow, Sir John, 48-50
Claxton, Robert, 82
Claxton, Thomas, 100
Clement VII, 43, 45, 47, 61-62, 64, 82
Cleveland, 17, 118, 189
Clifford, John, 16
Clifford, Roger, 82
Clifford, Sir Lewis, 51
Cobham, John Lord, 44, 53, 64, 80
Cockin, John, 76, 90, 100
Col, Walter, 55
Cole, William, 143
Collace, 143
Commons, House of, 29, 38, 44, 49
Constable, Sir Robert, 143
Constance, wife of John of Gaunt, 49, 80
Conyers Falchion, 117
Conyers, John, 91, 162
Conyers, Sir Robert, 100, 162
Courtenay, William, Archbishop of Canterbury, 36, 38, 64,
Coventry, 33, 124
Coventry and Lichfield, diocese of, 25, 37, 39, 57-58, 151
Crayke, 73-74
Croft-on-Tees, **116,** 117
Cross, William, 166, 168, 175-176
Cumberland, 48, 81, 104
Custeby, Robert, 3, 167, 168

D
Dacre, Lord, 51
Dagsworth, Sir Nicholas, 46-47, 50-51
Dalton, Peter, 25, 36,
Dalton, John, 72, 175-76
Dalton, Robert, 85
Darlington, 72-73, 76-77, 84-85, 87, 98, 116-117, 173
Denia, Count of, 55-56
Devereux, Sir John, 44, 49-50, 64
Dinsdale, John, 111
Drax Priory, 18
Drax, Richard, 157
Dring, Peter, 77, 111, 147
Dunnington-Jefferson, Rev. J, 127-128
Durham, archdeacon of, 70, 78, 90, 105, 151, 153, 164, 165, 169
Durham, bishop of, 2-3, 5, 25, 35, 39-40, 62, 64-67, 69-70, 72-75, 77-78, 82, 85-88, 90, 94, 96-97, 100, 102, 104-106, 112-116, 127-130, 133, 137-138, 144-153, 156, 159, 164, 166, 179-188
Durham Castle,73, 75, 97, **113**
Durham Cathedral, 22, 64, 69, 86, 88, 93, 95, 103, 106-107, **108,** 109, **110, 113,** 117, 133, 145,**149,** 150, 152, 154, **155,** 157, 159-160, 178, 189
Durham City/County, 48, 73, 76-78, 85, 90, 94, 98-99, 102-107, 111-119, 154, 184, 188
Durham College, Oxford, 94-95,160,178
Durham diocese, 9, 40, 62 -78, 82-93, 97, 105,137,151-53, 159-160, 164, 166, 169, 183,
Durham House, Oxford, 9
Durham House, London, 35, 70, 73, 75
Durham, Palatinate of, 65, 97, 99, 100, 103-06
Durham Priory, 8, 64-66, 72, 75, 78, 82, 84, 87, 88-96, 105, 111, 113, 133, 146, 148-154, 160, 162, 177
Durham, University of, 73, 75, 133
Durham, William of, 9, 184

E
Eaglesfield, John, 143
East Riding of Yorkshire, 1-3, 14, 17-18, 21-26, 53, 84, 106, 120, 127, 143, 183
Eccleshall Castle, 57
Edward I, 65, 98, 105, 117, 122, 180
Edward III, 2, 9, 18, 21, 26, 29, 30, 42-43, 79, 81, 135,
Edward VI, 27, 109
Ellen, wife of William Skirlaw, 3, 160, 171, 174

Ellerker, Sir Ralph, 143
Elmeden, William, 100
Elvet, 89-90, 94, 98, 112, 147
Ely, bishop and diocese of, 39, 40, 62, 64
Erghum, Bishop Ralph, 40, 62
Eure, Sir Ralph, 72, 77, 91, 162, 177

F
Faringdon, Sir William, 54,
Farne, 87
Fauconberg family, 1, 3
Felbrigg, Sir George, 46-47
Felbrigg, Sir Simoon, 47
Fenton, 14
Ferriby family, 3, 8, 23-24
Ferriby, North, 3
Finchale Priory, 77, 87, 93, 113
Fishburn, 99
Fishburn, John, 64
Fishburn, Thomas, 161, 165,
FitzHugh, Sir Henry, 80, 142
FitzWilliam, Sir William, 80
Flanders, 41, 43, 46-48, 50
Flanders, Count of, 43, 47-48
Flint Castle, 53
Fordham, John, keeper of the privy seal and bishop, 29, 39, 40, 58, 62-63, 85-86, 105, 113, 187
Framwellgate Bridge, 112, **113**

G
Gateshead, 73, 76, 98
Gaunt, John of, 15, 29-32, 35, 37-40, 45-53, 58, 62, 80, 154
Gielgud, Sir John, 184
Ghent, 43, 48
Gilbert, Bishop John, 39, 42, 46, 48
Gille, John, 172, 175
Glendower, Owen, 81,
Gloucester, Duke of, (see also Thomas Woodstock) 37-40, 50-51, 58, 80
Good Easter, 4, 26, 37, 189-190
Goole Grammar School, 134
Gourney, Sir Matthew, 53, 80
Graundesden, W., 172
Gray, Sir Thomas, 72
Graystock, Baron, 51
Greatham, 70, 84
Gregory XI, 18-19, 29, 31, 43, 45
Greystoke, Lord, 80
Grimsby, 3, 137
Grosseteste, Bishop Robert, 6
Grosseteste College, 5
Guines, 52

H
Hagthorp, John 92-93
Hamelake, William, Lord Roos of, 52
Hangest, Jean de, 54-55
Harper, Ellis, 110
Harrington, Lord, 51, 180
Hartlepool, 82, 98, 109
Hatfield, Bishop, 9, 35, 62, 75, 94, 148
Hatfield, E. Yorkshire, 148
Hatfield Manor, 62
Havering-atte-Bower, 29
Hay, Elizabeth de la, 162, 165,
Hay, Peter de la, 57, 67, 76, 91, 137, 144, 146, 148, 151, 154, 156-157, 161, 164-69, 177
Hemingbrough, 8, 89
Hemingbrough, John, 91-93, 105, 153
Hemingbrough, Robert, 93
Henry I, 26
Henry II, 53, 102, 135
Henry IV (see also Henry Bolingbroke), 53-55, 79-81, 98, 103-05, 122, 137, 153-54, 184, 187
Henry V, 144
Henry VIII, 27
Hermesthorp, John, 18, 64
Heron, Gerard, 52
Heron, Sir William, 54
Hexham, 78, 84, 87
Hexham, John, 147
Hexham, Thomas, 175, 176
Hildyard, John, 151, 164, 169
Hilton (Hylton) Castle, 104
Hilton family, 103-104, 137, 142
Hoccleve, Thomas, 34
Holderness, 1-4, 10, 17, 135, 143, 148
Holland, John, 47-48, 51
Holland, Thomas, 46
Holme, Richard, 54, 69, 137-138, 144, 151, 164-69, 176-177
Holy Island, 87, 98
Holystone, 87
Hornsea, 1, 4,
Hotham, Sir John, 80
House of Lords, 38, 77
Howden, 74, 127, 130, 133-134, 145, 156-157, 184, **185**
Howden Grammar School, 133-134, 186, 188
Howden Manor, 73-75, 127-128, **129**, 145, 150, 164-66, 177
Howden Minster, 17, 25, 70, 74, 127, 130, **132, 133**, 145, 156, 157, 162, 173, 181, **182**
Howdenshire, 3, 73, 78, 133
Hull, (Kingson-upon-Hull), 1, 16, 30, 35, 45, 134, 181

Hull, Charter house, 16
Hull, Holy Trinity Church, 134
Hull, John, 100
Hull, William, 170, 176,
Hundred Years War, 29, 42, 43, 61, 104
Hyndley, Thomas, 109, 147

I
Ingelberd, Philip, 10
Innocent VI, 18
Innocent VII, 167
Isabella, (second queen of Richard II), 52-55
Isabella, (queen of Edward II), 21

J
Jarrow, 87, 92, 94
John IV, Duke of Brittany, 43-44
John, King of Aragon, 52

K
Kepier Hospital, 76, 84, 90
Keyingham, 10
Kilmore, 40, 62
Kirkham, Bishop Walter, 150

L
Lancaster, John, Duke of (also see John of Gaunt) 29-30, 38, 53,
Lancaster, Henry, Duke of (also see Henry Bolingbroke) 157, 180
Lanchester, 76, 84-86, 100, 164
Lanchester, Robert, 92,
Langley, Bishop Thomas, 69-72, 99-100, 107, 109, 112-113, 133, 137-138, 153-154, 166, 177, 180, 186
Langley, Edmund, (Duke of York), 37, 39
Laton, Sir Robert, 100
Leeds Castle, 47
Leo VI, King of Armenia, 49-50, 58
Leulingham, 47-51
Lewyn, John, 77
Lightfoot, Bishop Joseph, 154
Lincoln, 5, 24, 137,
Lincoln, Bishop of, 6, 9, 12, 29, 171
Lincoln Cathedral, 24-25, 37, 130,
Lincoln diocese, 6, 12, 25, 31, 33, 36, 72, 127, 152, 169
Lincoln's Inn Fields, 32
Lincoln, University of, 5
Lincoln, William, 163, 168,
Lollards, 8, 53, 58, 78, 81-84
London, 17, 19-20, 23, 25-33, 36-37, 39-47, 50, 53, 55- 56, 62, 70, 73-75, 79-80, 83-84, 92, 96, 100, 143, 159-64, 167, 171, 174-179

London, Bishop of, 26, 33, 35, 64, 70, 81, 162, 164, 166, 170-171
Long Riston, 4
Lords Appellant, 39-40, 49, 61-63, 187
Louth, Nicholas, 22-24
Lumley family, 94, 98, 100, 103-104,
Lumley Castle, 104
Lyth, Thomas, 146, 148, 177

M
Man, Isle of, 40, 65
Mansfield, Robert, 23
Mapilton, Thomas, 109
Mappleton, 17
Marches, Scottish, 15, 45, 48, 51, 104
Margaret Roding, 183
Marnhull, W., 76, 172, 174
Markham , John, 100
Maxwell, William, 143
Meaux Abbey, 2, 4
Medford, Richard, 34, 59, 63
Melton, Sir William, 80
Merciless Parliament, 40
Merton College, Oxford, 7-8
Metham family, 133, 167
Middleton, John, 111
Middleton Laurence, 189
Middleton, William, 90
Milton Ecclesia, 37
Monkton, 146-147, 154
Monkwearmouth, (see also Wearmouth), 89, 92
Montague, Sir John, 35-37
Montague, William, 37, 42, 44
More, Robert, 172, 175
Mortimer, Sir Edmund, 81, 180
Mowbray, Thomas, 39-40, 51, 180
Myton, 16

N
Neasham, 87
Neville, Alexander, Archbishop of York, 16-20, 23-26, 33, 38, 40, 61-64, 75, 78, 133
Neville, Anne, (wife of Richard III), 33
Neville, Sir John, 64, 94, 103-104
Neville, Ralph, 104
Neville, Sir William, 48, 51,
Neville's Cross, 79, 114
Newark, Alan, 52
Newcastle, 45, 75, 83-87, 102, 105, 109, 116-119
Newminster, 84, 87
Newton Aycliffe, 184
Newton, John, 154, 162

Newton, Sir John, 52
Norham Castle, 73, 98
Norhamshire, 73, 97-98
Northallerton (see also Allerton), 73-74, 98, 116, 189
Northumberland, 7, 30, 65, 70, 72-73, 81, 83-84, 87, 97, 104
Northumberland, Earl of (also see Percy family), 50-56, 64, 80-81, 184
Norton, 76, 84-86, 174
Norton Richard, 91
Nottingham, 17, 30, 39
Nottingham, James, 84

O
Orleans, Duke of, 53
Oswald, Bishop of Whithorn, 70, 153, 162, 174
Otford, 57
Otterburn, 8, 49, 62, 105
Oxford, 5, 9-12, 183-184
Oxford diocese, 12
Oxford, Earl of, 37
Oxford University, 5-14, 94-95, 122, 137, 149, 160, 163, 176, 178, 181, **182**, 183, **184**, 188

P
Pagula, William, 10
Paull, 10
Patrington, 143
Patrington, Stephen, 165-167, 171
Payntour, William, 148
Peasants' Revolt, 32
Penryn, 44
Percy family, 104, 180, 181
Percy, Henry (Earl of Northumberland), 50-56, 64, 99, 104-105, 184
Percy, Henry junior, 64
Percy, Sir Ralph, 52
Percy, Sir Thomas (Earl of Worcester), 44, 48, 51, 54-55
Philip VI of France, 42
Philip, the Bold (Duke of Burgundy) 48, 50
Picardy, 44, 48, 50, 52
Piercebridge, John, 147
Pisthorn, William, 159, 164, 166-171, 175
Plessington, Sir Robert, 36, 58
Pole, Sir Edmond de la, 48
Pole, John de la, 25
Pole, Sir Michael de la, 16-17, 25, 35-39, 45, 49, 58, 63, 99, 187
Pole, Sir William de la, 17
Pontefract Castle, 54, 187
Portugal, 49, 50

Poupaincourt, Jean de, 55
Preston Bissett, **11**, 12, **13**, 14
Punde, Catherine, 166

R
Raby, Lord, 94
Rasyn, John, 109
Ravenser, 3, 53,
Ravenser family, 3
Ravenser, Richard, 17, 19-25, 28, 31, 127
Redington, John, 52
Redness, John, 137
Richard I, 65, 102
Richard II, 24, 29-31, 33-43, 45-55, 57, 58, 63, 78, 81, 85, 99, 103-105, 122, 179, 186-187
Richard III, 33
Richardson, T M, 112
Richmond, Surrey, 29
Richmond, Yorkshire, 17, 58, 64, 189
Riplingham, Robert, 183
Ripon, 48, 127
Ripon, Richard, 93, 152
Ripon, Robert, 93, 153
Ripon, Roger, 23
Rise, 1, 3
Robert II, king of Scotland 45, 51
Robert III, King of Scotland, 52
Romania, 46
Rome, 8, 43-47, 63, 78, 152, 156
Rome, Thomas, 153
Ronhale, Richard, 37, 49-51, 63
Rushook, Bishop Thomas, 40, 62
Ryall, Thomas, 152-153
Ryall, William, 86, 169, 171, 174
Ryton, 75, 77, 89

S
Sadberge, 64-65, 73, 97-99
Salisbury diocese, 36, 40, 62, 69
Salisbury, Earl of (also see William Montague), 37, 42, 44, 47, 50
Salisbury, John, 29
Savill, John, 80
Saville, Thomas, 35
Savoy Palace, 46
Say, Sir John, 50, 54
Scarborough, 1
Scarborough, John, 20
Scrope, Archbishop Richard, 78-81, 84, 122, 137, 180-181, 186
Scrope, Lord Henry, 99,
Scrope, Sir Richard, 35, 45, 64, 79,
Scrope, Sir Stephen, 80
Sedgefield, 70, 105

Page 221

Segrave, Sir Hugh, 35-39, 42-46
Selby Abbey, 145, 157
Sheppey, John, 30, 42, 48, 50
Sherburn, Archbishops' Manor of, 121
Sherburn Hospital, 84-85, 93, 154
Shincliffe, 107, 113
Skirlaugh,1-4, 134-41, **141, 142**, 143-144, 145, 146, 161, 172, 178, 186
Skirlaw family, 2-4, 32, 137-39, 150, 160, 166, 171
Sheffield, Ellen, 167
Snaith, Henry, 20, 23, 25, 130
Southwell, John, 91,
Southwell, 189
Spurn Point, 1, 3, 53
St. Andrews, 20, 23, 25, 40, 52, 59-64, 67, 82, 106, 159, 164, 167
St. Augustine, 72, 136, 138, 140, 143, 145
St. David's diocese, 17, 27, 42
St. Leonard's Hospital, York, 19
St. Leonard's Priory, 91
St. Malo, 44
St. Martin Prebendary, Beverley, 20, 23
St. Martin-le-Grand, 20, 25-33, 36-37, 42, 45-46, 63, 189-190
St. Mary's Priory, York, 16, 22, 87, 189
St. Mary's Priory, Bridlington, 84
St. Omer, 51
St. Oswald, 67, 90, 106-107, 122
St. Paul's Cathedral, 23, 25, 27, 37, 81, 153
Staindrop, 84, 89
Stapleton, Peter, 18
Stapleton, Sir Brian, 44, 64
Stockdale, E., 134
Stockton, 73, 76, 98, 117, 119
Strech, John, 162
Stretton, Robert, 57
Stynte, James, 143
Sudbury, Archbishop Simon, 32
Sunderland, 98, 104, 119
Swine Priory, 1, 2, 3, 4, 9, **135**, 136-40, 144-45, 161, 166, 174, 177-178

T
Texchen, Duke of, 46, 47
Thearne, Richard, 23
Thirkleby, 144
Thirning, William, 100
Thoresby, John, Archbishop of York, 3, 5, 8-9, 12, 14, 17, 19, 22-26, 120, 181, 186
Thornton Abbey, 1, 135, 137, 139
Thornton, John, 10, 124, 127
Thrislington, William, 64, 93
Thwing, St. John, 84
Tirwhit, Ada, 166

Trinity College, 95
Tudowe, John, 147
Turnbull, Bishop Michael, 117
Tyler, Wat, 32-33
Tynemouth, 87

U
Ughtred, Thomas, 80
Ulceby, 137
Umfraville, Sir Thomas, 100, 103
Underwoode, Robert, 143
University College, Durham, 73
University College, Oxford, 9, 10, 183, **184**
Urban V, 18
Urban VI, 43, 45, 47, 59, 61, 64, 85- 86, 120

V
Vache, Sir Philip, 29
Valois, House of, 55
Vardy, Peter, 186
Vere, Robert de, 37-39, 55
Vere, Sir Aubrey de, 42
Visconti, Duke of Milan, 42, 46

W
Wadley, John, 109
Waldby, Archbishop Robert, 79
Walden, Roger, 80, 156
Waltham, 3,
Waltham, John, 8, 16-17, 35-36, 39-40, 45, 58, 62, 64, 69
Waltham, William, 25, 162
Walworth, Robert, 64, 75, 91-92
Walworth, William, 33
Washington, 184
Washington family, 104
Wearmouth, 69, 87, 92, 164, 189
Wellingborough, John, 23-24
Wells, 7, 29, 35, 37, 40, 59, **60**, 61-64, 77, 90, 151, 173, 178
Wenceslas, (son of Charles IV), 45-47
Westminster Abbey, 40, 47, 57, 62, 87
Westminster, Palace of, 8, 17, 29-30, 33, 35-36, 45, 49, 75, 78, 90, 153
Westmorland, 81, 104
Westmorland, earl of (also see Neville, Ralph), 53, 80, 94, 104
Weston, Thomas, 70, **71**, 90, 92, 105, 137, 148, 151, 153-54, 156-57, 164-69, 177
Westwick, Hugh, 72, 102
Wheel Hall, 73-77, 166-68
Whitby Abbey, 35
Windsor Castle, 10, 39, 49, 75
Wolviston, 146-147, 154
Wonderful Parliament, 38, 63

Page 222

Woodstock, Thomas, (also see duke of
    Gloucester), 30, 37, 39, 51, 64
Worcester, earl of, (Sir Thomas Percy), 44,
    53-55, 80
Worcester, bishop of, 29-30, 44, 53-55, 80
Wright, Bishop Tom, 117
Wyche, Richard, 83-84, 150, 187
Wycliffe, John, 8, 83
Wycliffe, Robert, 75-76, 90-91, 102, 105, 164
Wykeham, Bishop William, 28, 39-40, 78,
    181, 183
Wyott, Thomas, 159, 164, 167, 172, 175

Y
Yarm, 117, **118, 119, 120,** 184
Yarum, William, 162
York, 4-5, 15, 19, 22, 45, 61, 64, 74, 78-79,
    116-18, 120 128, 179, 181
York, Benedictine Priory, 61
York, Carmelite Priory, 165
York diocese, 3, 5, 8-9, 14-23, 26, 29, 38-40,
    58, 61-62, 64, 74, 77-79, 81-82, 86-87,
    91-93, 122, 136-38, 153, 159-60, 162,
    164-67, 169, 174, 177, 181, 183, 186, 189
York Minster, 8, 14, 16-18, 22, 24-25, 130-31,
    45, 54, 69-70, 78, 82, 86, 89, 107, 109,
    120, **121,** 122, **123,** 124, **125, 126,**
    137-40, 146, 153, 156, 160, 162, 165-66,
    173, 177, **180,** 181, 186, 189-90
York University, 5, 159
Ypres, 43

Z
Zetles, Sir Bernard van, 46